PLAY BETTER GUITAR

PLAY BETTER GUITAR

DAVID BLACK

Quercus

CONTENTS

Welcome to PLAY BETTER GUITAR

The guitar is a fabulous instrument that, in the hands of a maestro, is capable of producing sublimely beautiful and highly complex music. It also happens to be one of the most beginner-friendly instruments in the musical armoury. Even if you have never touched a guitar in your life, you can pick one up and start to make pleasingly harmonious noises within hours – or even minutes.

IF YOU ARE **LEFT-HANDED**

Left-handed guitarists have the choice of buying a left-handed guitar or else learning to play like the right-handed majority. Both options will work fine, but if you choose to learn to play right handed then you will have a greater choice of instruments to play later on – you will also find it easier to borrow someone else's guitar if you need to. If you decide to learn in the right-handed position, you will probably find that it makes little or no difference to your progress. If you decide to play left handed, the book will still work for you, but you will have to reverse all the left/right directions in the book, which has been written for the standard right-hand position.

Play Better Guitar has been designed to help you do just that. It is a practical guide that will enable you to make music from the very first lesson. It consists of tried-and-tested lessons based on the author's own practice as a professional classical and electric guitarist.

Unlike some guides, this book does not shy away from musical theory, which is always introduced at a helpful juncture. The point of these theoretical asides is to help you with your playing and musical development. But if you would rather pass them by, then you can still usefully work your way through the book. Many fine guitarists, after all, cannot read music, and would not be able to tell you exactly what a 'seventh chord' is.

Play Better Guitar is divided into three sections. 'The Basics' provides an introduction to chords, strumming and reading tablature notation (tab); 'Moving On' deals with learning to improvise, with fingerpicking and with finding your way around the fingerboard; 'Being Creative' helps you to hone the techniques you have learned, and explores advanced techniques such as slide guitar and different tunings, as well as giving some pointers on composing your own music.

The best way to use this book is to work through it in sequence, and at your own pace. Move on when you feel ready, allowing each new idea to settle in before you go on to the following topic. Study the photographs and diagrams closely and master each set of exercises before proceeding to the next. At the beginning, as little as ten or fifteen minutes' practice a day will ensure steady progress and lead to remarkable results. The book covers both acoustic and electric styles, but each lesson has been designed to work on either instrument – you won't need to buy both to get the most out of this guitar programme.

Guitar hero Jimi Hendrix was a self-taught guitarist. His playing included elements of blues, jazz and rock – all combined with a highly theatrical performance style.

Learning any instrument requires time and patience. This book can't guarantee to turn you into a pro by the time you get to the end, but it will enhance your enjoyment of the guitar, make learning a pleasure and give you the tools that you need to become the guitar player you would like to be.

THE BASICS

The great thing about the guitar is that you can make a good sound almost straight away. Just strumming a chord or two can be very satisfying, and even a little bit of chord knowledge opens the door to a vast storehouse of popular songs. This section is designed to get you used to the sound and feel of the guitar. You will begin by learning the most common chord shapes and strumming techniques before moving on to single-string playing and reading music. By the time you reach the end of this section you will already be a competent guitarist with a useful array of techniques at your command.

BUYING A GUITAR

A good guitar can make all the difference to your playing, so it is worth investing in a well-made instrument. You don't have to spend a fortune, but it is important that your first guitar plays easily and does not hamper your progress in any way.

A high-end, expensive guitar will naturally feel and sound better than an entry-level model designed for beginners. But there are plenty of decent instruments at the cheaper end of the scale. Shop around so that you are sure you are getting value for money, whatever price you are paying.

Intonation test This is a way to check that the neck is not warped or crooked.

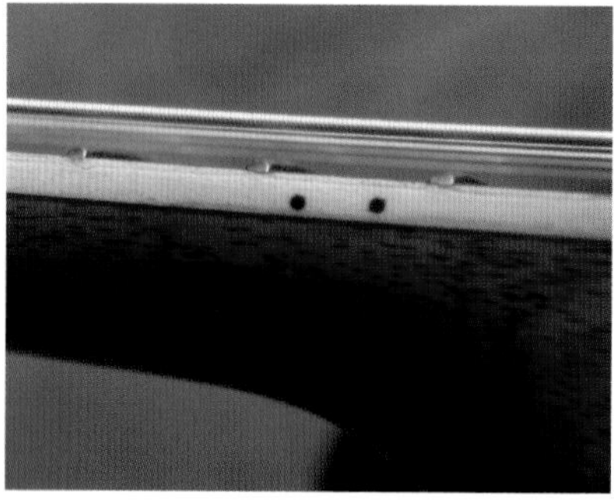

Guitar action The strings should lie close to the fretboard, to make fingering easy.

Check the general appearance of the instrument. Look for any scuffs and chips around the body. Assess the quality and finish of the materials used, and look for any sign of poor assembly or workmanship. Look carefully at the soundboard of acoustic guitars to check for hairline cracks and splits in the wood. These are serious problems that can get worse over time and are expensive to fix.

Intonation check

There are some things that you should check on any guitar that you are thinking of buying. The first of these is the 'intonation', which is the straighness of the neck and the correct placement of the frets along its length. Over time, changes in temperature and humidity can cause the neck of a guitar to warp. This can lead to tuning issues, especially higher up. Warping can also result if a guitar has been hanging in the shop for too long.

The best way to check intonation is to compare the harmonic against a fretted note at the twelfth fret (see page 154). Both the harmonic and the fretted note should sound exactly the same pitch. Test every string in this way. If all the notes sound out of tune it is likely that the neck is warped. If just one string seems out of tune, it may be just the string itself that is uneven. If possible, do this test with new strings, as they will be more accurate.

Action and set-up

The term 'action' describes the distance between the strings and the fingerboard. If a guitar has a high action, then you will need to press down with more force to play a note, making it harder work, especially on steel-string acoustics. If the action is too low, then the strings can reverberate against the frets causing a buzzing sound called 'fret buzz'. Most guitarists like the action to be as low as they can get away with. It is advisable to test every single note on the fingerboard to make sure there are no buzzy notes. Play the sixth string around the third, fourth and fifth frets to check that you can play at full volume without too much buzz. But bear in mind that all guitars will reverberate under pressure.

Buying electric

When buying an electric guitar, check that all the volume and tone controls work without crackling. Check also that the pick-up selector switch works correctly and that the jack input is secure and does not make any noise when you are plugged in. The tuning pegs should also turn easily and smoothly.

You will need a lead. Guitar leads come in different lengths but all use a ¼-inch jack plug. For guitars with the input jack on the front of the guitar – the Gibson 355, for example – there are right-angled plugs that fit flat against the body. For advice on amplifiers, see page 113.

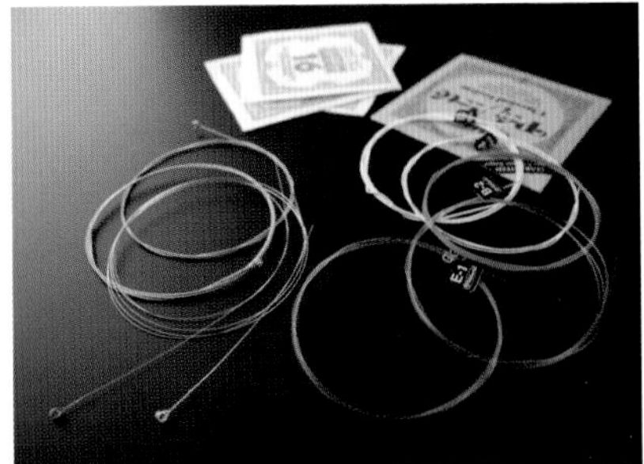

String theory The weight of the strings you use can make a big difference to the sound of your guitar.

Strings

Strings wear out, and the lighter ones can break, so you will be buying strings regularly. Steel strings come in a variety of gauges. (The term 'gauge' describes the thickness of individual strings, expressed in decimal fractions of an inch.) The top E string is likely to be about .011 of an inch thick, a bottom E around .046. In a pack of heavy-gauge strings, each one will be thicker than its equivalent in a pack of light strings.

Plectrums

Plectrums (picks) come in a huge variety of shapes, colours and thicknesses. They are usually plastic, but can also be made from stone, wood or metal. Many jazz guitarists prefer thicker plectrums for improved tone, while electric guitarists tend to opt for thin ones for speed playing – although Queen guitarist Brian May famously uses a pre-decimalization British sixpenny piece.

KNOW YOUR GUITAR

The mechanics of playing are the same for all kinds of guitar: the strings resonate audibly when they are plucked. But this simple principle – six strings stretched taut over a board – can produce a wonderful and almost infinite variety of music.

Many aspiring guitarists take their very first steps on a nylon-strung guitar. It is the ideal beginner's instrument because it is relatively inexpensive, is much easier on the fingers than a steel-string acoustic and it is simpler to use than an electric. But, unless you are planning to concentrate on classical guitar, you will soon want to invest in a steel-string instrument or an electric, like the ones illustrated here. These are the kinds of guitar that are most widely used in all forms of popular music – folk, blues, pop, rock and so forth.

The guitar, like any instrument, is a machine designed for making music. It is worth taking some time getting familiar with its construction, and learning the names of its several parts. You will certainly find it easier to follow the lessons in this book if you can distinguish your nut from your bridge, and your frets from your soundboard.

Acoustic-guitar parts

Acoustic guitars can have steel strings (as shown) or nylon strings (as on Spanish or classical guitars). The sound is created by the vibration of the strings. This creates a sound that resonates within the body

cavity and is projected outwards through the soundhole. A guitar's tone is determined by the quality of the build and by the woods used in its construction. On a high-quality guitar, the soundboard might be made of spruce or red cedar, the fingerboard of rosewood or mahogany.

ADVICE FOR THE **BEGINNER**

A steel-string guitar, acoustic or electric, is hard on the fingers at first. You will find that your thumb aches, and that your fingertips grow sore. But this stage is a temporary discomfort, like breaking in a stiff pair of boots, and it soon passes.

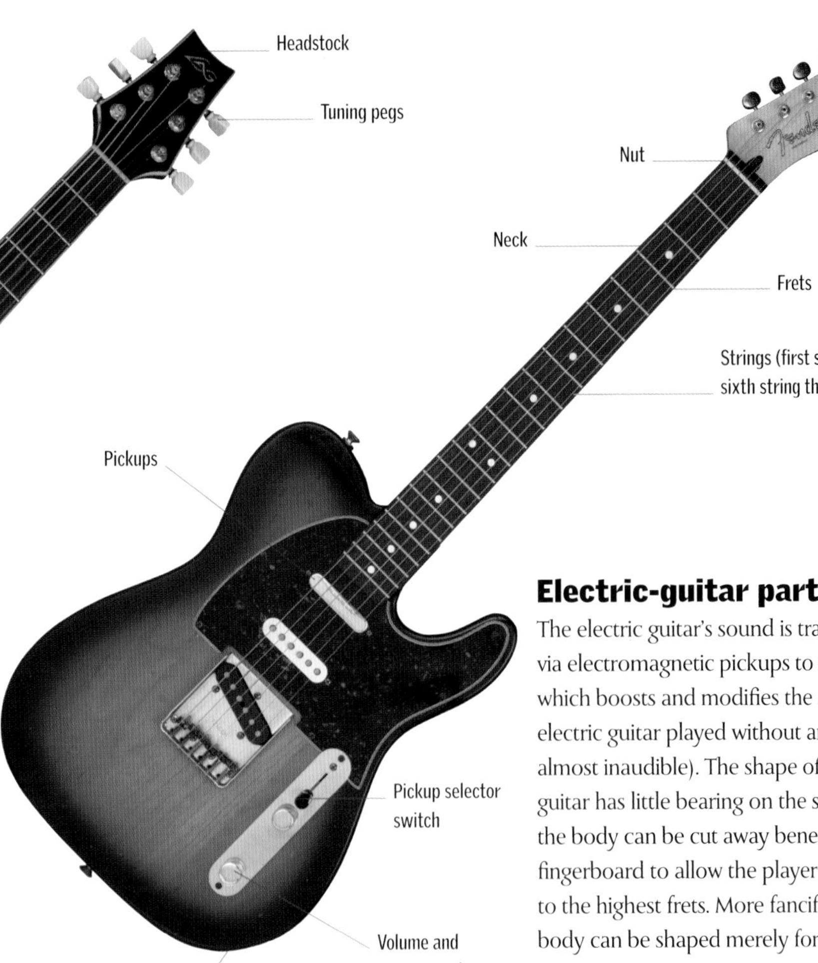

Electric-guitar parts

The electric guitar's sound is transmitted via electromagnetic pickups to an amplifier, which boosts and modifies the sound (an electric guitar played without an amp is almost inaudible). The shape of an electric guitar has little bearing on the sound, so the body can be cut away beneath the fingerboard to allow the player easy access to the highest frets. More fancifully, the body can be shaped merely for striking visual effect – a jagged star, or Gibson's *Flying V*, for example.

GUITAR MAINTENANCE

Keeping your guitar in good condition can extend the life of the instrument. The most common maintenance tasks are fairly easy, and don't require any specialist equipment. But there are some complicated jobs that are best left to the experts.

Get in the habit of wiping down the strings of your guitar after playing. This helps to prevent the build up of dirt and sweat from your fingers, and so slows the corrosion of steel strings. But strings will eventually need to be replaced, and you should know how to do it.

Two bridges On an integrated bridge (left) the strings are threaded through from the back. The independent bridge (right) has individual adjusters for the strings.

Changing strings

All steel strings have a 'ball end' that secures the string at the bridge. Most steel-string acoustics have bridge pins, like little pegs, that secure the ball-end of each string in its respective hole behind the saddle (the raised part of the bridge across which the strings are stretched). To change the strings, detach them at the headstock end first, then remove the pin, pull out the old string and insert the ball-end of the new string into the hole. Replace the pin to lock the string in place.

On electric guitars, the string commonly passes through the bridge. Some bridge units are integrated into the body of the guitar, and the string enters through the back of the instrument (most Fender guitars are designed this way). Other makes (Gibsons, for example) have a separate tailpiece through which the strings are threaded.

Capstans Vertical capstans on a Fender Telecaster (left); horizontal capstans on a classical guitar (right).

On steel-string acoustics and electrics alike, the other end of the string then passes through the 'capstan' winding mechanism at the headstock. There are two main types of capstan: horizontal and vertical. With a horizontal capstan (with the hole on the side) the string is threaded through the hole and passed around and under itself, locking the string in place when it is tightened. The excess string should then be trimmed. With a vertical capstan the string should be trimmed to length, leaving some spare for winding. Insert the string tip into the capstan and bend to one side before tightening. The string should be wound to the inside of the capstan.

The nylon strings used on classical guitars do not generally have ball-ends, and so need to be tied to the bridge. Pass the string through the bridge from the front (the soundhole side) and then back over the bridge. Loop the loose end underneath the string and knot. At the headstock end the string is passed through the hole leaving a little slack for winding. Pass the string underneath itself to form a loose knot.

Cleaning the fingerboard

While the strings are off you might like to take the opportunity to remove the build-up of dirt behind the frets. Wipe the neck with a clean, lint-free cloth and a tiny drop of fingerboard oil. Rub vigorously behind the frets with fresh cloth or a cotton bud to dislodge the dirt. Finally, clean the fingerboard with a small amount of oil, removing any excess with another clean, dry cloth.

Adjusting the action

Raising or lowering the action is easily done on electric guitars, as many instruments have individual screws at the bridge which adjust string height. Adjusting the action minutely changes the distance between the bridge and the nut, and this may affect the intonation. Test the intonation using the harmonic, as described on page 154. If a note played by pressing down at the twelfth fret is sharp, the string is too short and needs to be lengthened by moving the saddle back. If the note is flat, the string is too long and needs to be shortened by moving the saddle forward. Experienced players make such adjustments, but if you have any doubts about doing it yourself, consult an expert.

On fixed-saddle guitars (that is, on most acoustics) altering the intonation involves sanding down the saddle. This is a process that cannot be reversed and should definitely be left to a professional luthier (guitar maker). You should also be extremely wary of making your own adjustments to the metal truss rod that runs down the length of the neck and controls its curvature. If you have problems with the neck of your guitar, best take it to a specialist.

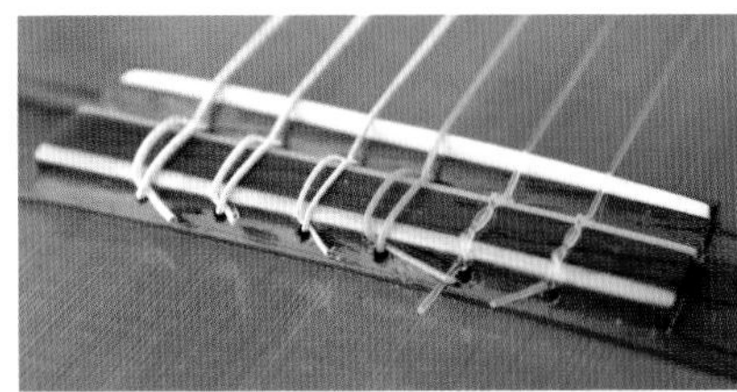

Tied knots The nylon bass strings of a classical guitar are secured with a single loop, trebles with a double loop (above). Steel strings (left) are held in place with a peg.

HAND POSITIONS

It takes a little time and practice to get the hands in the right playing positions. This is a matter of personal style as well as good practice. That is to say, you need to find a way of holding your guitar that allows you to play freely, and that feels comfortable and natural for you.

When you are preparing to play the guitar, both your hands should be poised in readiness over their respective parts of the instrument. They should be able to reach without straining the muscles of the hands and the arms. If you experience continued discomfort, you should review your positioning and adjust it.

Left hand

To position your left hand, curve your fingers around the neck in a loose 'C' shape, and press down on the strings with your fingertips. The left hand balances and pivots on the pad of the thumb, which rests on the back of the guitar's neck. Keep the tip joint of your thumb straight and try not to press too hard. Treat your arm and wrist as a flexible unit: if you do not feel comfortable, try moving your elbow forward. Your index finger should be able to reach the sixth string without discomfort or bending your wrist too much. Your fingers should be curled to the point where they can press down a string without making contact with the other strings.

Above and right The fingertips of the left hand should hang almost vertically above the strings). For instructional purposes, each finger is assigned a number: the index finger is first (1); the middle finger is second (2), the annular or ring finger is third (3), and the little finger is fourth (4).

Right hand

There are two techniques for the right hand: plucking the strings with the fingers and thumb (fingerpicking), and playing with a plectrum. Fingerpicking is commonly used by classical and folk guitarists but also by jazz and rock players. The use of a plectrum, or pick, is a technique generally associated with strumming.

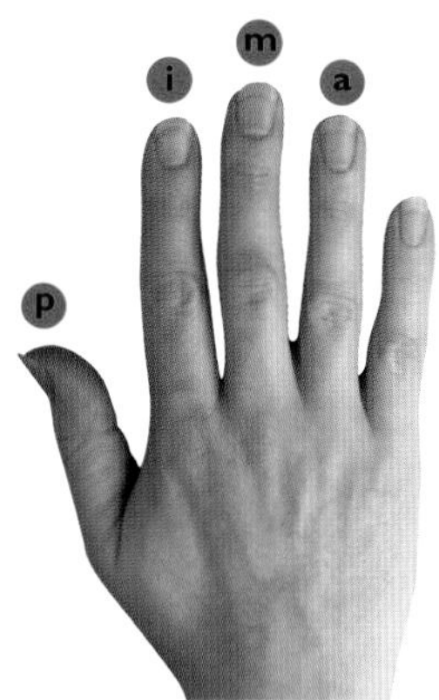

Left In guitarists' shorthand, the picking fingers of the right hand are assigned letters: the thumb is **p**, the index finger, **i**; the middle finger, **m**; and the ring finger, **a**. The little finger is not generally used for picking and so has no letter.

Fingerpicking stance

When you fingerpick, your thumb sits on the sixth string, 2cm (¾ inch) or so to the left of the fingers (from your viewpoint). The thumb plucks the string with the left side of its tip.

The index, middle and ring fingers curve under the third, second and first strings respectively. Think of a loose C-shape formed by your thumb and index finger. The fingers pluck the strings just to the right of the tip.

Your wrist and arm should be curved very gently over the body of the guitar. Don't rest your wrist on the front of the guitar; keep it up, as this helps the movement of the fingers.

Above The fingerpicking stance.

Above Playing with a plectrum.

Playing with a plectrum

The plectrum should be held lightly between the thumb and index finger of your right hand with enough of the point showing so that it strikes the strings cleanly. Some experimentation will be needed to work out how tightly to hold the plectrum: too tight and you will create a harsh tone; too light and your plectrum may fly out of your hands. Picks and plectrums are often used to play lead electric guitar, as well as for strumming.

PLAYING POSITION

The guitar, unlike more cumbersome instruments, can be played when you are sitting down, standing up or even moving around. But it is easiest to play sitting down, and this is how you should start. The most important thing is to adopt a position that is comfortable and relaxed.

When you sit down to play the guitar, choose an armless chair that is at a comfortable height for you. If your chair is too high, your guitar will slip down your knees; too low, and you will feel cramped and your movement will suffer. It is sometimes helpful to raise your right leg so that the guitar falls back into the body. If you use a music stand with this book it will help you keep looking straight ahead. You don't need a strap to play sitting down, but if you have one it might help keep your guitar stable.

Left The neck of the guitar should be angled slightly away from the body so that your left elbow is bent roughly at a right angle.

Sitting comfortably Your hands and arms must feel relaxed in order to play fluently and at speed. Try to maintain an upright posture when practising to avoid straining your back and shoulders.

STAYING IN TUNE

Guitars go out of tune all the time, especially when the strings have recently been changed. The very act of strumming stretches the strings and so makes the tuning go awry. Every player quickly becomes familiar with the ritual of retuning before each session.

For most purposes, you will tune the six strings of your guitar to the notes E, A, D, G, B and E (from lowest to highest). This is called 'standard tuning'. It is the configuration that underpins all the chord shapes and names in the 'Basics' chapter of this book, and it is the tuning that is used by professional guitarists in the vast majority of circumstances. (See pages 96–97 and 146–149 for alternative tunings and their uses.) The notes to which the strings are tuned in standard tuning are, from the bottom E, A, D, G, B, and E (two octaves above the bottom string). These notes can easily be remembered by using the mnemonic 'Even After Dinner Greedy Boys Eat'.

In practice, tuning is a painstaking process that can be frustrating for a beginner. You might spend some considerable time fine-tuning every string only to find that it sounds jarringly discordant when you come to play. A tiny tweak of a single tuning peg can make all the difference between a chord that sounds sweetly harmonious and one that is jarringly discordant.

The very act of tightening the lower strings can put the upper strings out of tune – even though they were right when you did them. So when you tune your guitar, be prepared to go through the routine several times before it comes out right.

Tuning to a piano

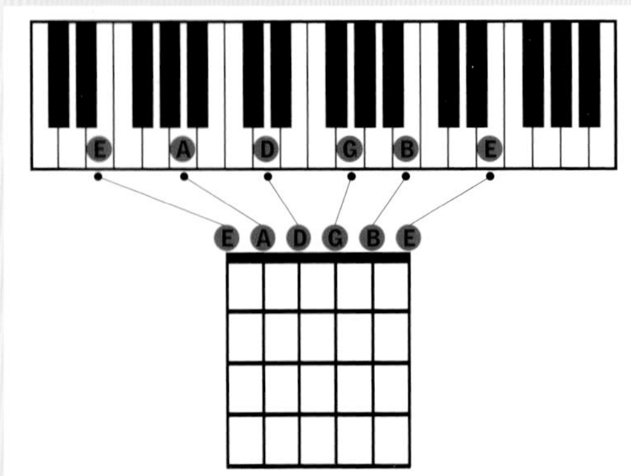

If you have a piano or other keyboard, you can tune your guitar according to this diagram. All the strings of the guitar apart from top E are below middle C. Using another instrument ensures that you will not be pitched too high or too low. This method also makes it possible to play along with other instruments that have more or less fixed tuning, such as a wind instrument or the keyboard itself.

Left Electronic tuners take most of the hassle out of the tuning process. They indicate when the tuning is spot on, meaning that you do not have to rely entirely on your own ear.

How to 'relative' tune your guitar

If you are playing alone, then it does not matter greatly if your guitar strings are not precisely tuned to perfect-pitch EADGBE, so long as all they are in tune relative to each other.

You do not need any external aids or instruments to tune your guitar. You can 'relative tune', which means that each string is tuned using the string below as a point of reference. This is to say that the sixth string, played at the fifth fret, should sound the same note as the fifth string played open. If the fifth string is low, tighten until they match. Now sound the fifth string at the fifth fret. It should match the fourth open; if not, adjust. Do the same for each string – but note that the third string should be played at the fourth fret, not the fifth, to get the correct pitch for the second string. Once you have relative-tuned all six strings, you will probably have to spend a minute or two fine-tuning.

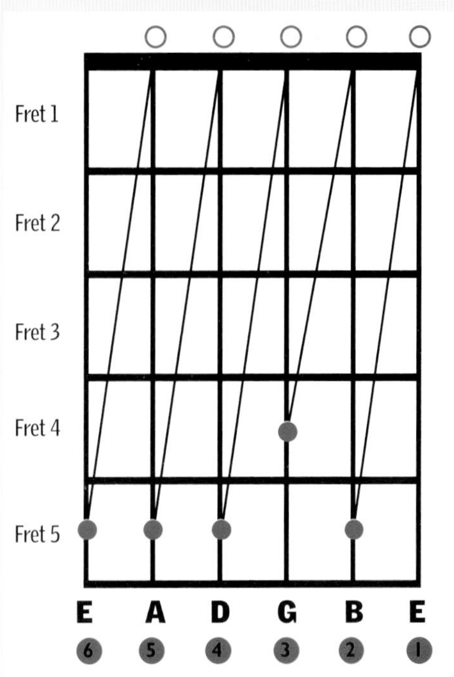

LEARNING CHORDS

Strumming chords is by far the easiest way to start playing. Learn a few shapes with your left hand and a whole world of songs opens up to you. Here we concentrate on the left hand; for more information on the role of the right hand in strumming, see lessons 5, 6 and 7.

Some chords are harder to reach than others – it is not necessarily the most fundamental chords that are the easiest to make. When you first begin to learn chords, you may have to stop strumming while you place your fingers on the right strings and frets, but very soon you will find that your fingers swiftly go where they are meant to be. Mastering chords is like learning to write – once you know the shapes, you no longer have to think about how to form them; it just comes naturally.

Interpreting chord diagrams

Chord diagrams are the conventional way of representing the shape and the fingering of any given chord. The grid represents the strings and the frets of a guitar viewed as if the instrument were standing upright. The vertical lines are the six strings, the horizontal ones are the frets. The circles show which string to press, and the numbers in the circle tell you which finger to use to do it. Empty circles at the top (by the nut, as it were) indicate open strings. An X in this position would indicate that a given string is not to be played when strumming this chord.

The chord shown here is E minor (often written Em), which one of the easiest chords to make. The photograph shows how the fingering should look. Press down close to the right side of the fret as you look at it – this helps avoid buzzing – and only press hard enough to make the notes sound clear. Avoid touching any other string with your left hand – arch your fingers so that the tip joint does not collapse, and the undersides of the fingers clear the open strings. Strum once or twice to check that the chord rings clear and harmoniously.

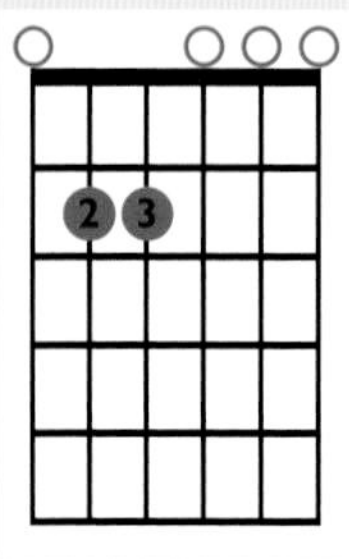

Some easy first chords

These are some of the most common chords. Don't worry about the names and what they mean for now; just have a go at making the shapes. All these chords will be introduced again in later lessons.

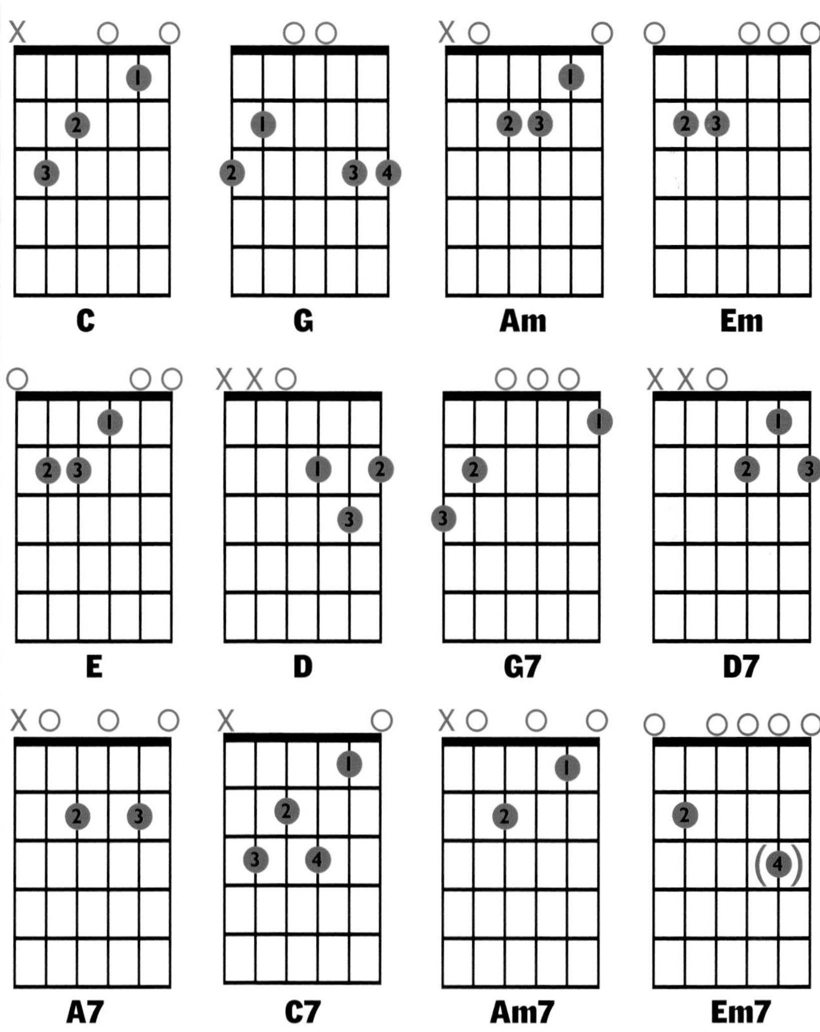

Note: There is a quick reference chord guide on pages 178–185.

PLACING AND MOVING FINGERS

Once you can form chords with the fingers of your left hand, you need to move them to different positions swiftly and neatly without missing a beat. By stringing chords together you will begin to construct the phrases which are the very language of guitar music.

Just as some chords are easier to make than others, so are some chord changes. The first step is to learn to switch back and forth between pairs of chords that sound good together, such as E minor and A minor, or E minor and C. Changes between these chords are very pleasing to the ear, and they are the subject of the practical exercise opposite.

As a general point, it is important to remember when changing chords that you are creating an accompaniment for a song: the timing and fluency of the chord changes should be the focus. Landing on the new chord in time but a little messily is preferable to stopping the flow of the music to look at your hands. Just try to keep going and trust that your accuracy will improve in time.

When strumming and changing chords simultaneously, you can buy yourself time by lifting your fingers a little early, one beat before the change. To get used to this, first try lifting and replacing the E minor chord without attempting to change chords. This will involve strumming the open strings briefly. Though the open strings don't sound great out of context, they go reasonably well when juxtaposed with this particular chord. When the exercise is up to speed it won't sound bad at all.

Left In any change, only move the fingers that you have to: there will often be common notes between the chords. When you move fingers, lift cleanly but not too far away from the fingerboard.

E minor to A minor

This exercise involves using E minor, the chord you learned in the previous lesson, and combining it with a new chord, A minor (Am). This new chord shape (see below) uses the second and third fingers in a similar way to the E minor but on the fourth and third strings.

When changing from E minor to A minor, try to keep the second and third fingers together and move them as a unit. The first finger of the left hand then joins the other two to complete the shape – be careful not to block the open first string with the underside of your first finger. Note that the sixth string should not be played in the A minor chord.

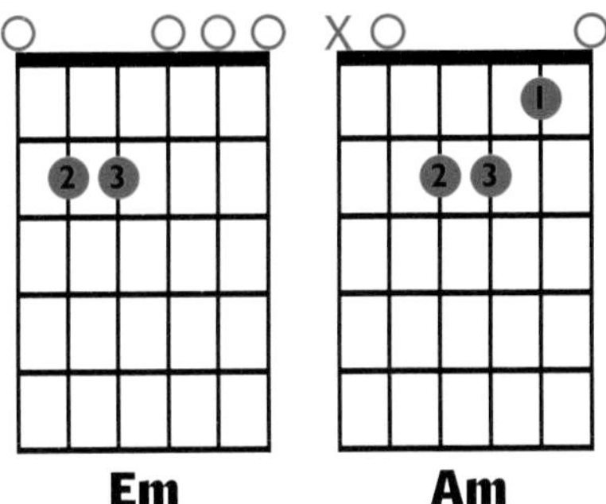

Above The A minor hand position. Avoid the sixth string in this chord. Though there is an E in A minor, it sounds better to base the chord on the A on the fifth string.

From minor to major

There is a major and minor form of every note in the scale. Major chords are often said to be 'happier' chords, while minor chords are melancholy. Major chords are normally named by the letter alone (C, D, A, etc.), while minor chords are denoted with a following 'm' (Cm, Dm, Am, etc.).

Certain pairs of major and minor chords are related harmonically, and this is sometimes reflected in the shape of the chord on the fingerboard. C major and A minor are one such pair; the difference between them is just one finger's position. C looks difficult at first, and it does involve a slightly wider stretch of the hand. To make the C major chord for the first time, simply hold an A minor shape, then move the third finger into position on the fifth string, third fret. Do this a few times, and once it begins to feel more comfortable try moving the third finger back and forth. You are now alternating between A minor and C major.

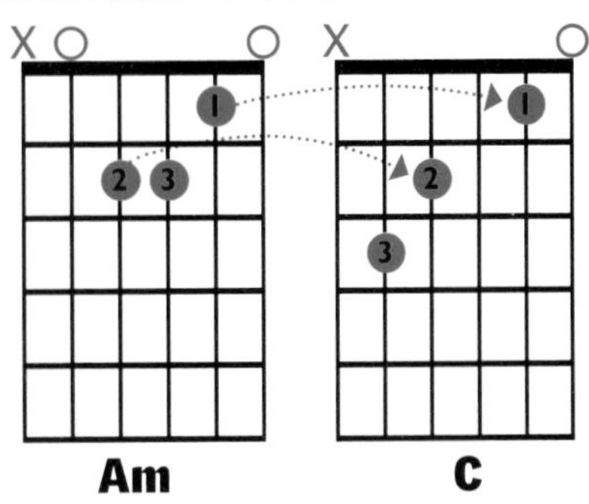

CHORD-CHANGE TECHNIQUES

Some changes are between chords that share notes, or between chords that require you to move a finger along the same string. There are techniques that make use of such 'overlaps'. Once you learn these methods, you will be able to take shortcuts between chords.

There are two useful chord-change shortcuts known as 'sliding connections' and 'pivot fingers'. A sliding connection means moving a finger to its new position further up or down the same string, and using that finger as a reference point for the others. The pivot-finger technique is simpler still: it means leaving a finger in place on the fingerboard if that note is present in both the chord you are starting from and the chord you are moving to.

Sliding connections

Sliding, or using a 'guide' finger, is useful for some of the most common changes. If you haven't practised these chords yet, familiarize yourself with their shapes using the chord diagrams below.

Slide from A to D

Your third finger is the slide. In the A-shape, it is already close to its destination, the third fret.

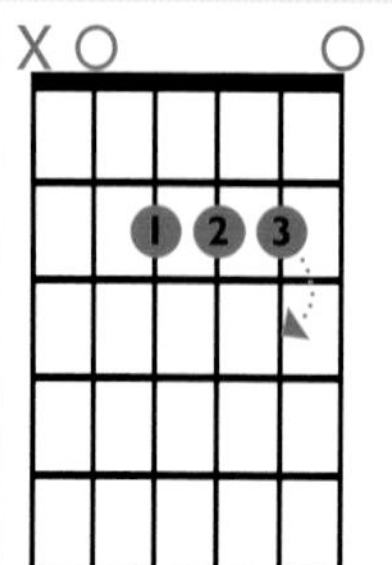

A major Three fingers have to fit in the second fret. Stack your fingers tightly, and don't let the third finger slip over into the third fret.

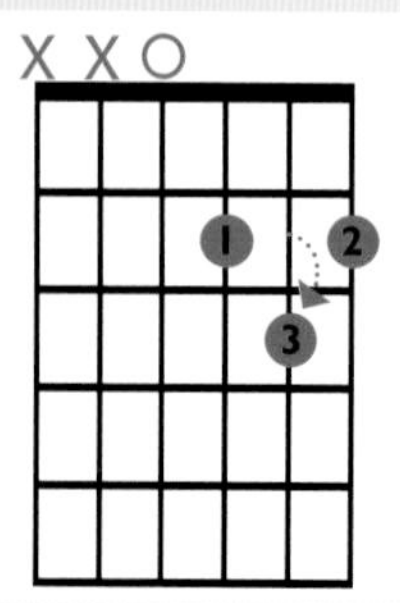

D major Try to be very neat with this chord. The most common problem is that the underside of the third finger can block the first string.

Slide from E to D

When you go from E major to D major, use the first finger to slide from the first fret to the second.

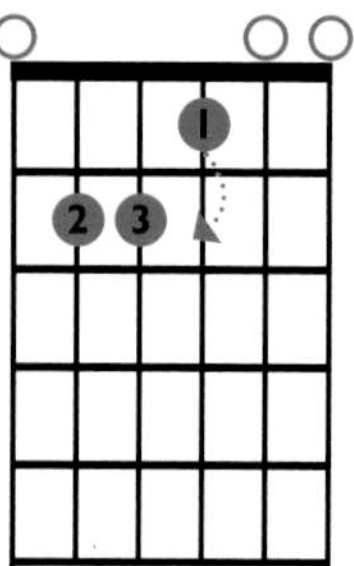

E major Form the chord in the usual way, but be prepared for the move. The second and third fingers have to be placed accurately.

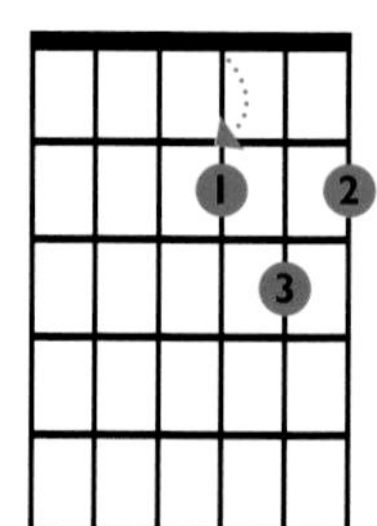

D major Lift the second and third fingers as you slide with the first. They come round the first finger, and land on the first and second strings.

Sliding is the most direct way to move between A major and D major, and between E major and D major (see below, left). For the change between A and D, the third finger is the connector. From the A chord, lift the first and second fingers and slide the third from the second to the third fret without lifting it from the string. Reposition the first and second fingers.

In the change from E to D, the first finger pivots on the third string, first fret. Try running all four changes together: A to D to E to D. A connection is available at each change, but you have to jump from D to A if you loop back to the start.

Pivot fingers

E minor to G major and D major to G major are changes where you might use one finger to pivot between two chords. When this chord change is coming up, you can give yourself a headstart by playing the E minor with the first and second fingers rather than the usual second and third. The pivot depends on it, since the first finger on the second string, second fret, is the one that doesn't move.

To make the change, lift the second finger over to the sixth string, third fret. The third and fourth fingers go on the third fret of the second and first strings respectively. This chord is literally a bit of a handful, since it uses all four fingers and spans the neck.

Try using the same pivot principle when moving from D major to G major. This time the third finger is the pivot finger. If you put the fourth finger down first, the third-and-fourth-finger unit is stronger, and less likely to buckle.

Pivot from Em to G

Your second finger has to move one way, while the third and fourth are pulling in the other direction.

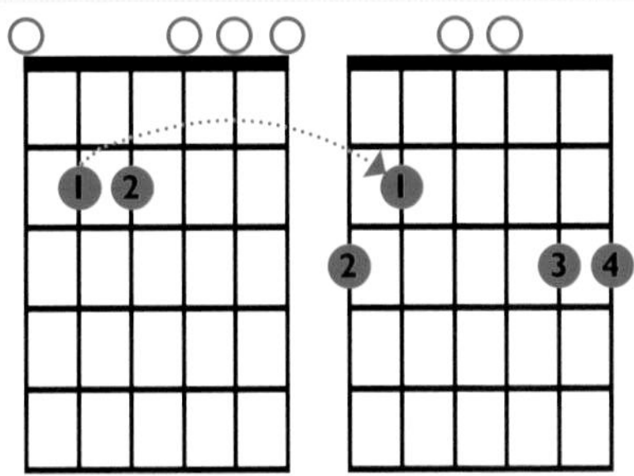

E minor Your first finger acts as the pivot, so long as you use the first and second fingers to make the E minor chord.

G major The third and fourth finger come into play. Have them poised ready, held close together, before you place them.

Pivot from D to G

The third finger is the stationary pivot; the first and second fingers move right across the neck.

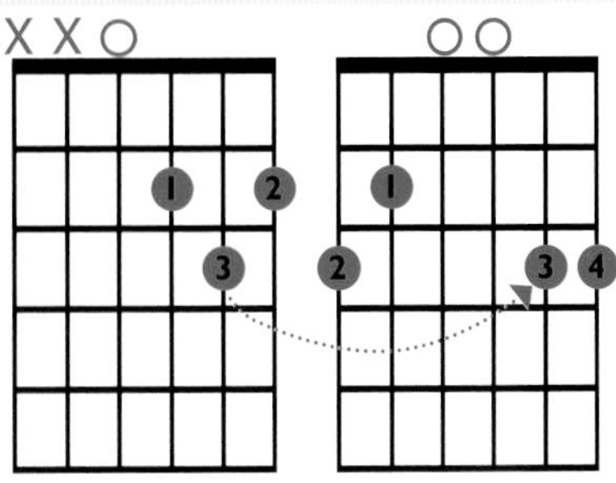

D major Anticipate the change to G by having your little finger ready, and putting it in place ahead of the others.

G major To make G, lift the second finger over to the sixth string; the third and fourth fingers pull in the opposite direction.

LESSON 4

TRICKY CHORD CHANGES

Sometimes there is no easy way to change from one chord to the next, and the only option is to make your fingers 'jump' and land accurately on the strings. This is not as hard as it sounds – as with many basic techniques, all it takes is a little regular practice.

So far we have been learning the tricks and 'cheats' that can be used when you are changing between the common chord shapes. There are occasions, however, where there just isn't a link, a slide or a pivot finger to take you from one chord to the next. The changes from A minor to D minor and from C major to F major are two commonly used examples, and these changes are discussed on the opposite page. Before you attempt the second exercise, you should practise the awkward F major chord. The box below tells you how to form this difficult shape.

Once you have completed this lesson you will have covered all the most common chord shapes. There are many more combinations and changes to learn, but you should be able to apply the methods you now know to any

F Major – two strings, one finger

The F major chord involves a new technique whereby you have to press more than one string with a single finger, and it can be a tough one to master. Start by placing the diagonal portion of the chord on the strings (third, second and first fingers). This is very similar to a C major, except that it starts on the fourth string rather than the fifth. Now try flattening the first finger over the first and second strings while maintaining the angle of the other fingers. When you strum, you should avoid playing the fifth and sixth strings.

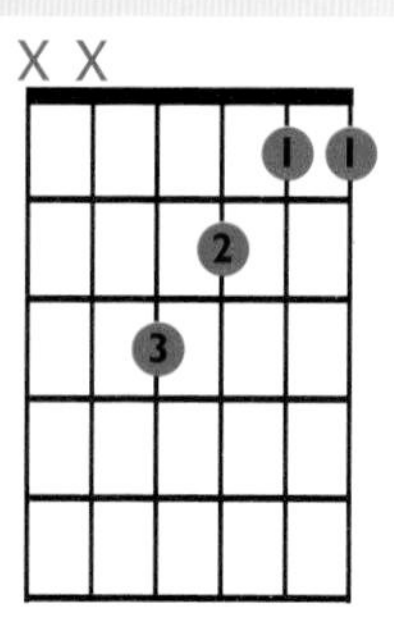

A minor to D minor

The change from A minor to D minor can be tricky, as many people find D minor a hard shape to form, at least at first. (Some players prefer to play the third-fret note with the fourth finger rather than the third. Try this if you are finding the stretch hard.) Practise very slowly at first and think of transforming the shape in mid air. Avoid placing the fingers down one by one, as this will take too long and disrupt the rhythm. Increase the speed only once you feel comfortable landing the D minor.

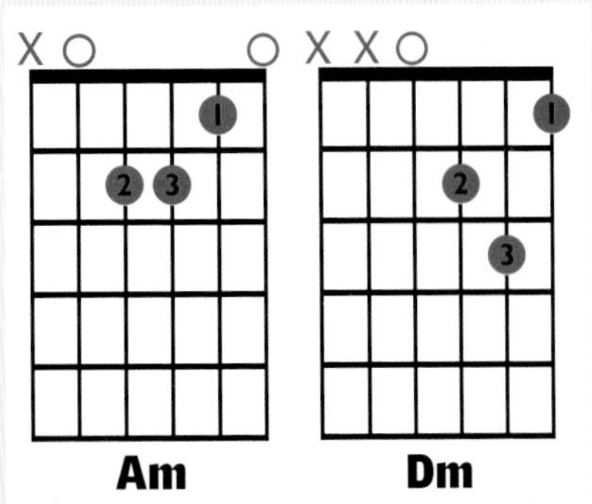

C major to F major

The obvious link between C and F is the first finger on the second string. As you change from C to F, flatten this finger across the first and second strings while simultaneously moving the second finger from the fourth string to the third, and the third finger from the fifth string to the fourth. Don't force the F chord, and remember that pressing harder is not necessarily the best remedy for a buzzy chord. Check the positioning of your fingers and make sure that no strings are blocked.

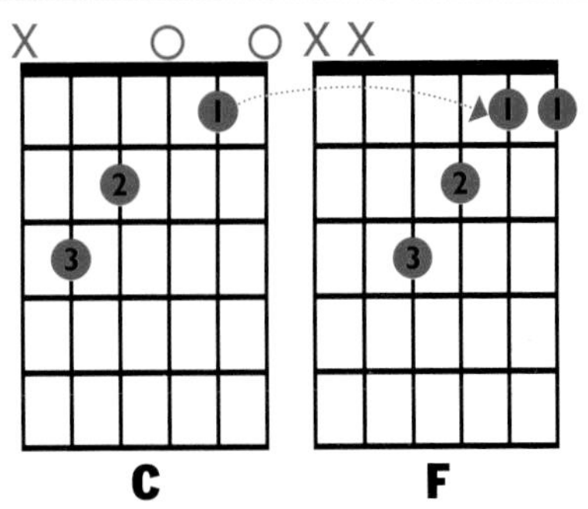

chord change. When you are playing you should always be on the lookout for slides and pivots – and also for jumps that involve similar finger combinations, such as the identical grouping of the second and third fingers when you are changing from E minor to A minor.

Bearing all these things in mind will help you to play more smoothly. Your fingers will become able to follow well-trodden paths from any given chord to the chord that follows.

WHEN A CHORD SOUNDS DULL

When attempting a new chord shape, strum slowly to check that each string rings clear. If some of the notes do not sound right, the problem is often that the back of one of the left-hand fingers is lightly touching the adjacent string, and so damping the sound. Fingernails can also spoil a chord. Guitarists should always keep their nails trimmed short, so that the tips of the fingertips can press down on the strings unimpeded.

LEARNING TO STRUM

So far we have concentrated on the left hand. Now we turn our attention to the work of the right hand and take a closer look at strumming. As with chords, there is notation that you can learn – but the main way to improve is to practise and experiment.

Strumming is the characteristic right-hand technique for the guitar. It gives a full sound that is not achievable on instruments that have fewer strings, such as those of the violin family or even the bass guitar. The rich harmony of a strummed guitar makes it a perfect accompaniment to a solo singer. What is more, it is not very difficult to achieve an impressive effect.

When you strum, you strike some or all of the strings both on the way down towards the ground (downstrokes), and as your right hand comes back up towards your face (upstrokes). Downstrokes are generally heavier sounding and are used on the main beats; upstrokes fit in between the main beats – on the 'offbeats' – and are lighter in feel, often only catching the top few strings of a chord. Using upstrokes and downstrokes together creates the possibility of a wide variety of rhythmic patterns.

Below Pete Townshend of The Who is a virtuoso strummer of the guitar. He achieves powerful effects by striking the strings energetically at lighting speed and by using rhythmic, almost percussive, patterns of downstrokes.

Introducing strum diagrams

To understand the strumming exercises that follow, familiarize yourself with the symbols below. The main symbols are fairly self-explanatory: arrows pointing downwards mean downstrokes, arrows pointing up mean upstrokes.

The harder part to grasp if you are new to strumming is the rhythm. This is indicated by numbers written above the arrows. The trick is to count evenly spaced beats as you play, as if you were counting seconds. Strum in time to the numbers. Most of the exercises on the following pages are in groups of four beats. This is a very common, solid sounding rhythm.

Each exercise is also marked with a repeat, and should be looped continuously to create the pattern. In addition to learning the symbols shown here, be sure to read the notes for the exercises as these will explain what to do more clearly.

↓	Arrows pointing downwards indicate a downstroke. Strum down towards the floor.
↑	Arrows pointing upwards indicate an upstroke. Strum up towards the ceiling.
↓ (underlined)	Arrows with a line underneath indicate a stressed beat. Emphasize these beats in the strumming pattern.
1 & 2 & 3 & 4	Counting: measure the length of each strum by counting the numbers above as you play. Keep an even beat.
(3)	Numbers in parentheses: these are main beats that are not played. Count these beats but don't strum.
(↓)	Arrows in parentheses: the right hand moves in the direction of the arrow but does not play the strings. This help to keep the momentum of the strumming hand.
‿	Phrase marks (curved lines underneath the strumming directions) group repeated strumming patterns together to make reading easier.
rep	Repeats: most exercises are designed to be repeated many times. Loop the strumming pattern without disrupting the rhythm.

GETTING BETTER AT STRUMMING

Now that you have learned the basics of upstrokes and downstrokes, it is time to improve your strumming technique. Then you can get your two hands working in harmony by strumming fluently while simultaneously effecting accurate chord changes.

The way you strum goes a long way to creating the mood of the music you play. The guitar is a versatile instrument in this regard: you can strum loudly or softly, with a driving rhythm or a gentle lilt, with heavy accents on certain beats, or in an unobtrusive way that allows a singer's voice to hold centre stage. You have already practised various ways of changing chords. Now it is time to integrate neat changes with smooth strumming. When jumping between chords, use the strumming pattern to propel the change. In any chord change the goal should be to land the fingers simultaneously. Aim to transform the shape in mid-air rather than placing the fingers one by one.

Strum some different rhythms

Here are some easy strumming exercises that involve different rhythms. Practise on a single chord – the easiest is E minor – so that your concentration is focused on the right hand.

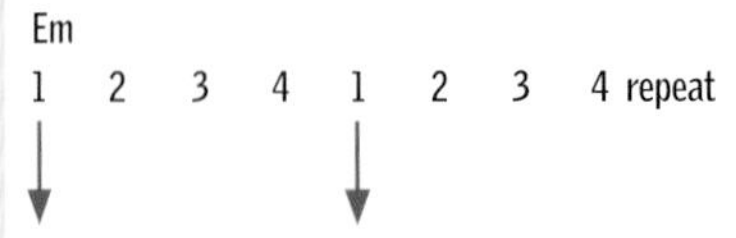

Using downstrokes, count to four as indicated and strum on each count. Focus on counting evenly and making a consistent sound on each strum.

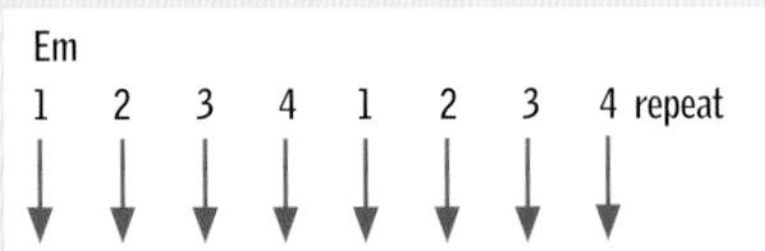

Strum on every beat. Keep the strumming evenly spaced and try accenting beat one to give the strumming a structure.

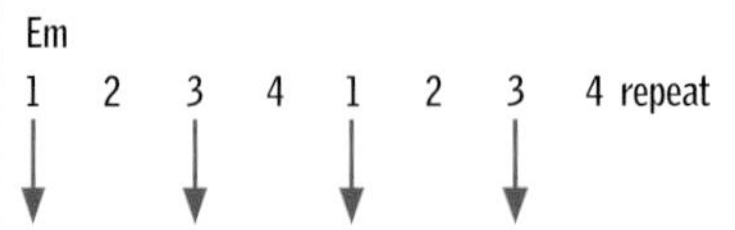

This time strum on beats one and three.

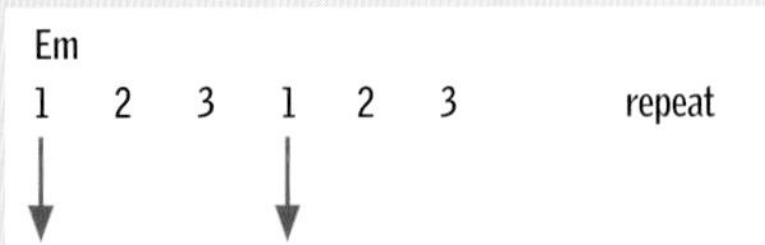

Strumming in groups of three – keep the counting even.

Simple changes

The aim of these first exercises is to make smooth chord changes as you strum. It is all about timing the change correctly and carrying it out swiftly – without missing a beat or placing the fingers wrongly.

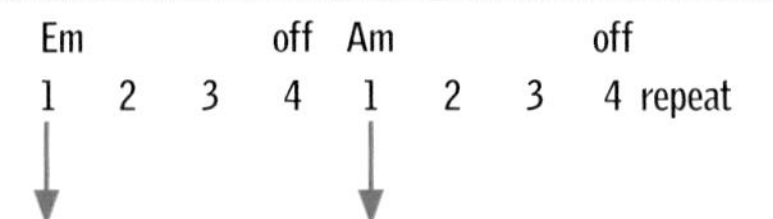

Strum once and count four beats. Let the chord ring and try to change without leaving a gap in the rhythm.

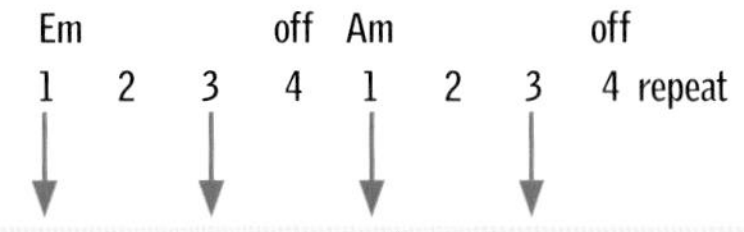

Strum on beats one and three, leaving gaps for beats two and four.

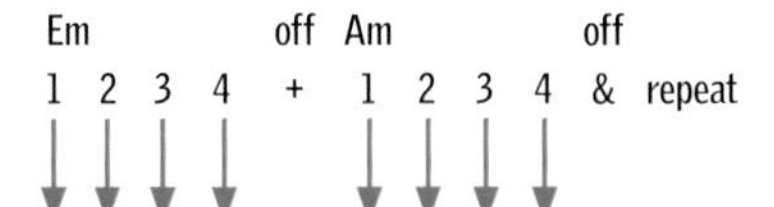

Strum on all beats, keeping an even speed. Here there is less time for the change. Lift the chord between beats four and one. Count 1-2-3-4-& to get the timing for lifting the chord.

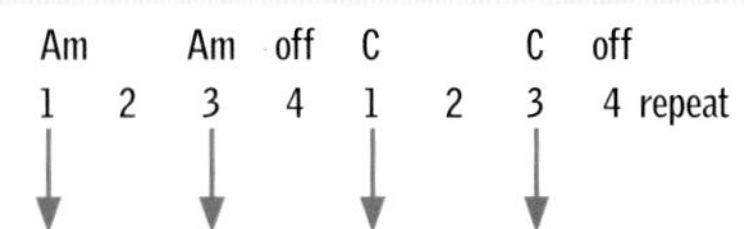

Strum on beats one and three. Lift the third finger on the fourth beat and reposition it for the new chord on the first beat. The sixth string is not part of either chord, so strum from the fifth string.

Strumming and sliding

Look back at Lesson 3 if you need to remind yourself about this chord-changing technique.

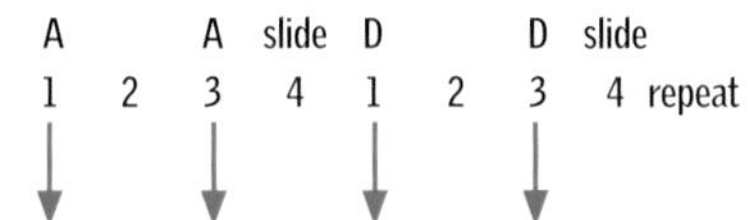

A major to D major. The third finger is the connecting finger for this change.

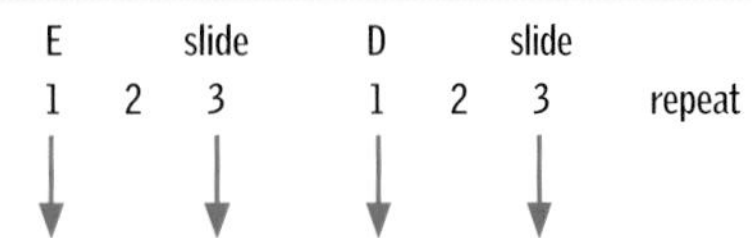

E major to D major. Use the first finger as a slide finger here.

Strumming and pivoting

This chord-change technique was learned in Lesson 3, too. Now your task is to execute it mid strum.

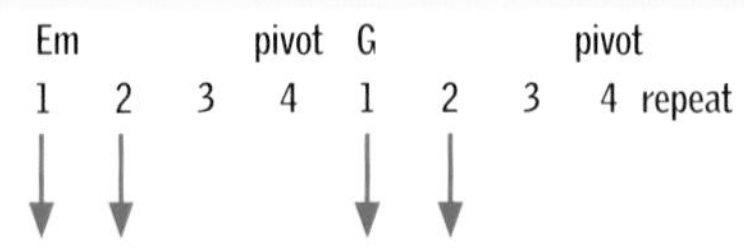

E minor to G major with a pivot on the first finger. Strum on beats one and two. Let the chord ring over beat three before moving on beat four.

D pivot G pivot
1 2 3 1 2 3 repeat

D major to G major. This change uses the third finger as the connector. The strumming pattern is the same as in the Em to G major exercise, left.

MORE STRUMMING PATTERNS

Strumming simple rhythms should be becoming second nature to you by now. You may even have begun to devise patterns of your own. In this lesson you will encounter a few more useful strum patterns that you can learn and experiment with.

A strummed guitar is often fulfilling an accompanying role, and the focus should be on keeping in time and changing chords without upsetting the rhythm. As you practise, tap your foot on the numbered beats (imagine playing along to a drum beat) and slot the upstrokes evenly in between those beats.

If the music is in groups of four there will be four downstrokes for the main beats and four upstrokes for the offbeats, so eight in all. To keep the momentum up, the left-hand fingers still need to lift slightly before each new chord. Try doing this on the offbeat, before the change. This will tie in with an upstroke in your right hand. Don't worry if you end up playing some open strings on the final upstroke. When the exercise is up to speed this will sound more natural than an unnecessarily quick jump or change with the left hand.

TIP

Keep your right hand moving in time across the face of your guitar even if the pattern requires you to miss out a strike. This will help you to maintain the rhythm.

Left With practice, you will find that you can alter the pattern and the mood of your strumming as naturally and unthinkingly as you modulate the tone of your voice. In time you will evolve a strumming style that is distinctively your own.

Variations on the strum

The exercises below are designed to get you strumming more rhythmically. They start simply and gradually get more complicated.

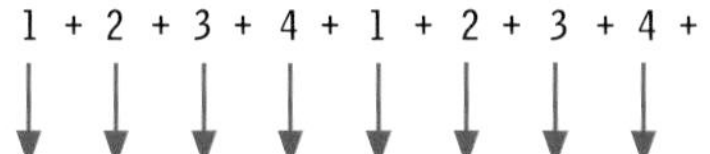

Your right hand here goes down and up, and this momentum should remain no matter what strumming pattern you are playing. Any strumming pattern will have this as its basis, and – as you can see in the following example – you will simply be dropping certain strokes to create gaps in the rhythm.

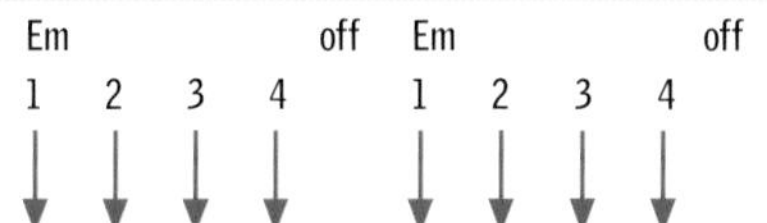

This is a basic 1-2-3-4 strumming pattern using the E minor chord. Strum on the beat and lift the chord between beats four and one to get the hang of the technique.

Dm off F off
1 + 2 + 3 + 4 1 + 2 + 3 + 4 rep

The second finger can connect the D minor to the F. Be careful not to strum more than four strings. Upstrokes need only be the top two or three strings.

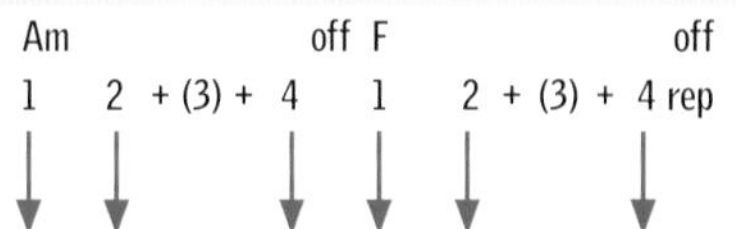

Beat three is missing in this exercise, which creates a syncopated rhythm (where the rhythm is interrupted). Make sure you feel beat three (tap your foot in the gap) and allow your right hand to travel downwards, missing the strings, so that you are on the correct side to play the following upstroke.

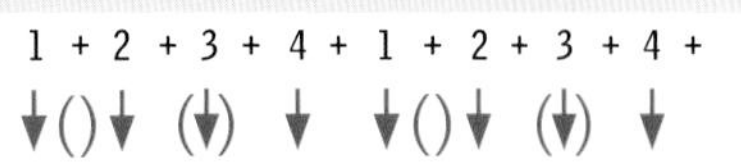

Once you master this there is no pattern you can't play. Even if you make a mistake, the up-down motion will ensure that your strumming is the right way round at the beginning of each cycle.

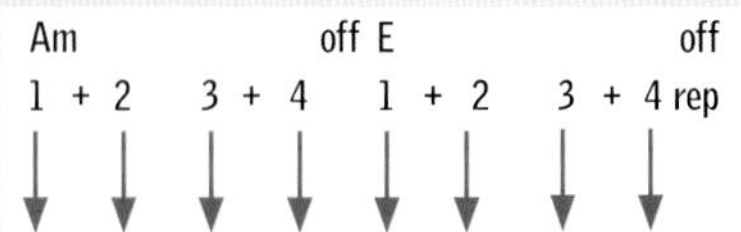

This is essentially the same shape jumping up and down by one string. Try to move your hand as a unit, keeping the shape rigid when jumping across the strings. Here the upstrokes slot between beats one and two then three and four. It helps to say the rhythm out loud as you play.

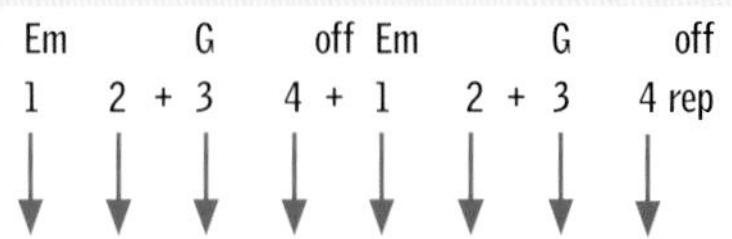

Use the first and second fingers for the E minor this time, so you can connect to the G chord by leaving the first finger on the fifth string, second fret. Use the last upstroke before the change to help you move – only the first finger should still be pressing at this moment; all the other fingers will be in transition as you strum the upstroke.

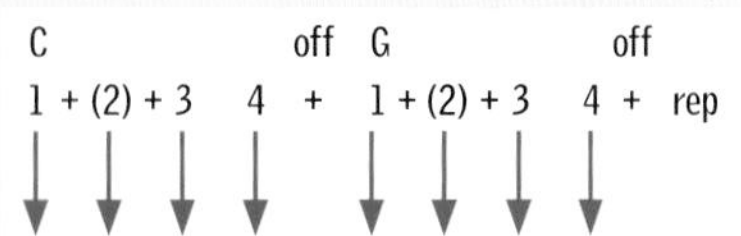

Beat two is missing here. As before, play a silent downstroke to keep the momentum of your strumming arm. Use the upstroke before the change of chord to help the transition.

THE THREE-CHORD TRICK

An astonishing variety of songs – from 'Silent Night' to 'Blue Suede Shoes' – use only three chords. There are thousands of songs you can play so long as you know the 'three-chord tricks' required, and this lesson introduces you to some of them.

There are many three-chord tricks. They occur in every key of the musical scale and in various combinations of major and minor chords. One three-chord trick consists of major chords corresponding to the first, fourth and fifth note of the scale (see pages 84–85) and a large part of the rock'n'roll canon is based on this progression. Both the major progressions given opposite are examples of this trick, in different keys. The minor progression below often crops up in folk songs. The rock progression (opposite, below) will sound good played on electric guitar.

A minor-chord progression

This exercise has an overwhelmingly minor feel even though it starts on C major. This three-chord trick is a fixed-finger progression – you can connect the chords by leaving common fingers down at each change.

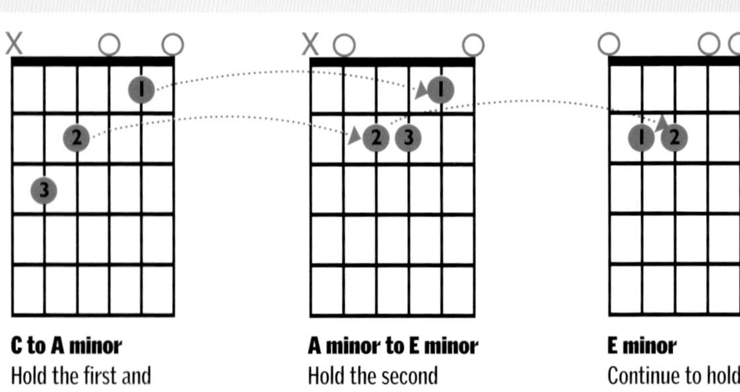

C to A minor
Hold the first and second fingers. Only the third finger need move in order to make the Am chord.

A minor to E minor
Hold the second finger. Move the first finger to the fifth string to make the Em shape. Stay on Em for two strumming cycles.

E minor
Continue to hold the second finger on the fourth string, and reposition the first and third fingers to return to the C chord.

Two major progressions

A D E

A-D-E. You can connect each change here with a slide. This is the most efficient method, as your hand does not have to let go of the strings (until you loop back from to E to A).

G D C9

G-D-C9. This fixed-finger chord progression features C9, a lovely chord, like a bell's chime. It often occurs with G, and is a similar shape: you just move your first two fingers up one string.

A rock progression

Play using short downstrokes and aim more for the bass strings. This will give you a driving, grungy sound. If you are playing an electric guitar, experiment with the volume and tone for different effects.

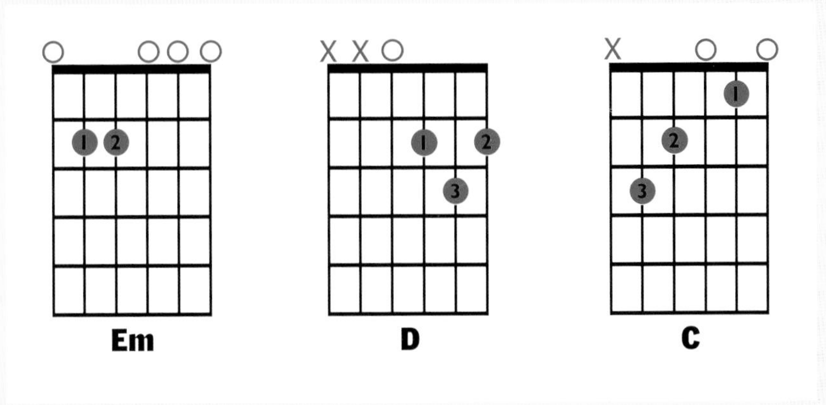

LONGER CHORD SEQUENCES

Not all songs are three-chord tricks, but in most popular songs there is a recurring chord progression. In this lesson you will begin to play some well-known songs. If you know the tunes or the words, hum or sing along as you play, and see how the guitar's sound can enrich a melody.

The main exercise in this lesson is to learn to play 'House of the Rising Sun', a tune you will surely know. The guitar part consists of five chords, all of which you have already encountered. Your task is to learn the progression and play it in a smooth, flowing manner. Once you have got the hang of it, play it through several times over without stopping.

As a kind of slow warm-up for 'House of the Rising Sun', have a go at playing 'Amazing Grace' (below). It is a fine example of a great tune that is based on a very simple chord progression.

'Amazing Grace'

This well known hymn uses C, F and G. Keep a steady three beats to the bar and concentrate on changing chords smoothly. Link the C and F chords using the method learned on page 29. There is no link to the G chord, so you will need to jump cleanly, lifting all the fingers at once.

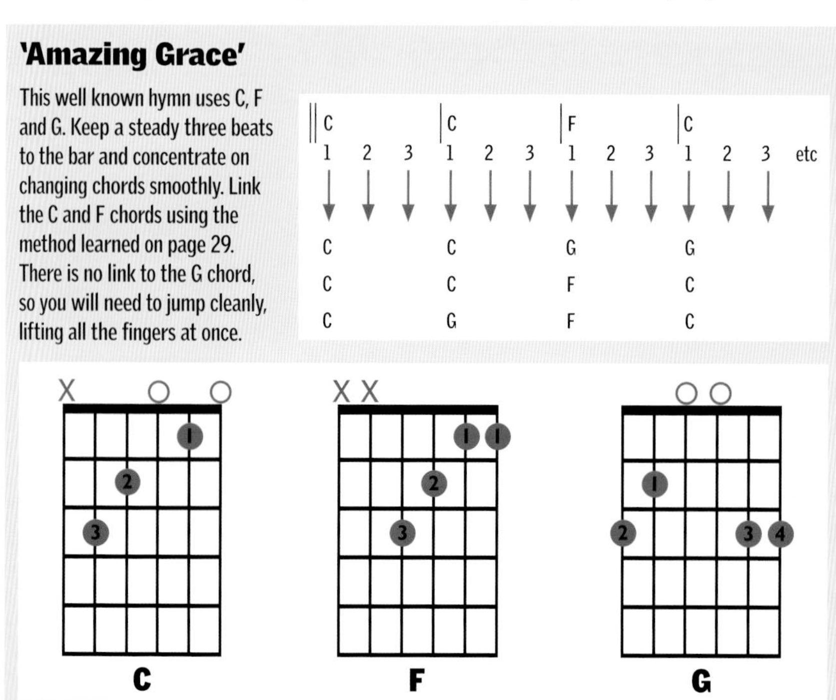

The Animals In The Animals version of this song, there was a slow build-up of volume and urgency from verse to verse. See if you can achieve a similar effect by strumming harder and more emphatically each time you repeat the sequence.

'House of the Rising Sun' – a five-chord song

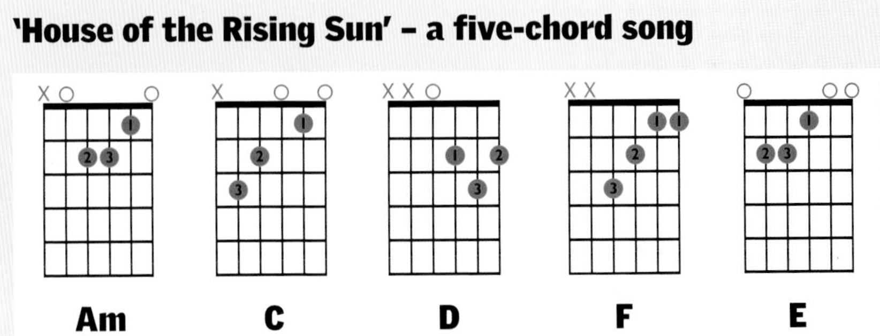

Start by practising this piece with just one stroke per chord, at least until the chord progression is fixed in your mind and reasonably fluent. The chords come in quick groups of three. Play the home chord, A minor, when you come to the end of the piece.

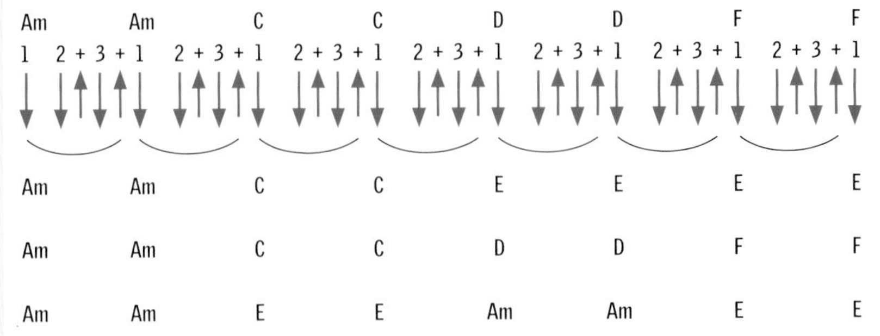

The strumming pattern needs to be light at first, with the emphasis on beat one all the way through. You may find it easier just to tap your foot on the first beat of each group once it is up to speed. Repeat the piece over many times to improve the strength of your left hand.

SINGLE-STRING PLAYING

On a guitar you can do more than strum an accompaniment; you can also pick out a tune. The next few lessons deal with playing a melody on a single-string, and introduce you to 'tablature' ('tab' for short), a system of musical notation used for fretted string instruments.

Playing a tune on the guitar is a rather different skill from strumming chords, and there is no escaping the fact that it is a harder task. But if you can master it, you will enrich your playing enormously and open up a whole world of musical possibilities for yourself as a guitarist.

Above With the right hand anchored on the little finger, the plectrum is poised within reach of all the strings.

The two hands

When you use your right hand to strum, the lower arm is in constant motion. But when you play a tune with a plectrum, the right hand stays almost still so that you can locate the right string. Some players anchor the right hand with the little finger resting on the soundboard. Do this lightly, as there needs to be plenty of flexibility in your arm, hand and fingers.

The left hand should be still, too, and in a pose where all fingers are available to play. The first finger should be at the first fret, second in second, and so on. This initial arrangement of the fingers is known as 'first position'. Once you have your hand in first position, you should try to keep it stationary (as much as the music you are playing allows it). The stiller your hand remains, the more likely you are to land on the notes accurately.

As with so many other aspects of playing guitar, you will find with practice that adopting first position comes naturally, and that your fingers will go to their respective frets without you even having to look.

Left In first position, the fingers of the left hand are spaced so that each one is assigned to its own fret.

Introducing tablature

Tablature is a form of musical shorthand used for the guitar, and for guitar-like instruments such as the banjo. It looks like a musical stave, but is in fact a graphic representation of the fingerboard. The highest horizontal line represents the top E string, the second the   string, and so on. The numbers on the lines represent the frets (they are not telling you which finger to use, as in chord diagrams). So, for example, a figure 3 on the fourth line means 'pluck the D string while fingering the third fret'. You scan tab from left to right, as you would read a line in a book, or a piece of music written in standard notation.

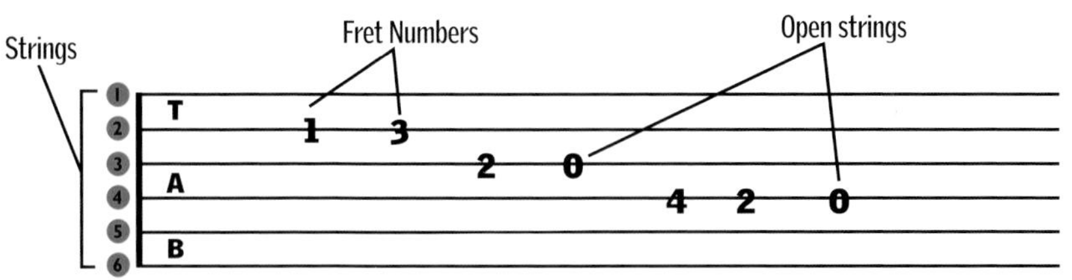

First-position exercises

Tab may appear baffling at first, but it is very popular precisely because it is easy to understand, once you get used to it. Try the exercises below, none of which requires you to move your fingers from first position: it is strictly one finger per fret. You will be surprised how soon you learn to play as you read.

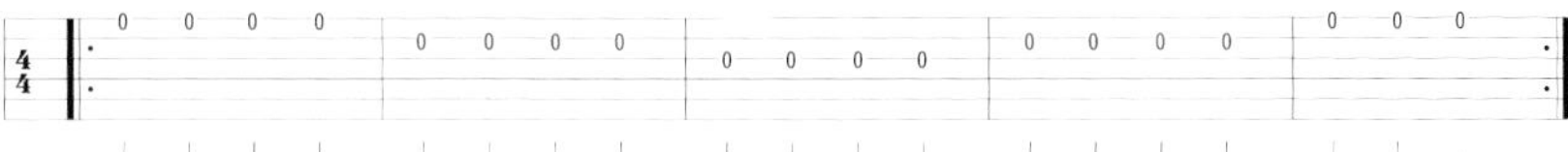

Open strings Keep a steady beat throughout, and concentrate on finding the correct strings without looking at your right hand.

One finger Use the first finger in the first fret and get used to timing your left-hand movements – if you move too soon you will hear the sound of the left hand pressing or releasing the string.

The first and third fingers Use the first finger in the first fret and the third finger in the third fret. Hold down the first finger while pressing the third finger. This will develop the stretch, and will also help you find the first finger again quickly.

LESSON 11

GETTING BETTER AT TAB

Tab does more than just tell you which note to play. There are ways of letting you know how long to hold a note, and how the note should sound on the ear. In this lesson and the next, you will learn new things about tab that will help you to improve your guitar playing.

In tab there is a way of indicating whether you should be plucking upwards or downwards. A downstroke is indicated by a ⊓ beneath the stave and directly below the note in question; an upstroke is indicated by a ∨ below the note.

When using a plectrum, you will be able to play twice as fast on one string by alternating downstrokes and upstrokes than if you play downstrokes alone. But downstrokes will always be the heavier stroke, and as such will play the main beats. The plectrum exercises for open strings (opposite) will help you get used to more complex plucking patterns.

The difficulty with much guitar playing is that your two hands are asked to do separate but equally complicated tasks. your hands have to move fast and remain in perfect sync. The second set of exercises on the opposite page will help you to develop that skill.

Tab exercises for four fingers and all the notes

These exercises are a little harder than the ones in the previous lesson. In both exercises, stay focused on using one finger for each fret and play without looking. This is excellent practice for developing speed and coordination.

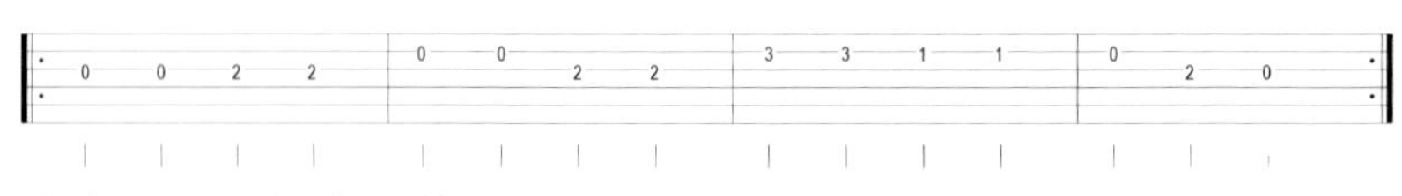

The first, second and third fingers Use one finger per fret.

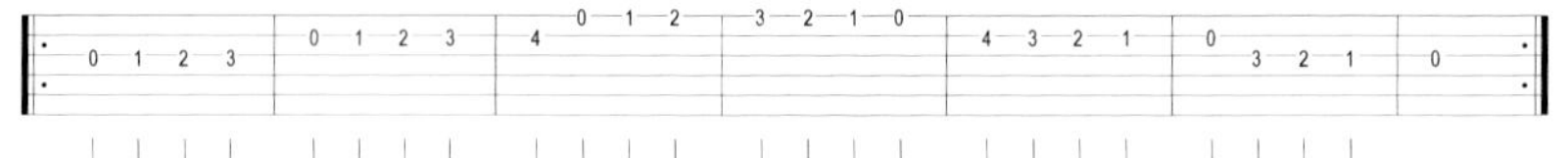

The chromatic scale The chromatic scale involves going up and down an octave a semitone (one fret) at a time. Crawl up each string, keeping the left-hand fingers as close as to the strings as you can. This is an excellent warm-up for your left hand.

Plectrum exercises for open strings

Remember to do these exercises without looking at your right hand, as it is important that you develop a feel for the strings.

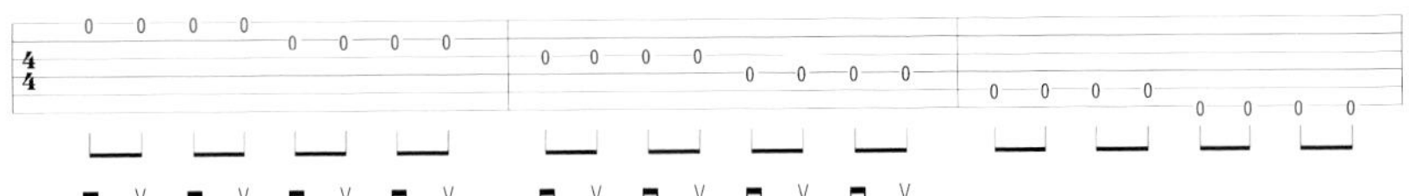

1. Four notes on each string Make sure the string changes are clean and decisive. The move to each new string will begin with a downstroke.

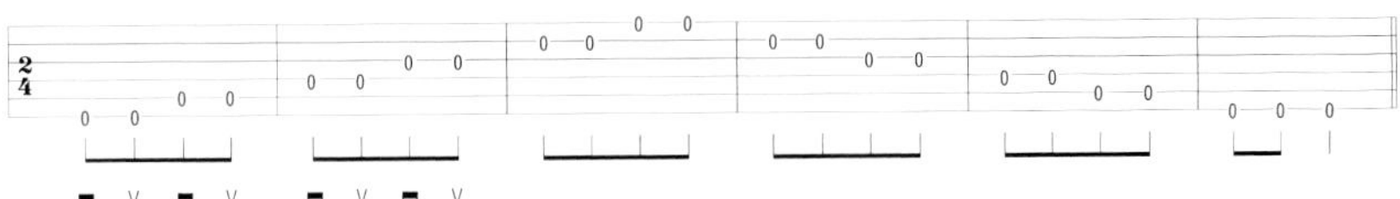

2. Two notes on each string Remember that the goal is to do this without looking at your hands.

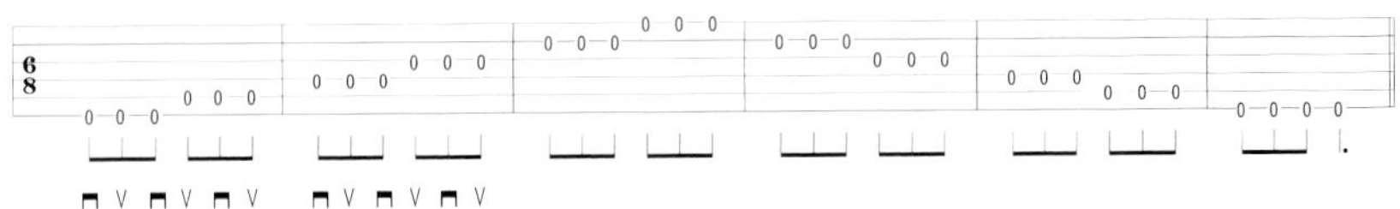

3. Three notes on each string Each group of three will change its plucking direction. This phrase should have a fluent, rolling feel once you are up to speed.

Exercises for coordination with the left hand

Play slowly enough so that you can think carefully about each movement. If you find yourself stumbling or making the same mistakes repeatedly, slow down.

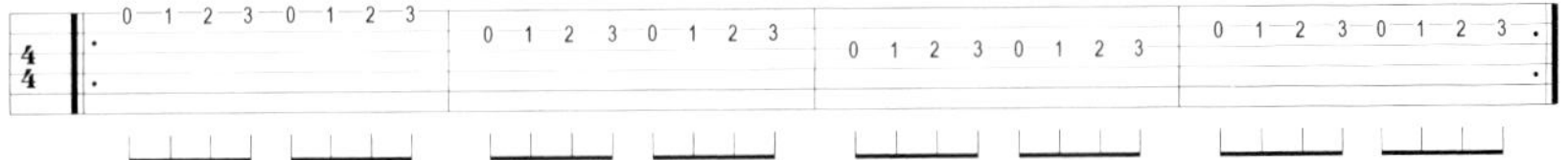

1. Left-hand fingers Keep your fingers as close as possible to the strings, with your fingertips pointing down towards the string to be played. Add fingers on the string as you go – the first, second and third fingers will be on the string at the end of the first group.

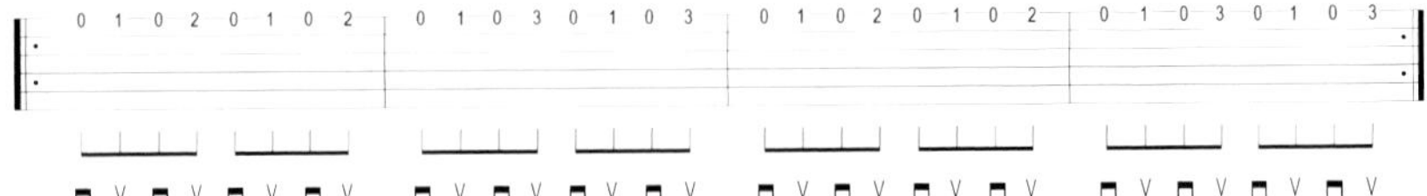

2. Gentle pressure Focus on pressing just hard enough to make the note – and no more. The lighter and more relaxed your fingers are, the faster you will be able to play. Be sure to keep each finger in first position on the corresponding fret.

READING RHYTHM

When reading music you need to know which notes to play – and you also need to know how long to play them for. Tab, like standard musical notation, has its own way of indicating the length of a note. Learning to read this element of tab language is the aim of this lesson.

The rhythm of any musical piece is made up of beats, which are the basic unit of measurement for notes. A note can last for one or more beats, or for fractions of a beat: a half, a quarter, or a shorter time. A single beat is equivalent to a crotchet. (It is also known, confusingly, as a quarter note, because in many pieces there are four beats to a bar.)

In standard notation, the length of a note is conveyed by the tadpole-like symbols variously named minims, quavers, semi-quavers, and so forth. In tab, the length of the notes is conveyed by the way they are spaced on the stave, and also by a system of lines drawn beneath the stave.

The symbols and their equivalents in standard notation are given below. Study the chart, then have a go at the tunes in the exercise opposite. Even if you are unfamiliar with musical notation you will see where the longer and shorter notes fall, and begin to grasp the system.

Tablature and standard notation

In this chart, standard music notation has been included alongside tab for reference. Rests (silences) have the same symbols in both tab and standard notation.

No of Beats	Tablature	Standard notation	Rest	Name
4				whole note (semibreve)
3				dotted half note (dotted minim)
2				half note (minim)
1				quarter note (crotchet)
1/2				eighth note (quaver)
1/4				sixteenth note (semi quaver)
1/8				thirty-second note (demi semi quaver)
				tied note

Exercises for reading and playing note length in tablature

Here are some exercises to get you used to playing longer and shorter notes. They are all tunes you are likely to know well – which should give you a headstart.

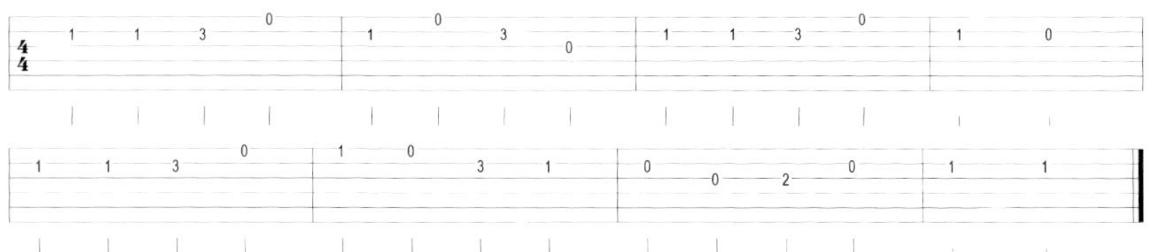

'Yankee Doodle' Keep your eyes on the page when playing and feel for the notes. The rhythm here is fairly constant, using mainly one-beat notes. There are two-beat notes in the fourth and eighth bars – be sure to leave a gap of one beat between each note in those by counting 1-2-3-4 and playing on beats one and three. In other words, play them for twice as long. Start slowly and with a steady rhythm and then try to speed up.

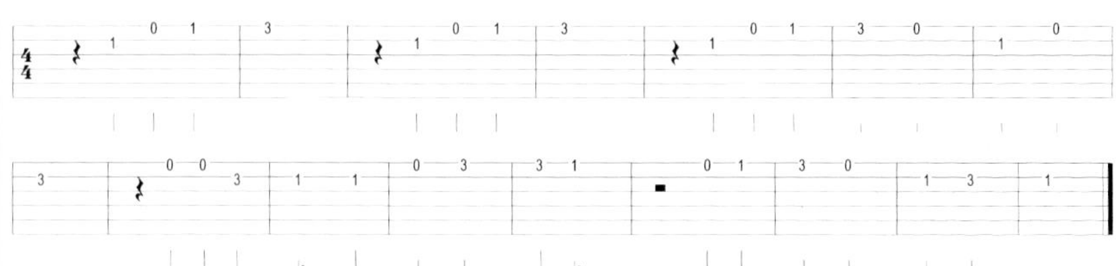

'When The Saints Go Marching In' Be careful of the rhythm here – wait on the four-beat notes and rests. Rests are musical silences, so make sure the sound is cut for the duration of the rest.

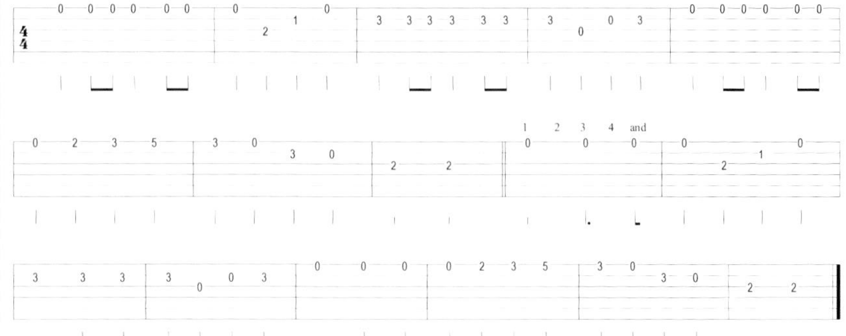

'What Shall We Do With The Drunken Sailor' In this tune the notes are repeated with a different rhythm the second time through. Take care over the complex rhythm in the ninth, eleventh and thirteenth bars. Remember: dotted-crotchet notes are one and a half beats. The rhythm of these bars can be counted as: 1 (2) 3 (4)& (leaving gaps for the beats in brackets). In the sixth and fourteenth bars the left hand should be one fret higher than usual so that the first finger is in the second fret, the second in the third, etc.

ADDING FLUENCY

To make your single-string playing sound more fluent you will need to learn some new tricks: the hammer-on, the pull-off and the slide. They are all ways of joining pairs of notes together smoothly and expressively, so achieving the effect known on other instruments as 'slurring'.

In all kinds of music it is common to blur the changes between different notes. Some instruments – the trombone, for example – are designed in such a way that sliding up and down the scale comes naturally. On the guitar, where each note is neatly and definitely divided from the next by a fret, some special techniques are required to achieve this effect.

With hammer-ons, pull-offs and slides it is the left hand that creates the slurred sound by moving on a string that is already vibrating. One advantage of these techniques is that your right hand has less work to do: plucking the string once gives rise to two or more notes. So, with practice, you should be able to play faster when slurring than when picking every note. In tab, slurs are indicated by a curved line, as shown in the exercises on these pages. Alternatively, you might see the abbreviations 'h.o.' and 'p.o.' (for 'hammer-on' and 'pull-off') between notes.

Hammer-on

Hammering-on is a technique for slurring notes upwards. In this example, the note slurs up from E to F. Play the open first string. As it sounds, use the first finger of the left hand to strike down firmly on the string in the first fret.

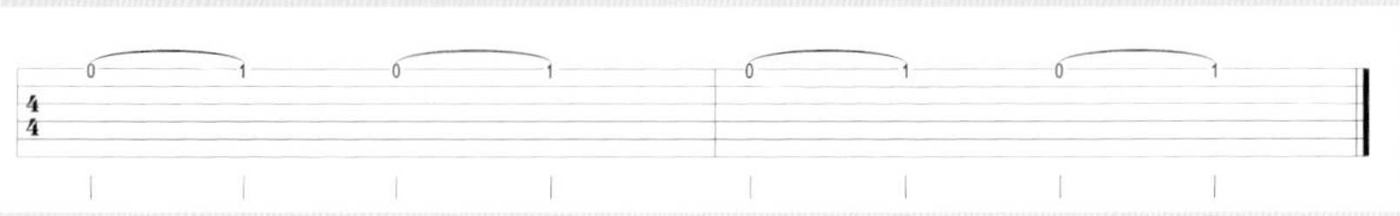

Pull-off

Pulling-off is a technique for slurring notes downwards. In this exercise you slur across two frets, and so two semitones – from C sharp down to B. Play the second string at the second fret with the second finger. After playing the note, pluck downwards with the second finger of the left hand, sounding the open string. The fingertip should come to rest on the first string.

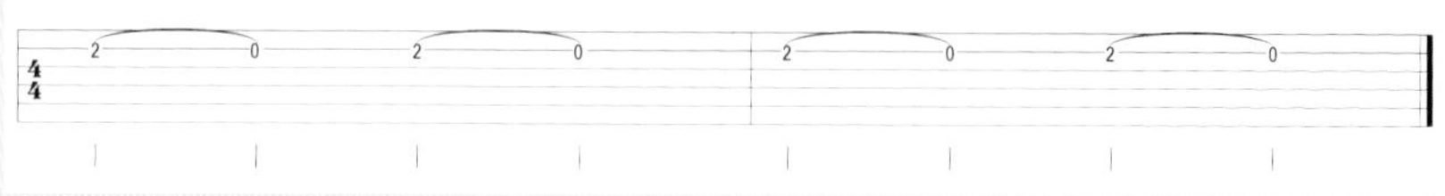

Slide

A slide connects two notes by dragging the finger along the string from one fret to another without releasing the pressure. You can connect any two notes this way – up or down – so long as they are on the same string. In tab, slides are indicated by a line connecting the two notes, either / or \ depending on whether the slide goes up or down in pitch.

In this exercise you slide up three frets (three semitones) from A to B and back. Using the second finger, play the second fret on the third string. After sounding the note, keep pressing the string and slide the finger up to the fifth.

Try this a few times. Move your whole arm as you slide and keep your thumb behind the second finger at all times. Pluck only the lower of the two notes. Try sliding backwards from the fifth fret to the second fret, too. Make the slide light and quick, so that you don't hear a jerky transition as you pass over the fourth and third fret wires.

Some simple slurring exercises

Here are some exercises that will help you to get used to hammering-on and pulling-off. Master the exercises that involve applying the techniques separately before moving on to the ones where they are combined. The final exercise requires you to do some tricky manoeuvres.

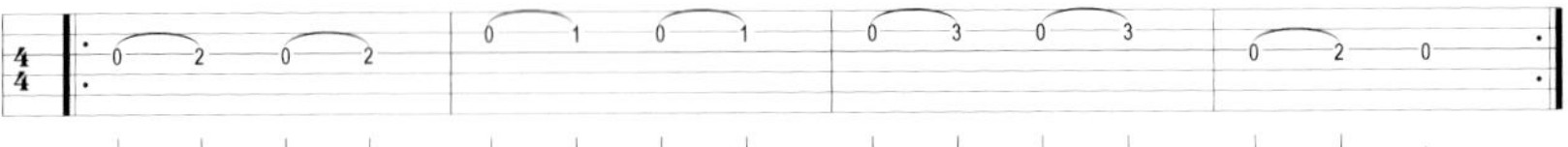

Melody using hammer-ons The aim here is to control the speed of your slurs and also to get an even sound from different fingers. You will need to work a little harder to get a solid sound from your third finger than your second, for example.

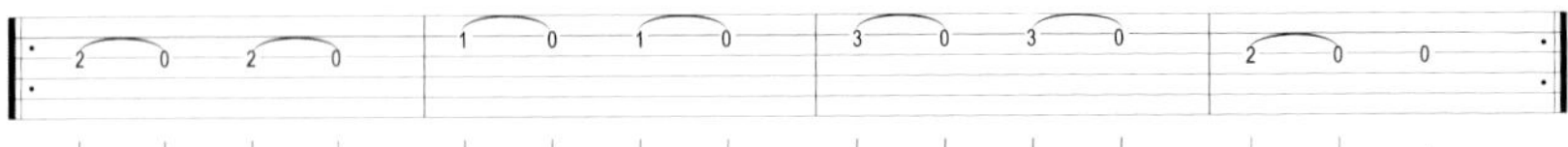

Melody using pull-offs Pull-offs are usually more difficult to control than hammer-ons. The focus here should be to pluck the string with the relevant left-hand finger as this will produce the best sound. Be careful not to let the finger slip through more than one string, and try to stay right on the fingertips throughout.

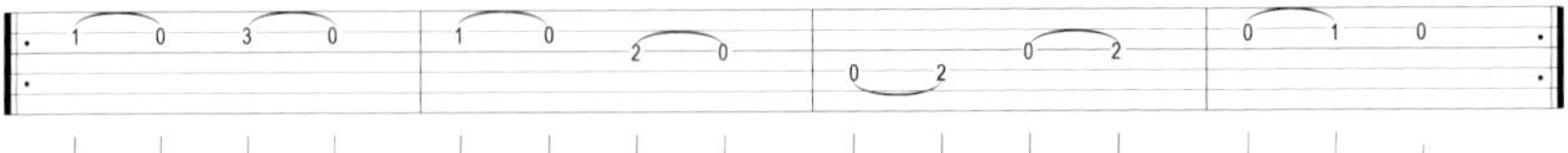

Hammer-ons and pull-offs combined Aim to even out the sound of both. As a general rule the plucked notes should be louder than the slurred notes.

Some difficult slurs Follow the rhythmic markings here, and be careful as the slurs in this exercise are less regularly spaced. In the second bar there is a hammer-on between the third and first frets. This is something you have not yet tried. To do this, hold and play the first fret and hammer the third finger on top – the first finger can stay in position throughout.

Blues licks

A 'lick' is guitarists' slang for a short series of notes that is often repeated when improvising or playing lead guitar. To put it another way, licks are short musical ideas, and also fixed finger patterns, that can be used as a kind of basic framework for a bluesy solo. Many blues guitarists construct all their solos from just a small repertoire of licks.

Hammer-ons, pull-offs and slides are one way of enlivening blues licks, and so are the focus of the exercises below. Pull-offs can sometime come out louder than hammer-ons, so listen carefully to the sound you make and try to gauge the pressure of your fingertips. For the slides, you will have to move your fingers out of position, then return to the normal shape.

An exercise in easy blues licks

For some more practice with hammer-ons, pull-offs and slides, try your hand at these easy blues licks. Wherever possible, stick to the first position (see pages 40-41) with your first finger in the first fret, second in second fret, and so on. Focus on getting an even sound.

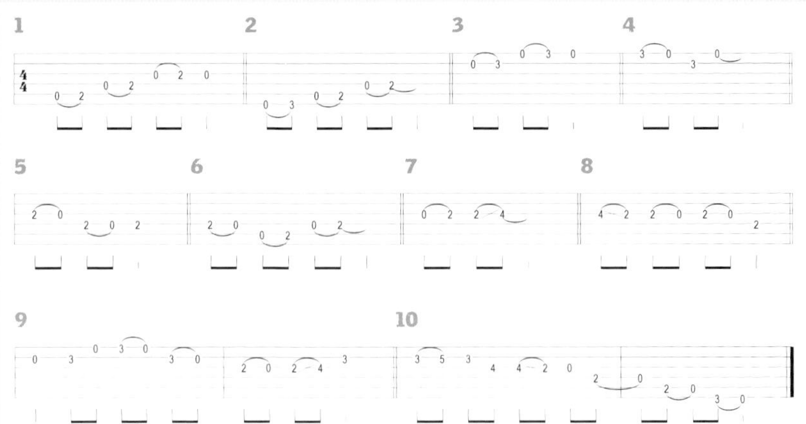

Simple licks, and not so simple licks These exercises begin easily, but numbers 9 and 10 here are harder because they require a change of position. At the close of example 9, slide up to the fourth fret with the second finger; use the first finger to press the second string at the third fret.

In example 10, start with the first finger in the third fret. Hammer on to the fifth fret with the third finger. Use the second finger on the third string, fourth fret, before sliding back to standard position for the rest of the exercise. The pull-offs are off the beat towards the end, but should be played exactly as before.

LESSON **14**

PLAYING CHORDS WITH MELODIES

Some very pleasing and varied effects can be achieved by strumming chords and picking out a tune in the course of the same piece of music. You are now ready to combine these two guitar techniques, and to learn to read chords in tab.

If you have already tried finding a tune within the notes of the chord you are playing, then you have experimented with combining chords and melody. But sometimes the notes of a tune are not in the chord that underpins it: you might have found that you have to seek out another note with your spare finger – a D on the third fret of the second string, say, when you are playing a C chord.

This kind of combination of chords and single notes is easily represented in tab, and if you are to play in an ordered, formal way then you will need to be able to read both. Chords in tab are written as stacks of numbers – which makes perfect sense, because you are being asked to play all six notes at once.

You will soon learn to recognize chords in tab just as easily as you can read chord diagrams. You will also begin to see that a run of notes is sometimes, in effect, a chord strung out over a bar or two. One way to play a sequence like this is to make the chord shape and pick the notes one at a time. As you get better, you may begin to feel that chords and single notes are not separate techniques at all, just part of the general business of guitar playing. And you would be right.

Reading chords in tab

When interpreting chords in tab, read from the first string down to the sixth. Play only the fret numbers written: a blank string is the equivalent of an 'X' in a chord symbol. Remember that the numbers represent frets not fingers.

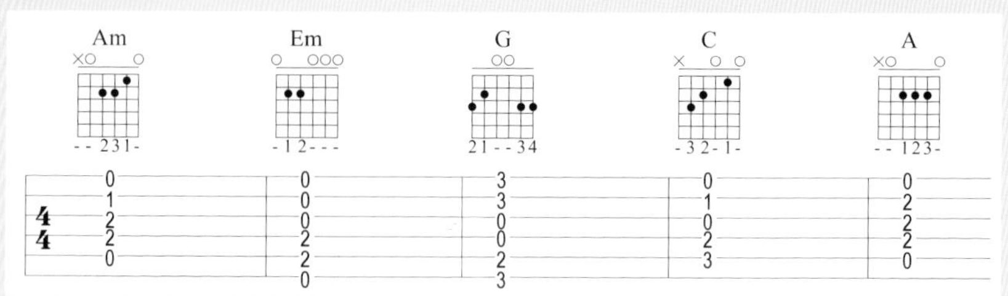

Simple combinations of chords and single-string playing

Here are three examples of tunes that can be played in combination with chords. This is an exercise in tab-reading as well as a new playing technique. Master each one before going on to the next exercise.

Tune on one string Strum each chord and hold for as long as possible. The melody is all on the first string until the very last chord. Miss out the first string on the final D chord.

Two-string melody Here the melody moves between the first and second string. In the second bar lift the first finger to play the open second string. In the third bar add the first finger to the E-minor chord to play the first fret on the second string.

Using all four fingers This exercise is a little more demanding. Use the spare fourth finger to reach the third fret while holding the C chord. In the second bar remove the first finger, then the third finger from the A-minor chord to play the open notes. In the third bar squash the first finger across the top two strings while holding the C chord as if preparing for the F, then use the fourth finger to reach fret three on the first string.

Right As a general rule, when combining chords and single-string playing, hold down the left-hand fingers for as long as possible, and so allow the notes to overlap. Your playing will have a less disjointed sound if you lift your fingers only when you need to. In this instance, the tune has been following a C chord, but is about to move on.

PLAYING ARPEGGIOS

'Arpeggio' is the proper musical term for a 'spread chord' or 'broken chord'. This is a technique whereby the notes of a chord are played individually: the notes overlap and ring together, but the feel and texture is very different from a straight strum.

A chord played slowly, string by string, is really an arpeggio. This is an effect that the guitar is very well suited to produce, as there are always six notes available to the player. Arpeggios can have a very simple structure – lowest note to highest, or vice versa – or they can take the form of intricately woven patterns of notes. Either way, a well-played arpeggio creates a beautiful and spellbinding effect.

The challenge in the exercises opposite is to play smoothly, so that the chords change without leaving an obvious gap in the sound. Care should be taken to follow the plucking directions precisely as this will aid the flow of your arpeggios.

Broken-chord exercises in tab

These exercises will get your right hand used to plucking the strings in turn.

C *let ring* C *let ring*

Play the C chord from the fifth to first strings like a slow strum. Then hold the C chord and pluck the strings in the order shown.

Em Am C Em

As you play the notes of the chord in sequence you will see that it is not always necessary to place the whole chord in one go. You can stagger the change by adding each finger in turn and then holding the chord. Look for connecting notes between chords – for example, the second finger from C to E minor.

Exercises in playing tunes with arpeggios

An interesting arpeggio is in effect a melody – one that drifts up and down the scale. Play these simple tunes with a plectrum, and follow the tab carefully.

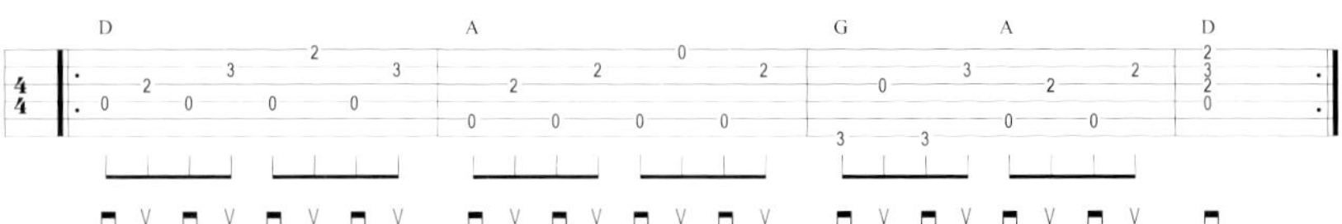

The plectrum returns to the bass note of the chord every other note, providing a pleasing drone. Finger only the notes that you need to play rather than holding the whole chord. For example, the G only requires two notes to be held. Use the second finger on the sixth string and the third finger on the second string.

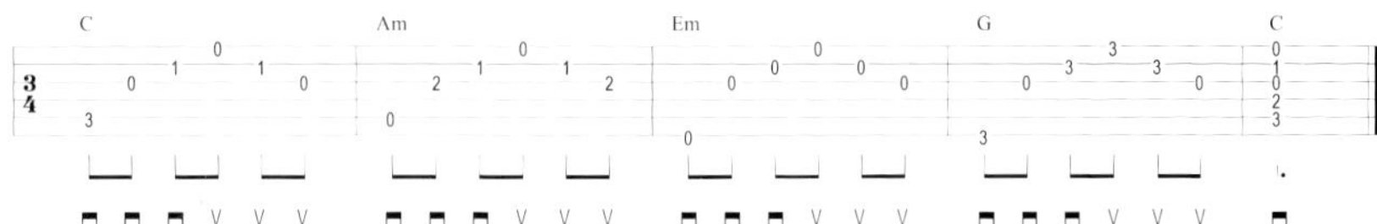

This is a very common arpeggio pattern with three downstrokes followed by three upstrokes to keep a circular motion. Note that the E minor does not require any fingers to be pressed down.

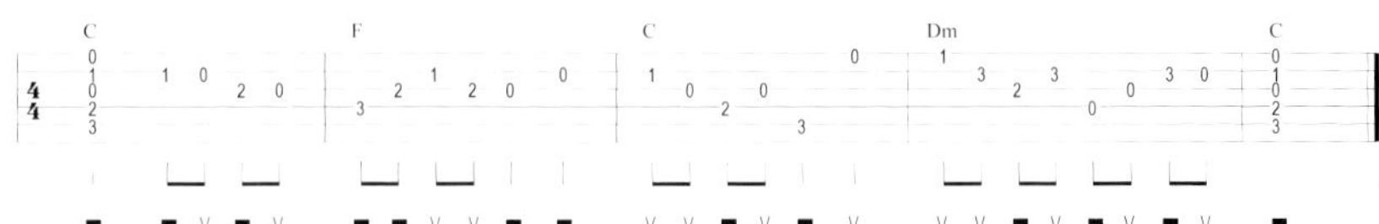

In this exercise we have a mixture of single-note and chordal playing. Follow the plucking directions exactly and hold the chord shapes where indicated. Let go of the chord completely for the second half of the first, second and fourth bars.

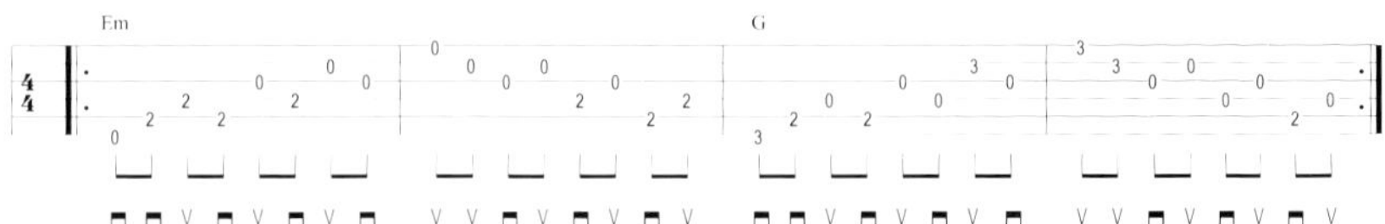

This is an excellent arpeggio picking exercise. Follow the directions accurately and gradually build up the speed. Notice how the right hand plays the same strings on both the Em and G chords. Play this one continuously and without looking at your right hand.

VOLUME
TONE

MOVING ON

This section is all about developing new skills. The lessons here will help expand the range and versatility of your playing, and so will pave the way to a variety of styles. Included in this section are some of the more common tricks of the trade – bar chords, soloing, string bending – along with tips on amplifiers and other electric gear. This section also covers the fundamentals of music theory; it contains a practical guide to reading music, and shows you how to apply fingerboard knowledge to your playing. Before embarking on this part of the book you should be strumming away confidently on the basic chord shapes, and also be ready for some new challenges.

BAR CHORDS

Bar chords involve using your first finger to press five or all six strings, and using the other fingers to form shapes. They allow you to play some unusual chords such as F-sharp (F♯) or B-flat (B♭), and also to form more familiar chords further up the neck of the guitar.

The principle behind bar chords is that you use the shapes you already know but use your first finger to raise the pitch. So, for example, if you bar the first fret and play an E-shape with the other three fingers, you have an F, which is a semitone higher than E. (This is a more advanced and versatile way of playing an F than the shape you have already learned). Once you can do bar chords well, you may well find it more convenient to use them for the common change from F to G (a barred E-shape on the third fret) than to move your fingers to different positions.

At first, however, you should expect the left hand to feel a little tired when practising bar chords, especially the thumb muscle and the bar finger. Your fingers will get used to it, and the chords will become easier with practice. Eventually bar chords will become one of the most frequently used techniques in your repertoire.

Forming a bar chord

We are using E major, one of the easier and most frequently used shapes, as an introduction to bar chords.

First play a standard E chord with the first, second and third fingers. Now play the same frets and strings but switch to the second, third and fourth fingers, leaving the first free. Slide the shape up one fret so that you are pressing in the second and third frets. Finally, flatten the first finger across all the strings in the first fret.

In this position, try to keep the first finger as flat as possible. Push your wrist further forward than usual so you can place the chord shape neatly on the fingertips. And don't press too hard: this is a common error that will place unnecessary strain on your hand and wrist. Only the sixth, second and first strings need to sound clear, so don't worry about the third, fourth and fifth. Make sure the thumb moves position with the fingers: keep it roughly behind the second finger. An E-shape played on this fret is an F major.

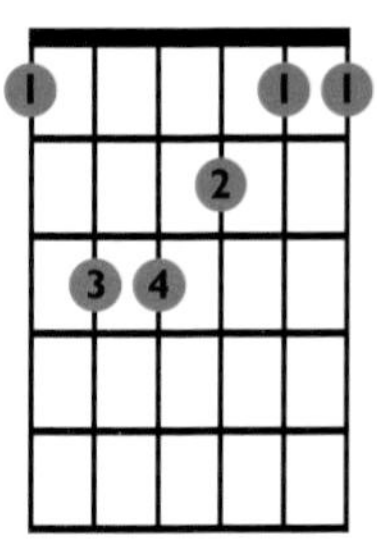

E-shape

Exercise: more bar chord shapes

Here are some more bar chord shapes to practise. The A-shape is by far the hardest, especially when played high up the neck, as you are required to do in the first exercise. Persevere: practice makes perfect, and effort invested at this stage will pay dividends later.

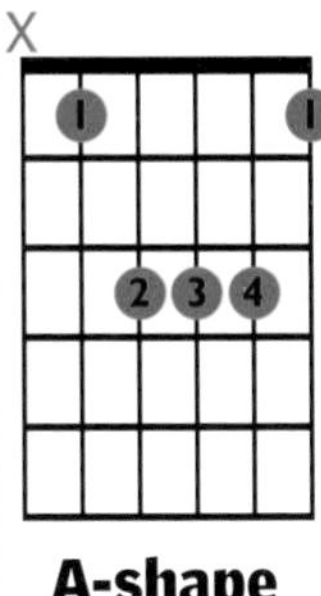

A-shape

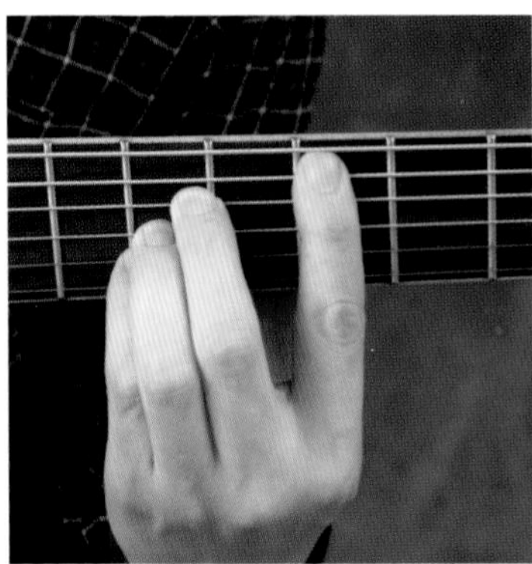

Here you are playing an A-shape bar chord on the fifth fret, making a D chord. First, play a standard A chord. Now play the same shape but use the second, third and fourth fingers. Slide the shape up five frets so that all fingers are now in the seventh fret. Flatten the first finger across the first to fifth strings in the fifth fret, not touching the sixth.

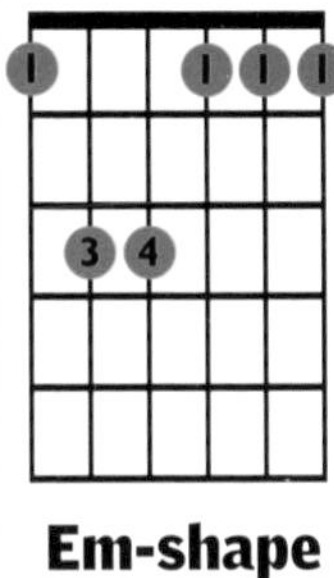

Em-shape

The E-minor shape is almost the same as the E-major shape but without pressing the second finger on the third string (which makes it easier). The important note here is the third string, as this will determine the minor sound of the chord. Pay extra attention to making this string ring clear.

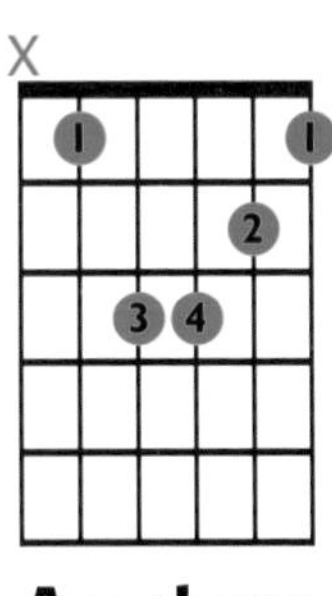

Am-shape

The A-minor bar-chord shape, like the E minor, is a little easier than the major. You can think of this as being identical to the E-major shape but with everything moved up one string. Remember to cut the bar down to five strings: the sixth string is not played.

MOVING THE BAR

Once you can make bar shapes, the next task is to be able to move the bar comfortably and cleanly from one fret to another. The learning process is exactly like mastering changes between chords: slow and difficult at first but easier and more natural the more you practise.

When moving from one bar chord to another you need to be able to get to the right fret and form the shape in the course of a single beat, so that you don't make a mess of the chord or (worse) interrupt the flow of the music. This is not an easy thing to achieve, and the aim of this lesson is to help you to get good at it. The exercises opposite are all about developing this key skill.

Sharps and flats

You'll need to back up the practical work with a little theory. One of the benefits of bar chords is that they allow you to play the sharps and flats. Most of the notes in a scale are a tone apart, which equates to a two-fret gap (see the diagram below). A one-fret gap is a 'semitone'. These in-between notes are known as either 'sharps' (indicated by the ♯ symbol) or 'flats' (indicated by the ♭ symbol). A sharp is one fret or semitone higher than the main note; a flat is one lower.

It follows that a note played at the fourth fret on the sixth string can be termed a G-sharp (a semitone above G, the third fret) or an A-flat (a semitone below A, the fifth fret). Which name to use depends on a particular musical convention, and for the time being we will stick to sharps to avoid confusion.

Which chord am I barring?

This diagrams shows the positions known as 'root notes'. It functions as a guide to bar chords because it tells you that an E-shape played at the seventh fret is a B, and an A-shape played at the fifth fret is a D. Note that there is no sharp between E and F, or between B and C. These notes are only one fret apart on the guitar, because they are one semitone apart in the musical scale.

String													
5	A	♯	B	C	♯	D	♯	E	F	♯	G	♯	A
Fret	0	1	2	3	4	5	6	7	8	9	10	11	12
6	E	F	♯	G	♯	A	♯	B	C	♯	D	♯	E

Practising bars in different positions

Here are some exercises to get you used to moving bar chords up the neck. You will find that the chords are harder to play cleanly the further up the neck you go.

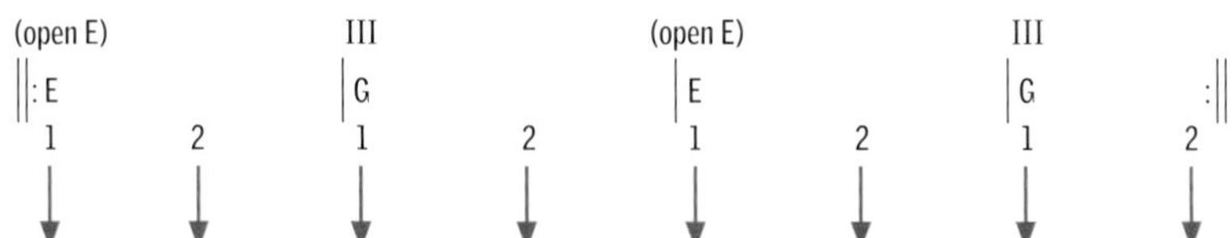

A simple E-shape exercise Start by playing an E chord, but with the second, third and fourth fingers. Slide this shape up the neck, and bar the first finger across the third fret. Release the pressure slightly as you slide up, but stay in contact with the strings and don't let the fingers come unstuck.

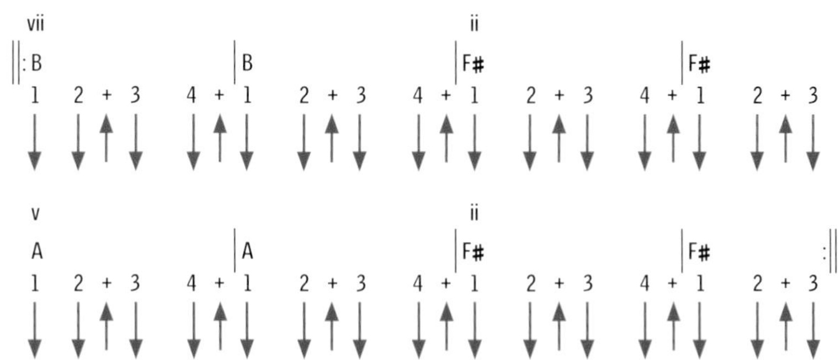

A harder E-shape exercise When shifting from the seventh fret to the second (marked here with Roman numerals), relax the pressure on the chord and glide down the string keeping the shape together. Make sure that the left-hand thumb travels with the rest of the hand, maintaining its position behind the second finger. This will reduce the effort involved in forming the bar.

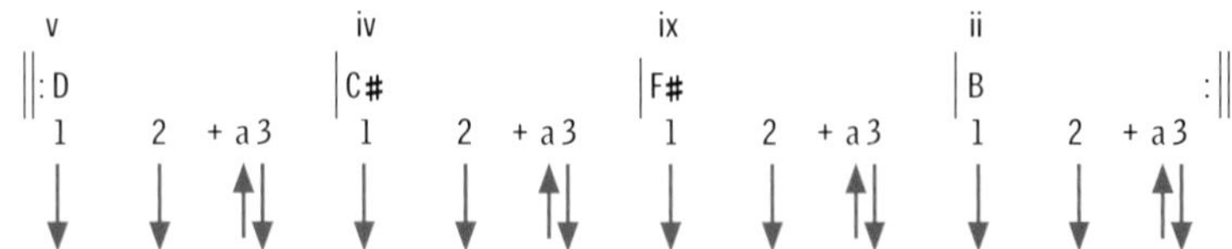

A-shape exercise The main focus in this difficult exercise is to keep the one-fret gap between the bar and the rest of the fingers. Be aware of the frets becoming narrower the further you go up the neck – you will need to adjust the shape accordingly, and make sure that the fingers are correctly spaced.

CHANGING BAR CHORDS

If you are to use bar chords freely in your playing, you need to get used to the changes from open chords to bar chords and from one bar chord to another. Once you can do this you will then be equipped to play all the most frequently encountered chords and progressions.

Bar chords are hard, but the ability to play them well makes a huge difference. Try playing a C by making a barred E at the eighth fret, for example. All the notes are higher, so this chord has a zingy quality that is not present when you play a standard open C.

At the level you have now reached, bar chords are more or less unavoidable. The change from C to F, for example, is one of the most common progressions in music: you should practise it until it is second nature. The move from E to B or B7 – an A or A7-shape played on the second fret – is another change that is frequently encountered, since it forms part of the 12-bar blues in E, the easiest key in which to play that kind of music.

The change from one bar chord to another is in many ways harder than the change from an open chord to a bar. It requires you to move cleanly while continuing to exert the right amount of pressure on the barred fret. You can often hear when a guitarist is struggling with such a move, because the chord sounds dull and muted.

Barred changes that remain on the same fret (say, F♯m to A♯m) are easier to pull off than ones that require you both to move the bar and to change the shape – say, B (an A-shape on the second fret) to G (an E-shape on the third fret). The exercises on the opposite page concentrate on this most tricky aspect of playing progressions using bar chords.

Left When you move from the E-minor shape to the A-minor shape, take the opportunity to relax your first finger for a moment. It is possible to keep contact with the string without depressing the string to the fret. This way you can still use the strings as a guide but your hand won't get as tired.

Exercise: bar chord sequences

Try these exercises here to familiarize yourself with moving between the major bar-chord shapes.

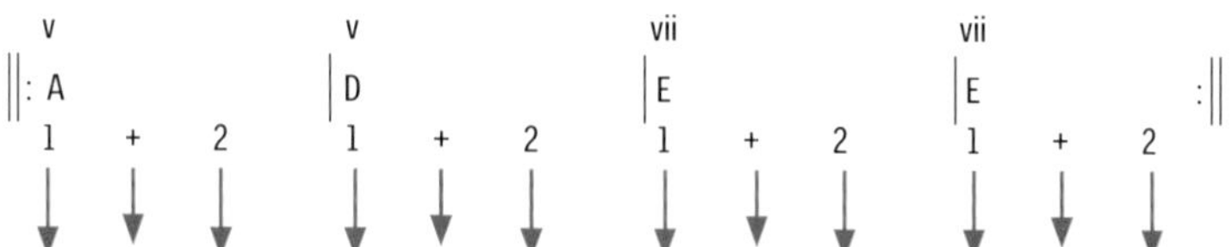

Combining E-shape and A-shape bar chords In this exercise, stick to downstrokes only. Jump cleanly across the strings and change the shape in mid air. Slide the whole shape two frets higher when changing from D to E.

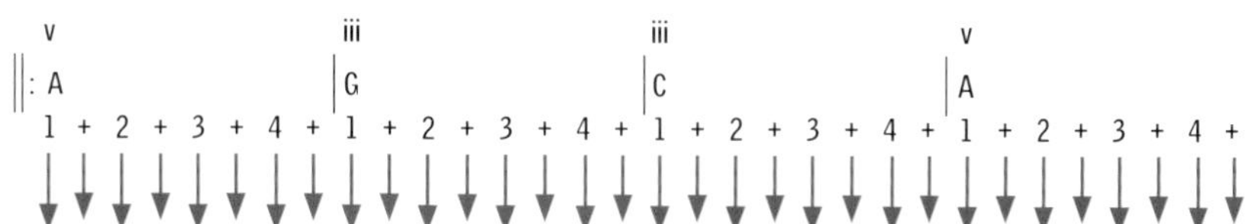

A standard rock-guitar progression For a slightly easier change, try playing the C chord with a flattened third finger in an A-shape over the fourth, third and second strings. This way of forming the chord is not quite as neat as the three-finger version but is fine for this style of music.

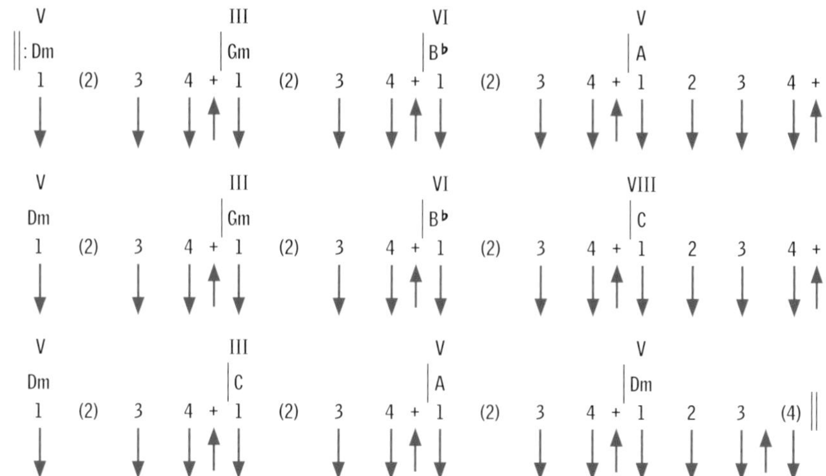

Combining all the bar-chord shapes Find the root notes first – you might like to write the fret number above the chord on the exercise as a guide. Use the fret dots on your guitar as a way of remembering the notes. If you know that the fifth fret is an A on the sixth string and a D on the fifth string, you can then use it as a reference point for all the other notes.

POWER CHORDS

A power chord is a kind of reduced bar chord that sounds best when played loud on an electric guitar. It is like a bar chord because the shape can move up and down the neck. You only play the lower notes, which makes for a hard, menacing sound.

Power chords are a really good technique to acquire if you are into heavier styles of music – punk or heavy metal, for example. They are of less use if you are only interested in playing folk acoustic. These chords sound great when played with distortion (see pages 112–114). If you do not have a preset distortion on your amplifier, you can achieve a similar effect by turning the gain up high. Turn the master volume down to compensate.

There are two main shapes – see the diagrams, above right. One of them starts on the sixth string and one on the fifth. Power chords are usually indicated by a '5' after the letter name – A5, D5. This shorthand refers to the fact that they are designed to consist solely of the first and fifth note of the scale: this is what gives them their grungy sound.

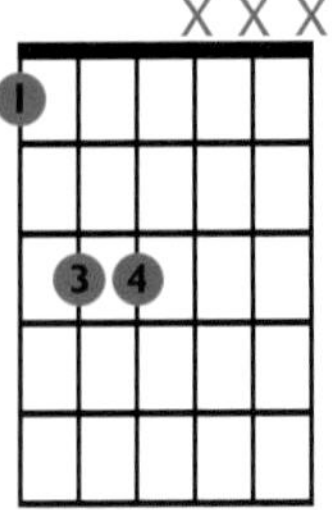

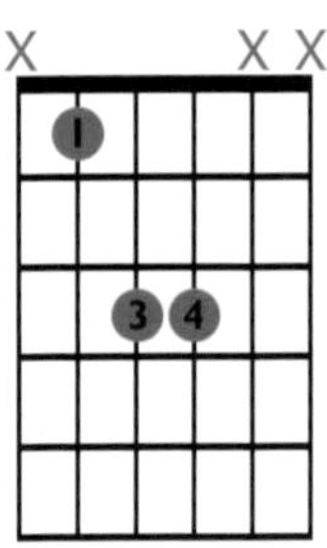

Above The two moveable power-chord shapes: sixth-string (left) and fifth-string (right).

Sixth-string power chord

When playing the sixth-string power chord, the top three strings should not sound at all. The first finger, although it is in the bar position, merely touches those strings to mute the notes. Angle your finger in such a way that it doesn't press down on them. The third and fourth fingers should be placed together as a

Finding the right fret

The letter name of the power chord will change depending on the fret covered by the first finger. In order to find your way around you will need to know the names of the notes on both the sixth and fifth strings.

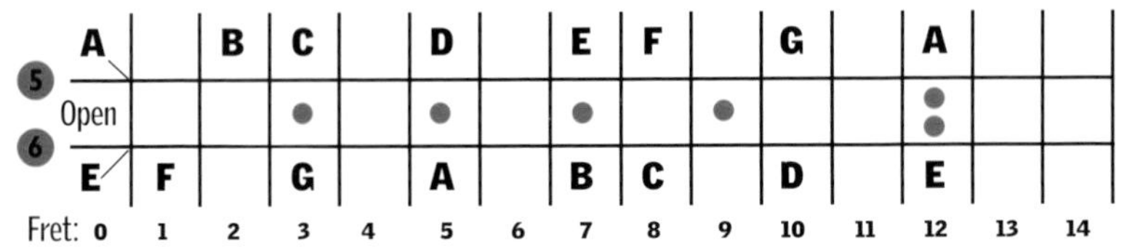

Above A power chord on the sixth string. Notice how the first finger of the left hand lies flat across the neck but does not press down on the higher strings.

unit on the fourth and fifth strings. The left hand is now covering all six strings, but when strummed only the fourth, fifth and sixth strings will sound. This allows the guitarist to play with maximum force without having to worry about limiting the scope of the stroke.

Fifth-string power chord

For the power chord starting on the fifth string, simply move the whole shape up one string from the sixth. The tip of the first finger can mute the sixth string as a safeguard, but the right hand should still aim to strike the fifth string directly. Only the fifth, fourth and thirds strings should sound when you play this chord.

A power chord exercise

Jump cleanly across the strings in the same fret. Keep the shape rigid and use the upstroke to help you change by playing the open strings while you move.

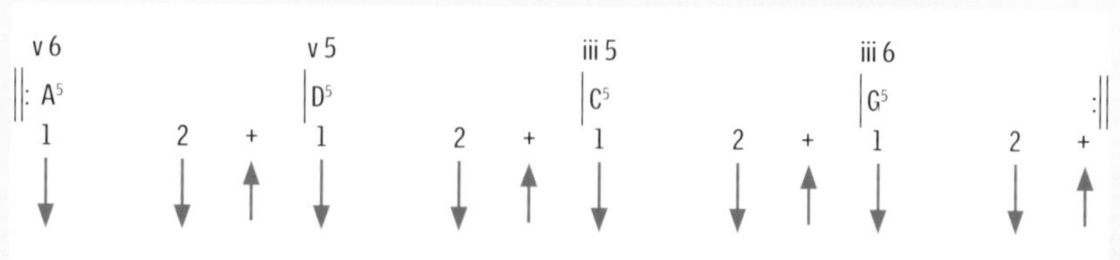

DAMPING

The technique known as damping is a means of stopping the vibration of the strings in a controlled manner. It is a skill that allows you to cut off the resonance of the guitar, or to create sharper-sounding rhythms when you are strumming.

Damping is most usually used to bring the guitar's sound to a crisp and definite stop at the end of a piece. It can also create a striking effect in the middle of a piece by engineering a beat or two of silence. Used this way before a big chord, it can sound quite dramatic.

Right-hand damping

To damp the string with your right hand, first try strumming an E chord with a downstroke. Once your plectrum has left the first string, immediately rest the heel of your right hand and the side of your thumb across all six strings, cutting the strings with one movement. The plectrum should come to rest at a point just outside the first string.

Left-hand damping

Left-hand damping can be performed in two ways. The first is simply to relax the fingers pressing the strings so that there is not enough pressure to make the note sound. The second way is to use a free finger to cover the strings – the slightest touch will be enough to cut the sound.

The first is used most effectively with bar chords and power chords. Try playing an A major bar chord at the fifth fret and releasing the pressure suddenly to stop the sound. Squeeze the chord when you want to hear the notes and empty the hand of tension to cut the sound crisply. To practise, keep the fingers in position on the strings at all times while simply squeezing and relaxing the hand.

The second method is commonly used when playing standard chord shapes. Most of these incorporate open strings which will keep on ringing unless you do something to stop them. To practise this method, play an E chord, lift and flatten your fourth (little) finger lightly across the strings to cut the sound while relaxing the pressure at the same time.

Whichever method of damping you use, be decisive about it. You should aim to cut the sound completely, and to avoid buzzy and over-ringing notes.

TIP

You can use damping to add colour to your strumming patterns. Do continuous downstrokes and upstrokes while playing bar chords, and release/apply pressure on different beats. Try damping over the fretboard for a sound like a snare drum.

Three ways to damp

With the right hand Note the finishing position of the plectrum, outside the strings.

With the left hand Play a bar chord, and then release the pressure on the strings to cut the resonation.

With one finger Lightly touch the string or strings you want to damp – the slightest contact will kill the sound.

Damping exercises

In these exercises you put the various damping techniques into a musical context, and so learn how damping can be used in a variety of ways. The instruction to dampen is denoted by a letter 'X' in the midst of the strumming pattern.

Use the side of the thumb and the heel of the hand to stop the strings, making sure that the plectrum stays outside the first string ready to perform an upstroke immediately afterwards.

This is a very common strumming pattern. Block the strings with the right hand as before. If you block the note with more force this can add a layer of percussion to the strumming, which makes for an interesting effect. Block hard enough so that the strings hit the frets.

G A B A

1 + 2 + 3 + 4 + | 1 + 2 + 3 + 4 + | 1 + 2 + 3 + 4 + | 1 + 2 + 3 + 4 +

X X X X X X | X X X X X X | X X X X X X | X X X X X X

Use two bar chords for this exercise (at the seventh and fifth frets). Strum continuously and relax the pressure on the chord where marked with an 'X'. This will create a 'scratching' effect.

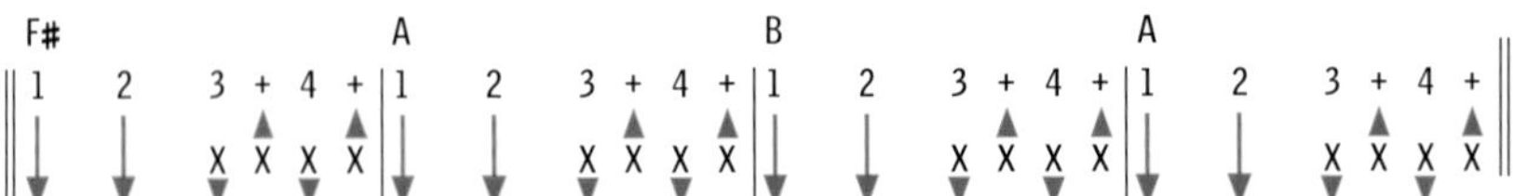

In this exercise we have three bar chords and a different rhythm. The muted notes should still be strummed – use them to help the change of chord by relaxing the pressure on the strings and then sliding the chord over beats three and four.

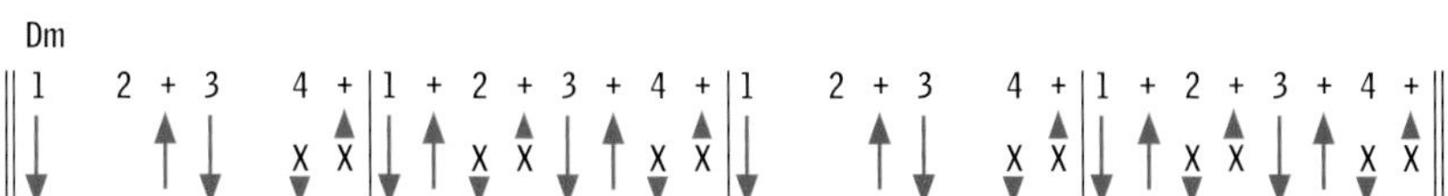

Use a D minor chord at the fifth fret, and squeeze the chord on and off to create this funky rhythm.

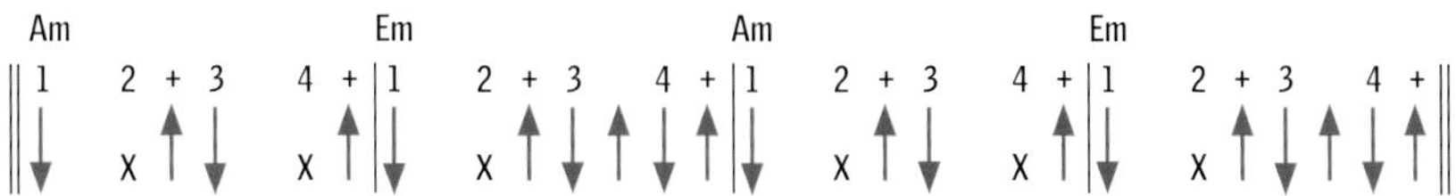

Use the little finger of the left hand to help damp the open strings. Release the pressure on the chord at the same time for a clean stop.

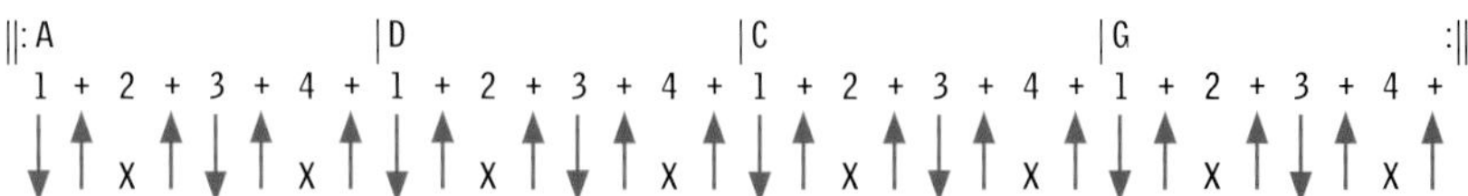

The little finger needs to work hard in this exercise. Practise very slowly at first before building up speed. Use a combination of left- and right-hand damping to ensure that the rhythmic stops are crisp.

Chelsea girl Damping can be used not only to put a stop to a sound, but also as a textural part of a strumming pattern. Left-hand damping is a feature of Joni Mitchell's song 'Big Yellow Taxi', for example. Right-hand damping can be heard in her song 'California'.

LESSON 21

PALM MUTING

Palm muting means using the right hand to suppress the vibration of the strings, inhibiting the sound without cutting it out completely. It is a way of controlling the sound of the instrument by preventing ringing and unwanted resonance, which in some situations can sound messy.

Palm muting is deployed in many styles of guitar playing, but it has a particular importance to guitarists playing distorted electric guitar. In this context, the muting provides a contrast in the tonal and dynamic qualities. A slight movement of the right hand allows a player to move instantly from a restrained, almost throttled sound to the explosive effect of full power.

The term palm muting is a misnomer, since it is not the palm of the hand that touches the strings, but the side of the hand closest to the little finger – that is, the part of the hand that normally hovers above the strings without touching.

To get in position for palm muting, place the hand alongside and fractionally to the left of the bridge. The hand should be above the strings and the plectrum should be at the ready to play. To mute the strings, rest the hand lightly and gently on the strings alongside the bridge. The strings should still sound when you play, but the resonance will be subdued and short-lived.

Above The right hand in position for palm muting. Place the hand vertically alongside the bridge so that it is covering the strings with the plectrum in position.

METAL **GUITAR**

Heavy metal has its origins in the 1960s and 1970s. It grew out of the high-energy blues-rock of bands such as Led Zeppelin. Early metal bands such as Black Sabbath were fond of using macabre imagery in their lyrics, which they combined with a somewhat doom-laden, guitar-driven sound. This set the template for the genre: metal is characterized by thick, distorted guitars played at speed and high volume with insistent rhythms and extravagant solo excursions.

Suggested listening

Deep Purple, Metallica, Slayer, Black Sabbath, Iron Maiden, Motörhead, Guns N' Roses, Kiss.

Exercises in palm muting

On open strings The letters P.M. above the stave stand for palm muting, which should continue for the duration of the dotted line. Practise playing the sixth string open. Listen to the sound and adjust the distance of your hand from the bridge. You should still be able to hear the pitch clearly.

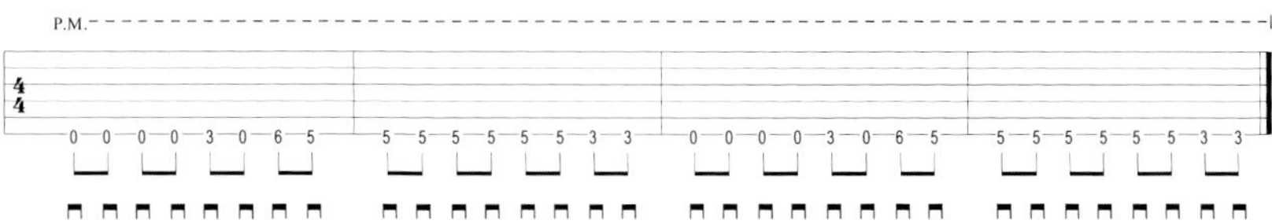

This is a riff all on the sixth string using only downstrokes. Keep the left hand in third position – first finger in the third fret, second finger in the fourth fret, etc. Work up the speed gradually and repeat many times.

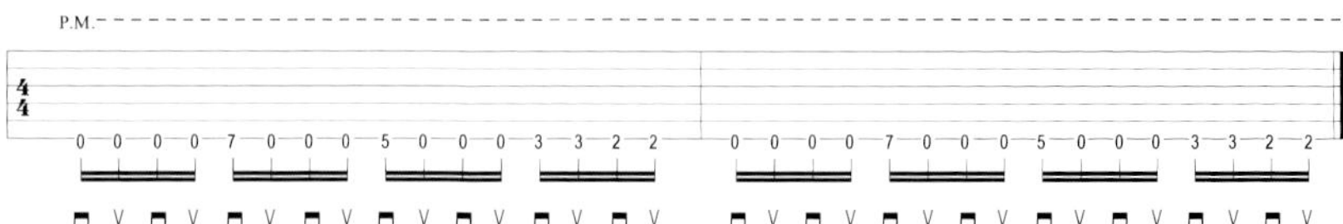

This exercise involves some jumping around of the left hand. Alternate downstrokes and upstrokes and keep the right hand stationary, muting the sixth string at all times.

With power chords Palm muting is often used with power chords and a distorted amp setting. This allows for a big contrast in dynamics. You can move from a restrained, almost throttled sound when palm muted to full power just by lifting your hand away from the strings. In the exercises below, lift the hand where indicated to let the notes ring.

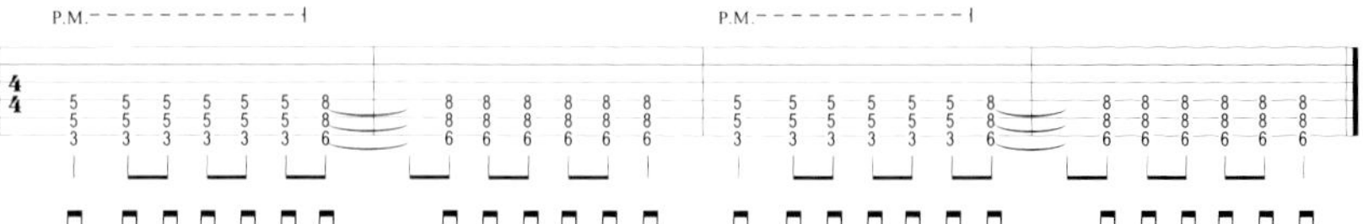

Palm-mute the G power chord (third fret) and release the right hand explosively on the change of chord. Be careful of the rhythm here and watch out for the notes tied across the bar line.

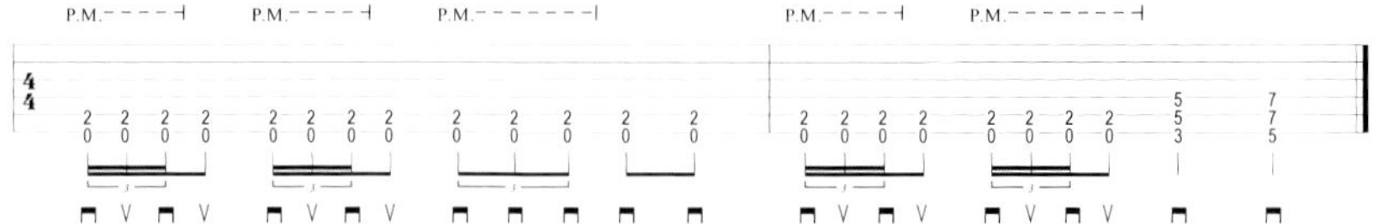

This is an example of what metal guitarists call 'galloping'. Galloping describes very fast short bursts of notes – the triplet groups at the beginning of this exercise are an example. Follow the palm-muting marks very closely and notice how the right hand lifts off at the end of each group on an upstroke.

EASY SOLOING

By now you may well feel ready to have a go at playing lead guitar. Improvising a guitar solo might seem like a daunting challenge, but it is much easier than you think. The key to it is to stick to the set of notes known as the 'pentatonic scale'.

The word 'pentatonic' means 'five notes', which is to say that in the pentatonic scale you play only five notes in each octave. On the guitar, this translates into a fixed-finger pattern that you can play at any point on the fretboard (that is, in any key). The pattern is easy to learn, and if you stick to it you will never play a bad note when you solo.

This is the simple secret behind nearly all the great guitar solos in rock music. Once you master the pentatonic scale, you should be able to play along with some of your favourite songs, and you will be able to jam a solo of your own when playing with other guitarists.

The finger pattern that you need to know is given in the first exercise on the opposite page. It can be moved anywhere on the neck. The root note is determined by the starting position of the first finger on the sixth string. So for instance, at the fifth fret the root note is A; start here and you will be able to improvise a solo to any song in the key of A or A minor. It is easy to spot the key in which any song is played: it is almost invariably corresponds to the satisfyingly conclusive chord on which it ends.

Above Left-hand spacing at the fifth fret. This one finger per fret approach helps you to keep your hand in position. The fourth finger will feel awkward at first, but it will grow stronger and more flexible as you use it.

Effective soloing

The exercises opposite are designed to get you playing fragments of the pentatonic scale and making use of the notes available. You don't need to play the whole scale when improvising – that would make for a very boring solo! Use just a few notes at first, perhaps starting on the middle strings and slowly moving further up and down. To get an idea of how it is working, get someone to accompany you with simple chord progressions – or make a recording of yourself and improvise along to that.

Exercises using the pentatonic scale

These exercises will help you to get familiar with the shapes of the pentatonic scale.

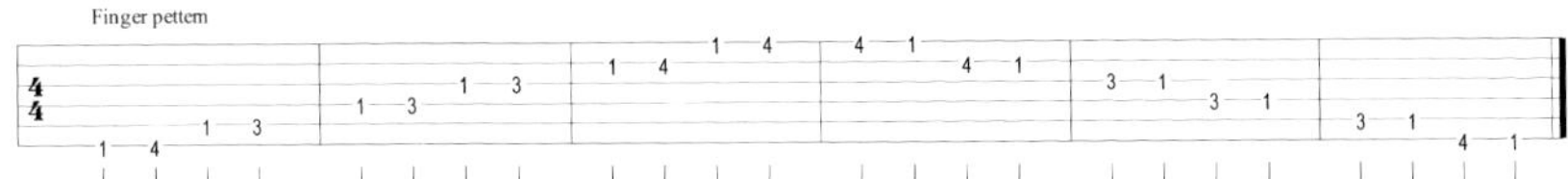

The pentatonic scale in tab showing the finger numbers Treat the tab here as finger numbers rather than fret numbers. Start with the first finger at the fifth fret and make sure your fingers are spaced properly with the second finger at the sixth fret, the third at the seventh fret, and so on.

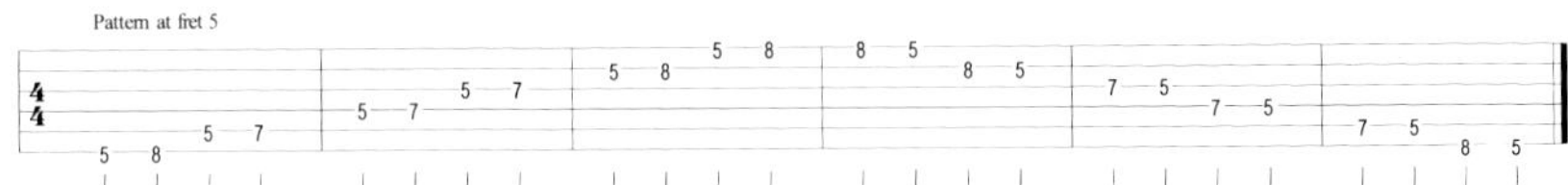

The pentatonic scale in tab showing the fret numbers Play through the scale using downstrokes until it feels comfortable. Then try alternating downstrokes and upstrokes. This works well as there are two notes to play on each string.

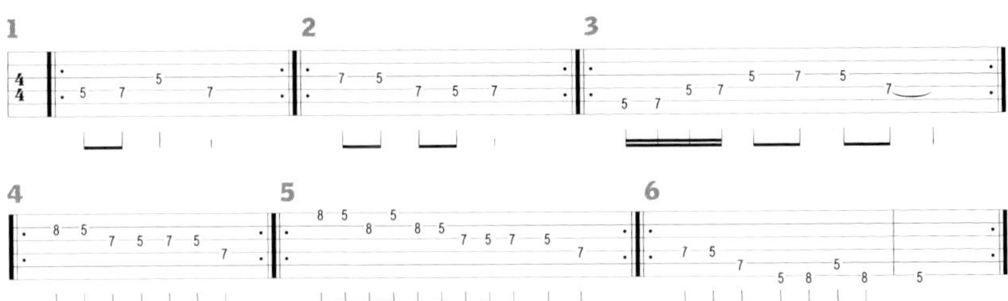

Six riffs Each of the six exercises above uses the seventh fret as its 'home note'. Each pass gets a little more adventurous. Remember to stick to the one-finger-per-fret rule.

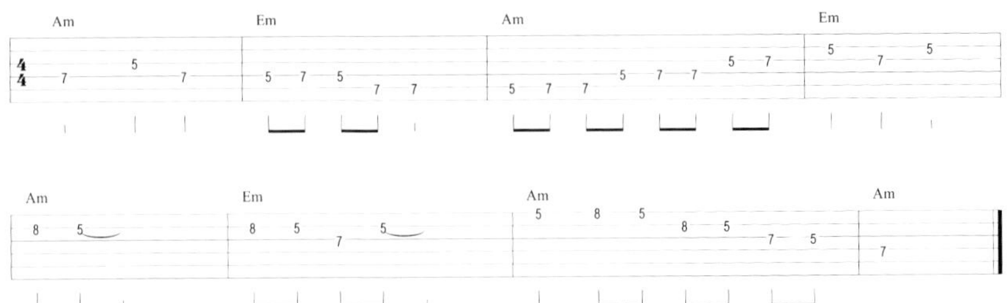

Improvising to chord progressions Use the ideas in the example above as a starting point and experiment with different combinations. Start on the safe ground of the middle strings before moving to a higher register to finish. That way, your solo will have a pleasing shape. This piece begins at the fifth fret (A). You could also try using the scale with the following chord progressions at the same fret: Am-G-F-G; A-D-E. This is a blues progression – see pages 84–85 for more on the blues.

SLURS IN SOLOS

The slurring techniques that you already know – hammer-ons, pull-offs and slides – are a vital part of any guitar solo. When performing for an audience, you should use them sparingly, mixing them in with single notes to vary the effect and highlight the solo tricks.

Less is always more when you are on stage, but not when you are practising. While you are learning the solo slur techniques, you should feel free to deploy hammer-ons and pull-offs as much as you like. Once you can bend notes (see page 76) you can incorporate that technique, too. But be minimalist occasionally: sometimes it can be very effective to play the same note repeatedly over a key change.

A very good way to improve your playing is to listen to some recorded guitar solos: you will be surprised by

Top and above The preparation and execution of a hammer-on. This is a smooth way of slurring up in a solo – in this case by one whole tone.

Top and above The preparation and execution of a pull-off, on the same string and fret as the hammer-on shown left.

Above Hammer-on and pull-off in one movement: making ready (left), execution two frets above the lower note (middle), final position of third finger (right).

how often a memorable riff is made up a very brief melodic line using a very small number of notes. Remember this when you are playing, and aim to repeat short ideas when putting your improvisation together. Playing in recurrent 'phrases' will make much more musical sense than an aimless and rambling stream of notes.

Both in one

When you feel confident, try hammering on and pulling off in one movement. This allows you to play three notes with one pluck of the string, and so creates an impression of speed. Bear in mind, though, that faster is not necessarily better. Don't try to play more swiftly than your technique will allow. You will naturally become more nimble fingered as you practise. The main aim for now is to make pleasing music.

ROCK **GUITAR**

Rock music owes much of its musical language to the blues. Many bands of the 1960s and 1970s took their inspiration from recordings of early bluesmen and adapted the style to electric guitar that could fill stadiums with sound.

Rock has evolved in many directions since then, but the blues influence is still there, like a family resemblance passed down through the generations. The familiar cadences and finger patterns of the pentatonic scale can be detected in the progressive-rock guitar-playing of David Gilmour (Pink Floyd), and the very different but equally virtuoso playing of artists such as Slash (Guns N' Roses).

Suggested listening

Jimi Hendrix, Eric Clapton (Cream), Jimmy Page (Led Zeppelin), Guns N' Roses, Pearl Jam, Red Hot Chilli Peppers, The Edge (U2).

Wish you were him Dave Gilmour plays a highly melodic and almost dream-like style of rock guitar.

Solo hammer-on and pull-off exercises

Here are some exercises in using slurs as a solo trick.

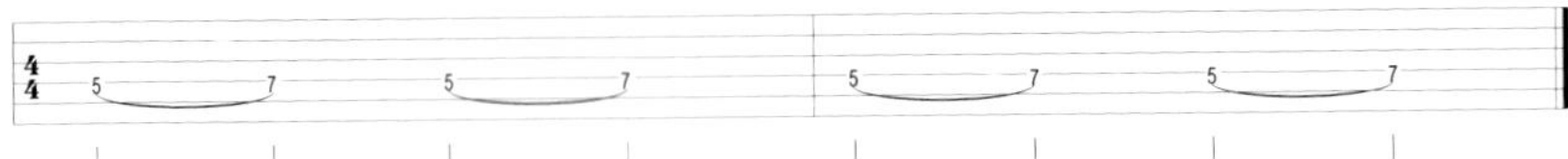

Hammer-on Play the fourth string, fifth fret. With the third finger of the left hand 'hammer' down on the fourth string at the seventh fret. The first finger can remain on the string.

A scale with hammer-ons Now try playing part of the pentatonic scale using hammer-ons on the fifth, fourth and third strings. After a little practice you should find that you can play this series of notes faster than if you were plucking them individually. Using hammer-ons helps with coordination and will make your playing sound a great deal smoother.

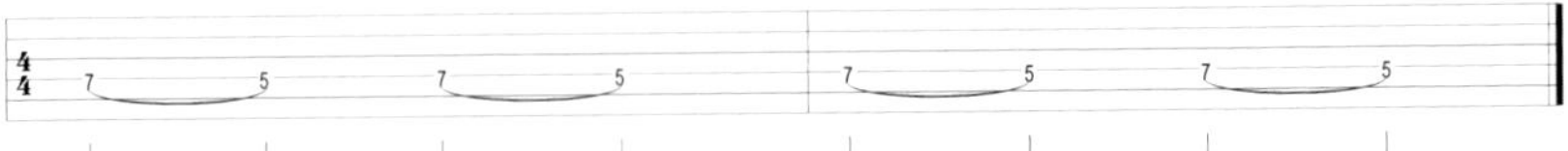

Pull-off Press the fourth string, seventh fret, with the third finger. The first finger should be ready at the fourth string, fifth fret. With both notes ready, play the seventh fret and pluck downwards with the third finger, sounding the prepared fifth-fret note. The third finger should come to rest on the third string. Try making this movement on other strings and other parts of the neck.

A scale with pull-offs Here is part of the pentatonic scale which you should play using pull-offs. Begin with the fourth finger at the eighth fret and work downwards. Make sure each pair of notes is prepared in advance, and that the higher finger plucks the string solidly before coming to rest on the string below.

Exercise in using slur techniques in the pentatonic scale

When you first tried using hammer-ons and pull-offs you were were going from open-string notes to fretted notes and vice versa. But now that you are working with the pentatonic scale, you will need to take the technique a step further and use it to make slurs between two fretted notes. Try the exercises below to get an idea of the possibilities.

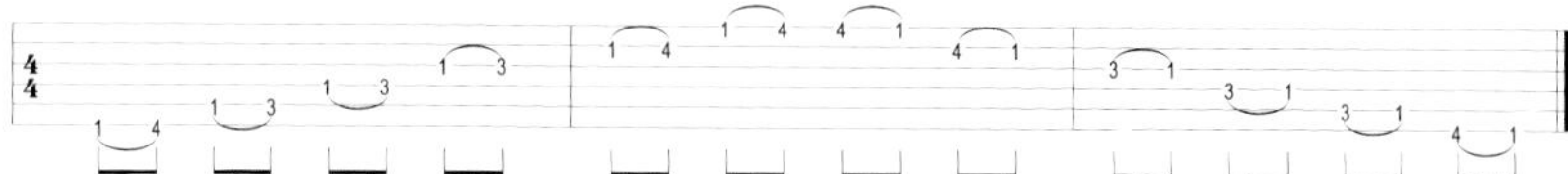

1. Warm up by slurring your way up and down the pentatonic scale.

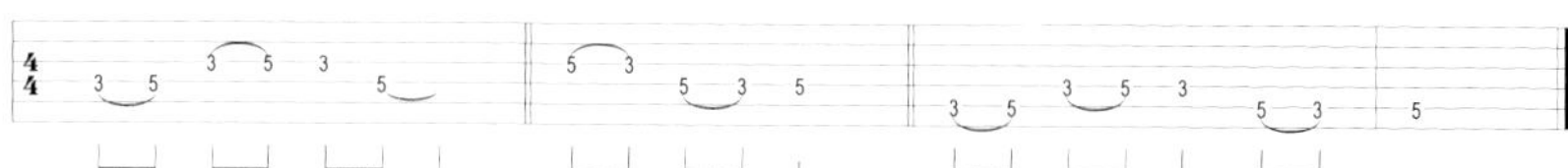

2. The following exercises are sample riffs using slurs. This one is in the key of G. Keep the speed of the hammer-ons and pull-offs the same. Press precisely on the tips of the fingers and concentrate on making an expressive sound.

3. Here is a riff in A. The fourth finger is often a problem at first. Treat it exactly like the other fingers – keep the finger curved so that it is pressing right on the tip. Accept that it is a weaker finger but that it will get stronger if you use it correctly. For the faster (semiquaver) passages, keep your hand relaxed. As the higher of the two notes plays, lift the first finger over ready to play the next string. This way you will avoid a gap in the rhythm.

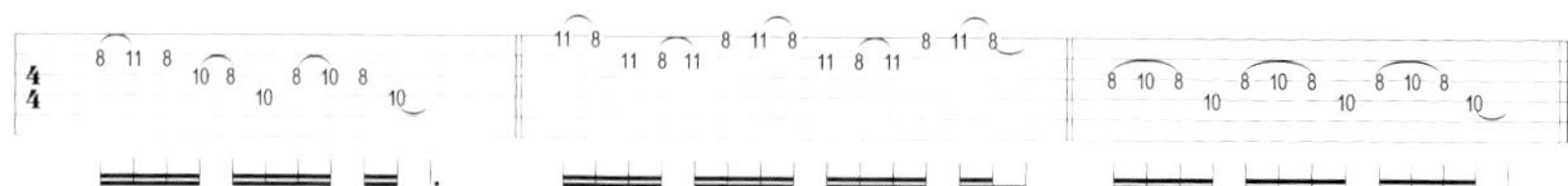

4. This riff is in C. Here the slurred notes occur off the beat. Their purpose in this instance is to make playing easier according to natural finger movements. This exercise uses a double slur, where you hammer-on and pull-off in the same movement.

BENDING STRINGS

Bending the strings is often associated with the electric guitar. It is easier to do on an electric's lighter strings, and it makes for an appealing, bluesy wail. But it is not just an electric trick. You can bend strings on all types of guitar so long as your technique is solid.

To begin our practice, we are going to bend the third string at the seventh fret, as in the photograph below. Begin by pressing the third string at the seventh fret. Place the first and second fingers on the third string behind the third finger. Play the third-finger note and continue pressing while gradually pushing the string up, using the first and second fingers to help bend the string. Make sure the third finger keeps enough pressure on the string to sound the note. The pitch will shift as the string is pushed up.

Bear in mind that not all the notes suit being bent; some notes don't sound good at all. The best notes to bend are on the thinner third, second and first strings.

Left A bend on the seventh fret. A half-tone bend should sound the same as the eighth fret, while a whole-tone bend sounds the same as the ninth.

Exercise using the pentatonic scale with bent notes

Try each of the licks below a number of times before moving on to the next. Use bending sparingly and for emphasis on certain notes.

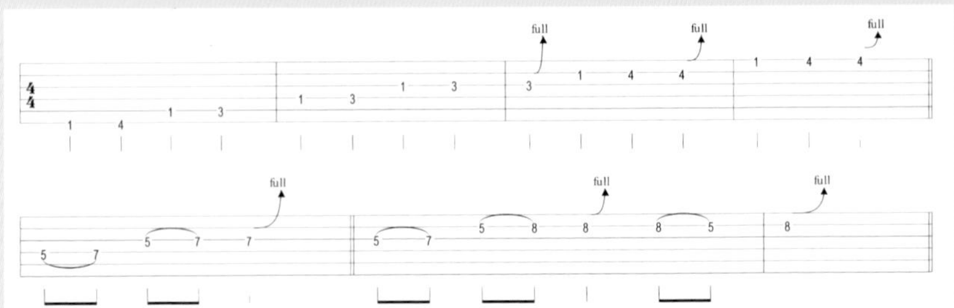

Remember to use hammer-ons and pull-offs where marked. Look out for bend/release signs: an arrow going up and down. If you see one of these you'll need to push the string up and allow it to relax down again while maintaining pressure on the string throughout.

Stone man Keith Richards of the Rolling Stones achieves fantastic effects by combining imaginative bends and slurs with an open-string tuning (see pages 148–149), backed up by a sparse and unpredictable strumming style.

TWO WAYS WITH VIBRATO

Think how a singer's voice might quiver gently on a sustained note. That resonant effect is vibrato, and instrumentalists have long sought to incorporate its vocalic quality in their playing. There are two ways to achieve this solo effect on the guitar.

Vibrato is an effect that can add great expression to your playing. Technically, it is a regular, pulsating change of pitch that can be altered in terms of its depth and speed. On fretless stringed instruments, such as the violin or the cello, vibrato is produced by manipulating the string with the left hand. Working from the precise point at which the note is played, the hand rocks rapidly and rhythmically, introducing a wobble into the note.

On the guitar this method of producing vibrato is not possible, because the pitch of any given note is determined by the position of the frets. So creating vibrato on a guitar requires a different technique, or rather two separate techniques, termed 'horizontal' and 'vertical', both of which demand that the string be stretched around a central pitch at the point where it touches the fret.

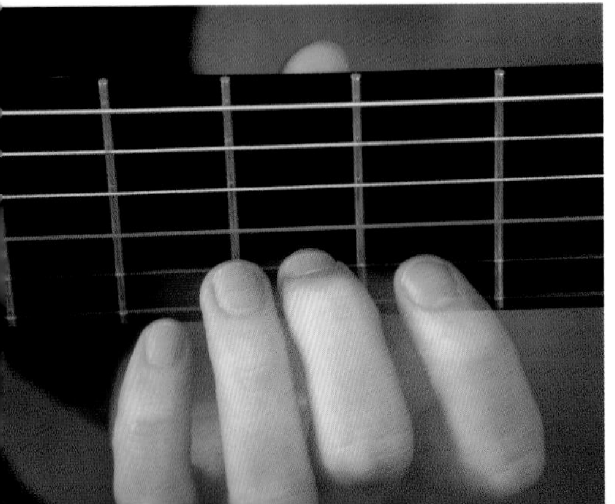

Horizontal vibrato

Horizontal or 'classical' vibrato is easier to perform higher up the neck. Start by anchoring the second finger on the fourth string, seventh fret. Play the string, and without letting the fingertip slide along the string, move the whole arm from left to right, pulling the string from side to side. Press hard on the second finger and listen for the change in pitch. As you move to the right the pitch will flatten; as you move to the left it will sharpen.

Keep a regular rocking motion and experiment with different speeds. Try using the other left-hand fingers at the same fret to get the same effect. Balance the hand solidly on the fingertip, and keep the thumb on the back of the neck behind the second finger.

Left Horizontal vibrato on a classical guitar. Here the second finger pulls the string from side to side to achieve the desired effect.

Vertical vibrato

Vertical vibrato is used by electric guitarists, and also in situations where the strings are difficult to move horizontally, such as low down on the neck in first position. With vertical vibrato, the pitch can only go sharp.

To perform vertical vibrato, anchor the first finger on the third string, fifth fret. Play the string and move it up and down with the first finger. This is a twisting action mostly using the wrist – the first finger should stay fairly solid. The faster you shake or twitch your hand, the more rapid the vibrato. With practice, it is possible to get very quick indeed.

Above Vertical vibrato on an electric guitar. The whole hand rocks rapidly back and forth in order to move the first finger up and down.

Vibrato exercises

Practise both forms of vibrato with these exercises. The wavy line above the stave tells you which notes and phrases you should use it on.

Vibrato scale

Folky vibrato

Blues vibrato

LESSON 26

VARYING THE TIMBRE

The colour, or 'timbre', of the guitar's sound can be affected in a variety of ways. We have already discussed vibrato with the left hand. This lesson will focus on a way of using the right hand to lend different qualities to the sound of your playing.

Generally speaking, the right hand strums or picks directly over the soundhole of an acoustic guitar. Striking the strings in this central position allows the natural amplifying effect of the hollow body to be felt to the full extent. But it is also possible to move the playing position of the right hand, and doing so will alter the quality of the sound that your guitar produces.

This is a technique common to other stringed instruments such as the violin.

Sul tasto Plucking or strumming in the sul tasto position makes for a warm, soft, rounded sound.

Ponticello Playing the strings in the ponticello position lends a hard, crisp, clear quality to the sound.

Consequently, Italian terms (Italian being the language of classical music) are used to tell a player when to move the playing position of the right hand. Those terms are 'sul tasto', which means 'over the fingerboard', and requires the performer to pluck or bow the string close to the high end of an instrument's neck; and 'ponticello', which means 'little bridge', and instructs the performer to play closer to the bridge of the instrument.

The quality of the sound can vary hugely between these two points. Playing tasto will give a sweeter, warmer sound, while ponticello will result in a harder, scratchier sound. It is up to the performer to choose the colour 'palette' according to the musical context: tasto, normal, ponticello and all points in between.

It is a good idea to get to know the particular timbre of your guitar, since every instrument is different. One way to do this is to move between the tasto and ponticello positions when you practise your scales. Try to find playing areas that sound good on your own guitar.

It is possible to vary the timbre more subtly by shifting the plectrum's angle of attack to the strings. By this method, the sound can be altered without moving the whole arm. Accomplished players will adjust the timbre from note to note to heighten the tension of a melody, say, or to sweeten the end of a phrase.

Exercises in tasto and ponticello

Try the first exercise below, and experiment by gradually moving the right hand from a normal (central) position towards the bridge and then back towards the fingerboard. Listen to the change in the sound. Then have a go at the next exercise, which requires you to hold an E chord and strum while moving the right hand to different positions.

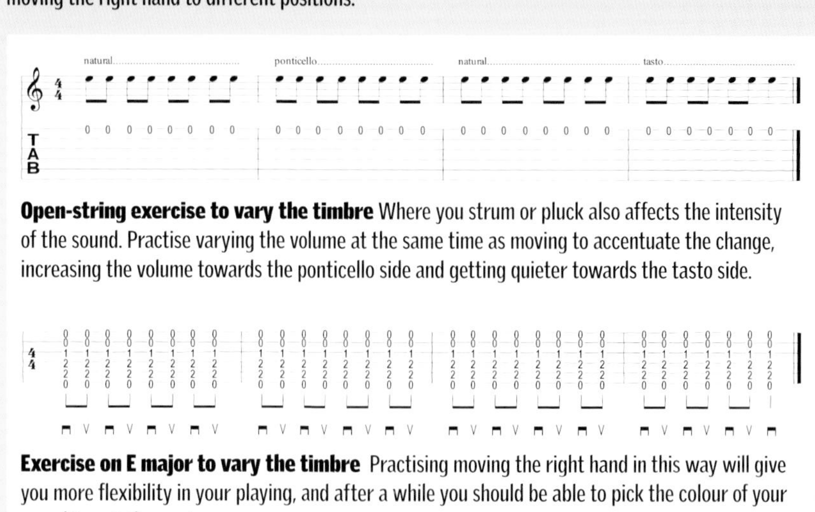

Open-string exercise to vary the timbre Where you strum or pluck also affects the intensity of the sound. Practise varying the volume at the same time as moving to accentuate the change, increasing the volume towards the ponticello side and getting quieter towards the tasto side.

Exercise on E major to vary the timbre Practising moving the right hand in this way will give you more flexibility in your playing, and after a while you should be able to pick the colour of your sound to suit the music.

SEVENTH CHORDS

We are now going to take a closer look at seventh chords. The term seventh means simply that the chord includes the seventh note of the scale alongside the first, third and fifth. Adding a seventh is by far the most common alteration of the standard chord shapes.

Adding a seventh to a chord sometimes makes it easier to play, and sometimes makes it harder. For example, the A7-shape is much easier than a simple A – especially if you are barring the chord. This is worth bearing in mind in your playing. Say, for example, you are strumming a twelve-bar blues in E major; you can always replace the B in the tenth bar with an easier B7, and it will sound better than the standard A-shape.

You will have encountered some sevenths in the gallery of basic chords on page 23. Your task in this lesson is to learn some more of them and to get to grips with new ways of incorporating them into your playing.

A major seventh has a wonderfully jangling and unresolved feel to it. It is an essential element of blues music – one might even say that it is the defining characteristic of the blues. That is why this lesson includes an easy bluesy three-chord trick made up entirely of major sevenths. Minor sevenths have a softer, more jazzy character that is no less attractive.

Seventh chords are less stable-sounding than the standard major or minors. As such, they tend to resolve to a more stable chord at some stage. Few tunes end on a seventh.

If you can get the hang of exploiting seventh chords in a clever and timely fashion, you will add a bright new colour to your guitar playing.

Blues exercise in the key of E

E^7 | A^7 | E^7 | E^7

1 + a2 + a3 + a4 + a1 + a2 + a3 + a4 + a1 + a2 + a3 + a4 + a1 + a2 + a3 + a4

A^7 | A^7 | E^7 | E^7

1 + a2 + a3 + a4 + a1 + a2 + a3 + a4 + a1 + a2 + a3 + a4 + a1 + a2 + a3 + a4

B^7 | A^7 | E^7 | B^7

1 + a2 + a3 + a4 + a1 + a2 + a3 + a4 + a1 + a2 + a3 + a4 + a1 + a2 + a3 + a4

Use a relaxed swing rhythm for strumming this piece. Count 1&a-2&a-3&a-4&a. If you count evenly and strum on the numbered beats and the 'a' the swing rhythm should emerge.

Forming the sevenths

Major seventh chords

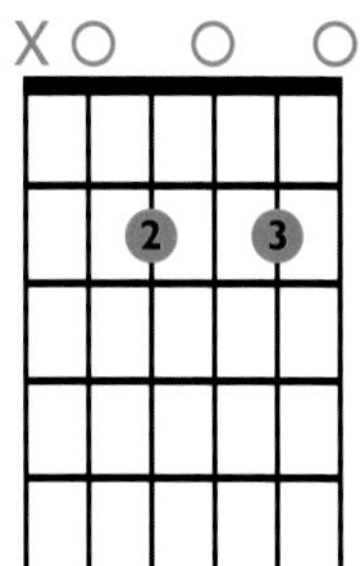

A7 This is essentially an A chord with the middle finger missing. The open third string should be heard clearly.

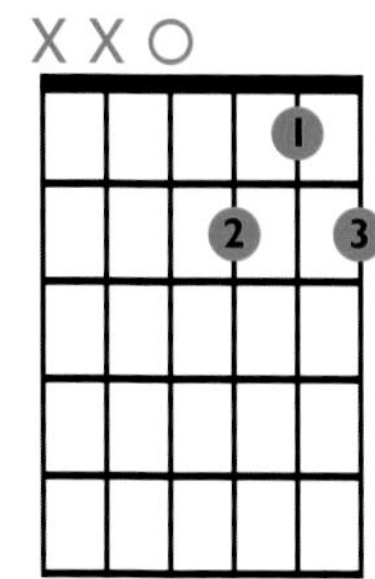

D7 Only the second-string note changes from standard D major, but the fingering has to change entirely.

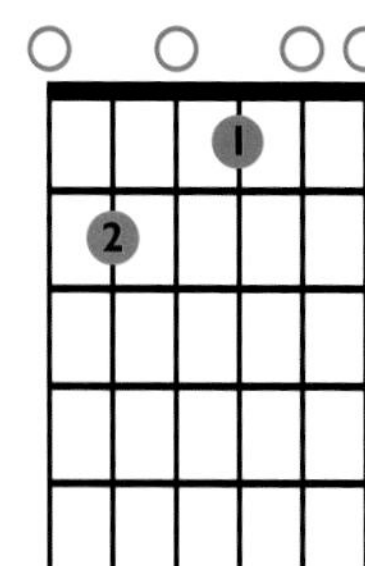

E7 This is a simple shape. Play a standard E major, then remove the third finger to make an open fourth string.

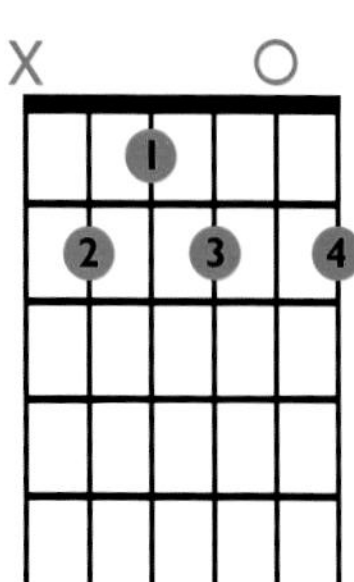

B7 This chord uses all four fingers but fits the hand well. The second, third and fourth fingers are all in the second fret.

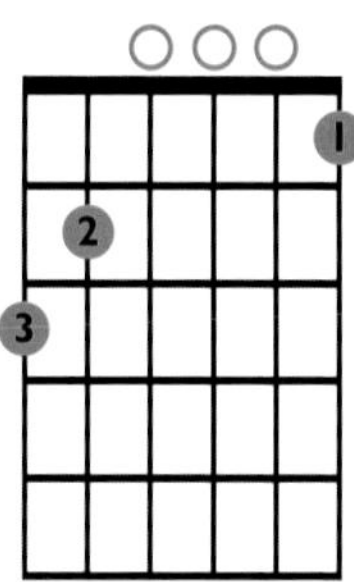

G7 (left) and **C7** (right) are two of the more tricky seventh chords. Make sure that the fingers are pressing on their fingertips and towards the right side of the frets. The stretches involved here do get easier with practice.

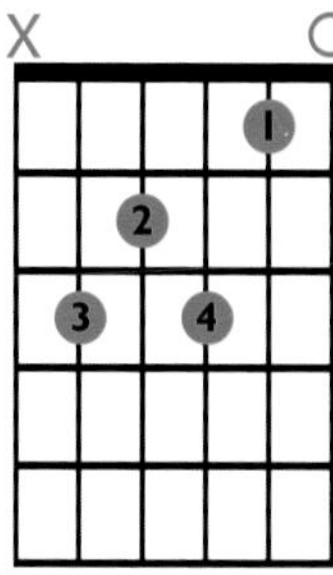

Minor seventh chords

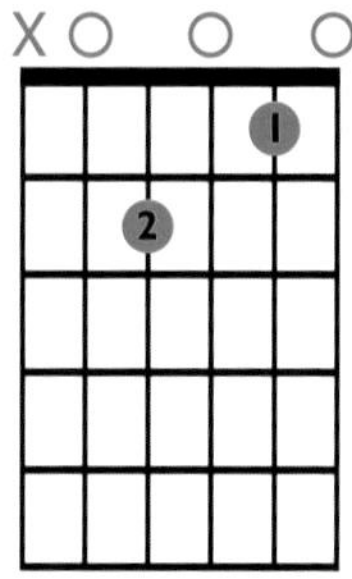

Am7 This is an easy chord: an A-minor shape without the third finger, leaving the open third string free.

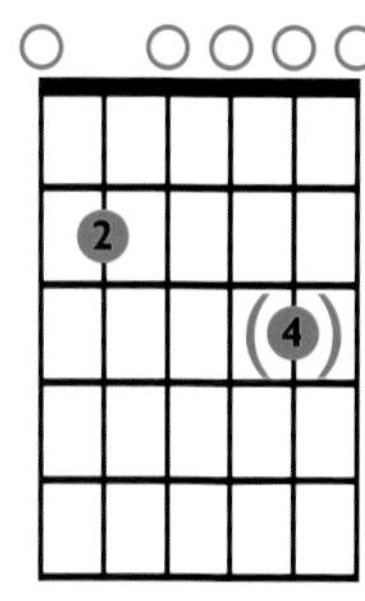

Em7 This chord can be played with the second finger alone, but the fourth finger reinforces the seventh sound.

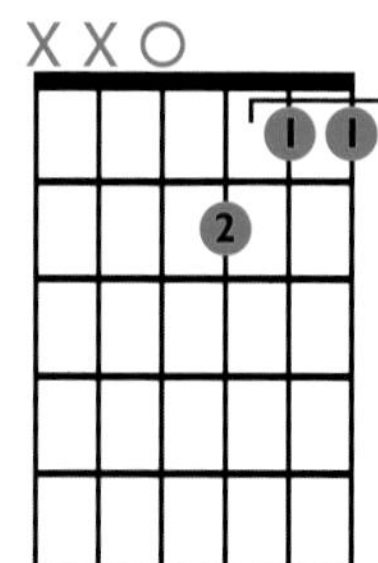

Dm7 The first finger needs to bar across the first two strings. Make sure all the strings ring clearly with this one.

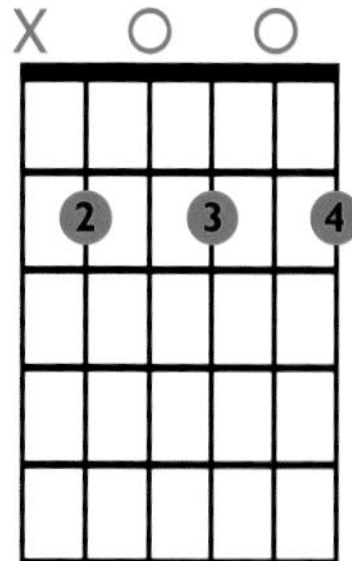

Bm7 This chord varies only slightly from B7. You only have to take the first finger off the fourth string.

LESSON 28

PLAYING EASY BLUES

You are now ready to start playing the blues. The seventh chords will give a gorgeous texture to any chord progression you play, and the pentatonic scale lets you weave a tune. The exercises on these pages are just a starting point for your own musical experiments.

Much blues music follows a structure known as '12-bar blues'. This is nothing more or less than a simple three-chord trick that uses the first, fourth and fifth chords in the scale. It takes twelve bars to reach a point where the cycle of chords begins again. The chords played in those bars progress as follows: I-IV-I-I-IV-IV-I-I-V-IV-I-I. You can play the 12-bar blues in any key, but in the key of E this would equate to this run of chords: E-A-E-E-A-A-E-E-B-A-E-E.

E is perhaps the most commonly used key for the 12-bar, and indeed for the blues in general, certainly when playing in standard tuning. This is because E is the easiest key to jam in: the low open sixth string is the root note, and all of the open strings form part of the pentatonic scale. You can hardly go wrong.

THE **BLUES**

Blues music emerged in the southern states of the USA at the end of the 19th century. It was an outpouring of the hard lives of the African-American people who made it. That hardship was expressed succinctly and eloquently in the plangent 'blue note' of the minor pentatonic scale.

Early blues can sound strange to modern ears, but it is interesting to listen to early recordings – mostly because they are wonderful pieces, but also because they are the antecedents of so much modern music. The songs of bluesmen such as Robert Johnson constitute the authentic archaeology of rock'n'roll.

Suggested listening
Robert Johnson, John Lee Hooker, Muddy Waters, B.B. King, Stevie Ray Vaughan.

Mister Lucky John Lee Hooker, blues songwriter and master improviser.

Two blues pieces

The first of these pieces is in the easy blues key of E major. The second is in A, but will work anywhere on the neck, so in any key. Both will sound good as a background accompaniment to a blues solo.

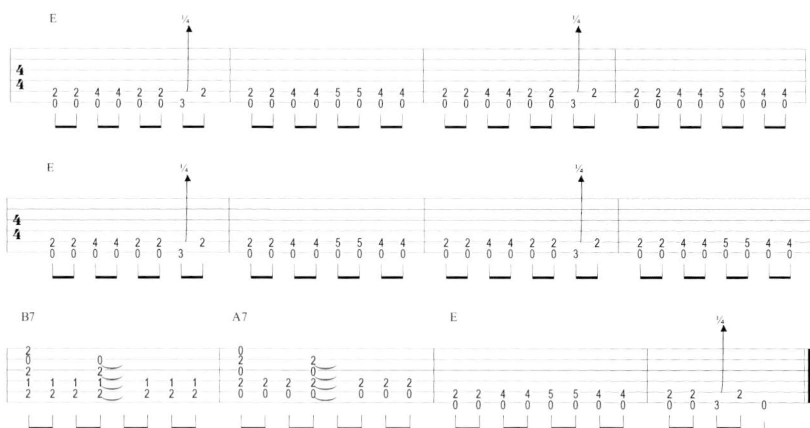

Blues in E Use a slow swing rhythm for this piece. The left hand is in second position and should be set out in the frets accordingly. Fifth-fret notes will be played with the fourth finger. Look out for the bent notes – a quarter bend (marked '¼') is just a subtle pull on the string. Try not to let them affect the rhythm. The last line changes the pattern – we have two strummed seventh chords (B7 then A7). Hold the full chords but try to pick only the strings shown and watch out for the tied notes.

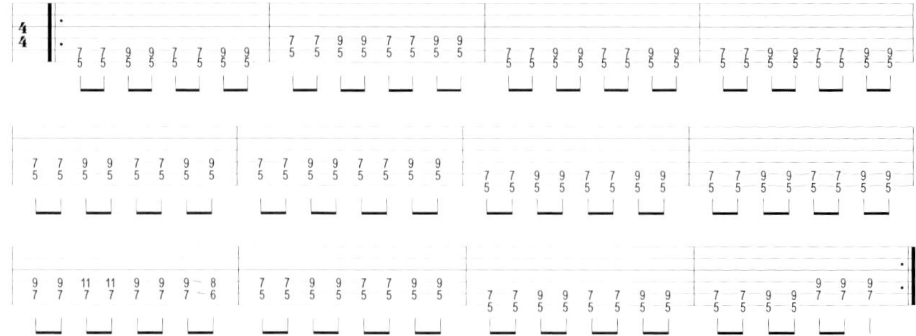

Moveable blues In this exercise, the shape of the left-hand is not dissimilar to a power chord. Using the first and third fingers, hold the first chord on the fifth and seventh frets. Without lifting the shape, use the fourth finger to stretch to the ninth fret. This is not easy but is an excellent workout for your little finger!

Copy this pattern in the second bar, but move up one string. In the first bar of the last line, move the pattern to the seventh and ninth frets on the fifth and fourth strings respectively. There is a quick slide at the end of the bar that helps you get back to the original position. Repeat this piece several times over. To finish, omit the last three chords and stay on the A chord at the fifth and seventh frets.

MODIFYING THE BASIC CHORDS

We have already looked at seventh chords, where a note one tone below the root note is added to the mix to create a particular effect. There are other ways to work notes into a chord while strumming – either to add interest or to create a melodic line.

The effect of adding or altering a note within a chord is best illustrated by doing it yourself. Pick up your guitar and strum a standard D chord. As you play, lift your second finger from the first string. Then, while still strumming, use the fourth finger to press the first string at the third fret. Speed up, so that you are changing the note on the sixth string every beat or two.

You are now, in effect, playing a simple melody consisting of three notes (E, F-sharp and G) on the top string, while the lower strings act as a pleasing background drone. To put it another way, as you were playing around with the D chord, a melodic line emerged almost incidentally on the top string. The point is that you can tease a tune out of your strumming by making small alterations to the shape of the chords.

That is what you are asked to do in the exercises on these pages. The first, below, uses the variations on D major that you have just been practising. Opposite are some more exercises in combining chords and a melody. As usual, they start fairly easy and then grow harder.

This kind of playing can come in useful when you are writing a song. It can serve as an instrumental introduction, or as a kind of final flourish at the end of the piece. You can also use this technique to echo a melody that is being sung, or else to harmonize with it.

D chord with a melody on the first string

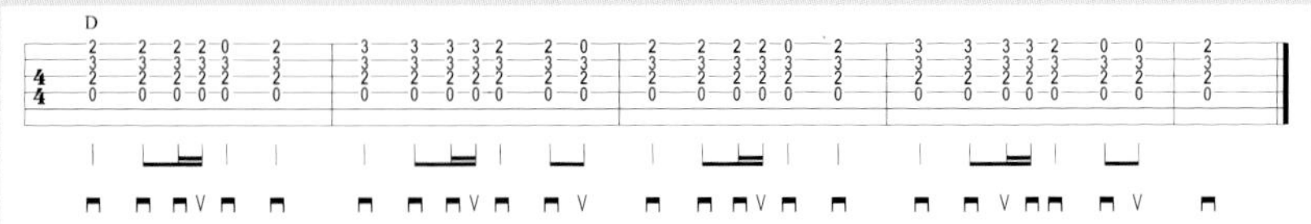

Hold a standard D chord. Follow the top line as you play, lifting the second finger and adding the fourth where required. The first and third fingers will remain stationary throughout. Follow the strumming pattern carefully.

Exercises in strumming a melody

Master each exercise before moving on. Loop the pattern to create a more extended practice session.

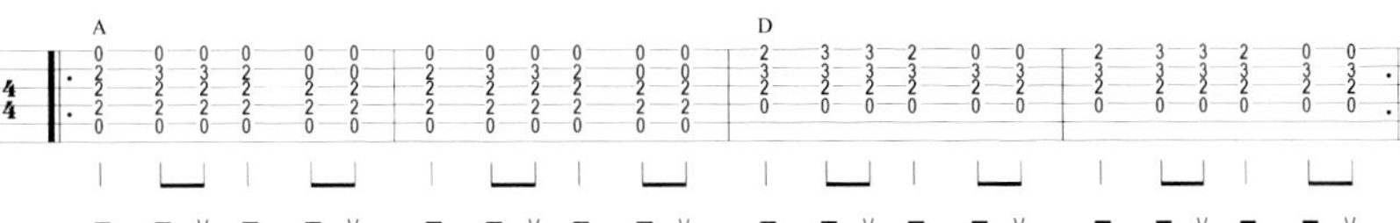

A to D with moving parts On the A chord it is the second string that changes. The third finger lifts off to leave the open string, and the fourth finger will play at the third fret. Change to the D chord in the third bar and follow the first-string changes as on the opposite page.

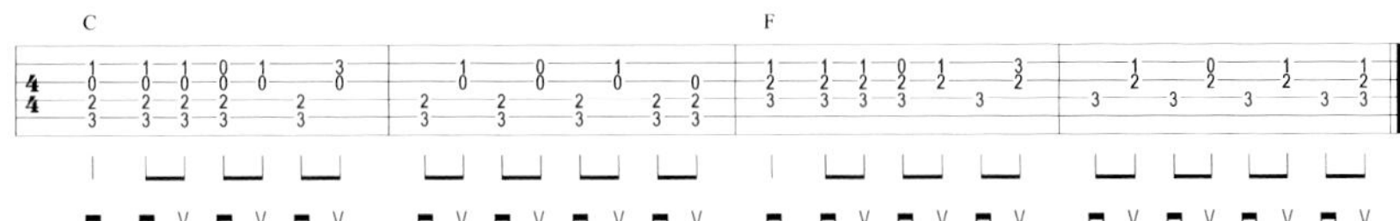

C to F with a melody on the second string The melody is on the second string and is the same for both chords. You will need to use the fourth finger to play the third-fret notes on that string. Only lift the notes on the second string and allow the lower part of the chord to ring over. Take notice of how many strings are to be strummed, but don't worry too much if you overshoot – the chord is covered by the left hand, and it is better to keep the strumming going here than to be overcautious. It will sound fine if you play the first string occasionally even though it is not indicated.

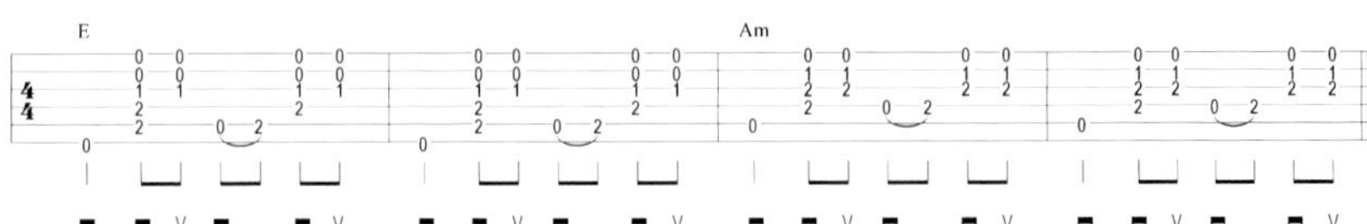

E to A minor with hammer-ons on the bass notes It is also possible to play a melody on the lower strings, and the aim here is to pick out the bass notes accurately while keeping the strumming sounding fluent and natural. To play the hammer-ons, simply lift the finger needed. In this instance, that is the second finger for both chords.

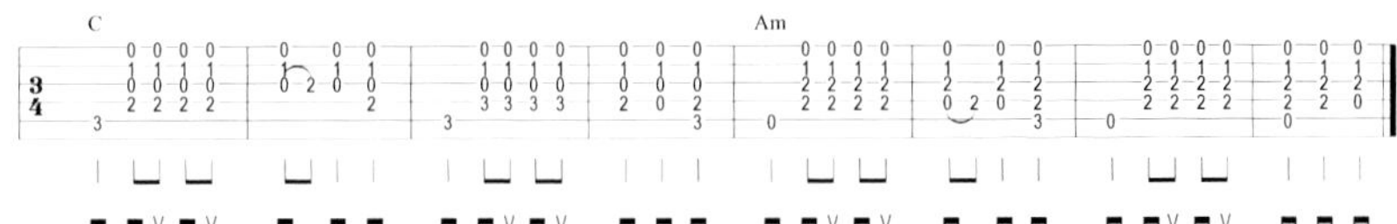

C to A minor with a combination of techniques This piece, based around C and A minor, includes picked bass notes, hammer-ons and added fingers in the chords. Read the tab carefully for the alterations. In the second bar, the second finger plays the hammer-on on the third string then returns to the fourth string. In the third bar add the fourth finger on the fourth string. At the end of the sixth bar add the fourth finger on the fifth string.

LESSON 30

PEDALS AND FIXED FINGERS

We have looked at using altered chords to create a melody. Now we are going to use the same principle to create a drone that is sustained across several chords. This effect is known as a 'pedal'. It is usually achieved using a technique called 'fixed fingers'.

In this context, the word pedal has nothing to do with the gadgets used by electric guitarists. Here the term suggests that the player has a fixed foothold that carries through from one chord to the next. The pedal or 'drone' note serves to unify a chord sequence in a way that can sound either interestingly jangly or ethereally beautiful. Pedals sound great on a steel-string acoustic, and they suit slow ballads and rock songs. Among the famous songs that make good use of pedals are 'If I Were a Boy' (Beyoncé) and 'Sweet Home Alabama' (Lynyrd Skynyrd).

Try the chord shapes below. You will see that they all have the same fingering on the first and second strings (in the case of F and A minor, just the first string). These two fingers make up the unifying pedal.

Seven chords, one pedal

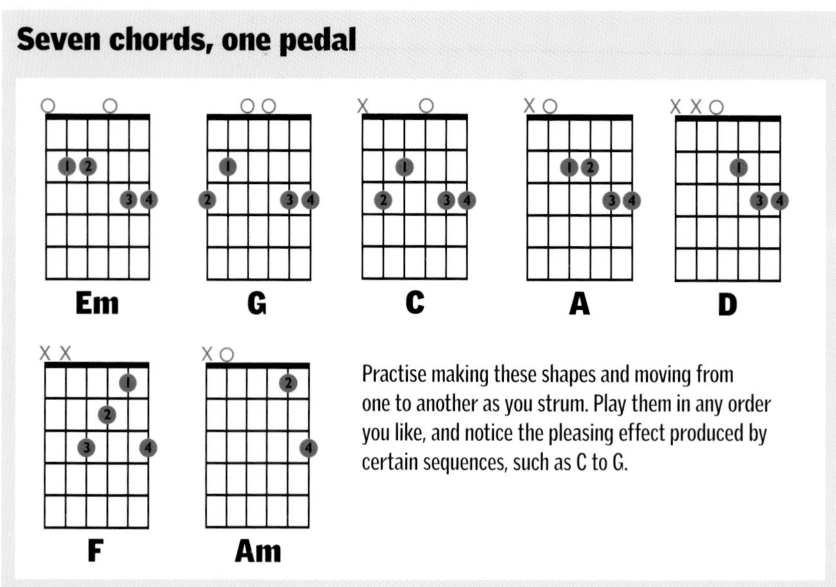

Practise making these shapes and moving from one to another as you strum. Play them in any order you like, and notice the pleasing effect produced by certain sequences, such as C to G.

Pedal exercises

These exercises demonstrate the variety of effects that can be achieved by using a pedal.

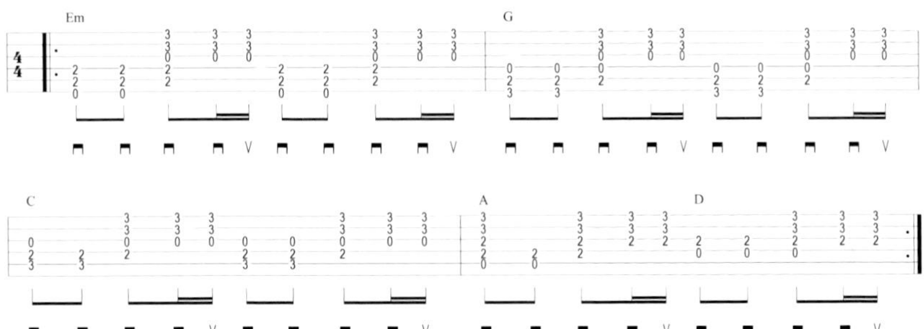

High pedal This exercise uses the chords on the page opposite. At first, the third and fourth fingers – the fixed fingers – will feel the strain of being held down for so long. Keep them together as a unit and remember to press just hard enough to make the notes ring.

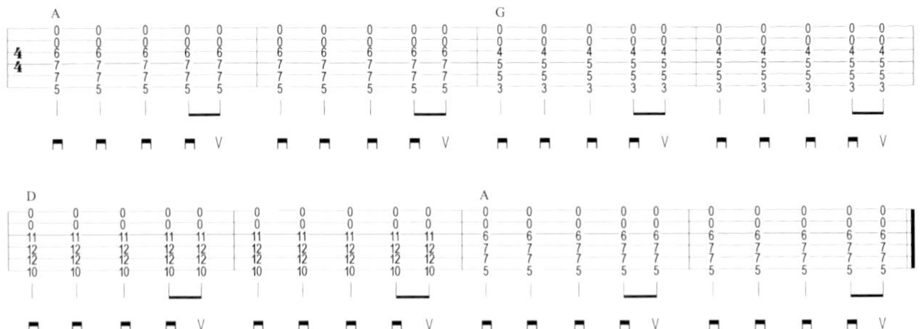

Open-string pedal This is a very effective technique that uses bar-chord shapes, but with the bar lifted from the top two strings. Since no fixed fingers are involved, you can slide the shape freely right up the neck of the guitar.

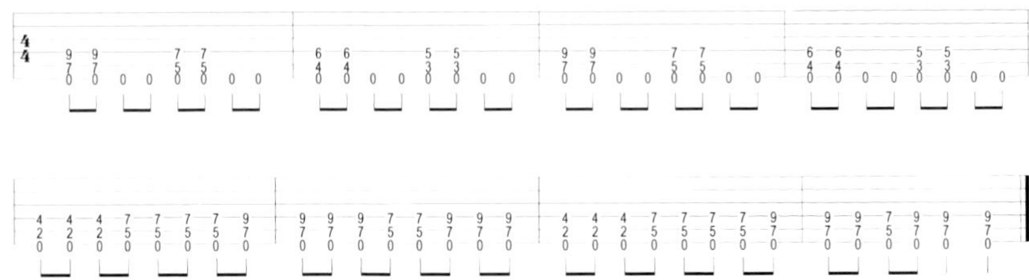

Bass pedal Playing a constant note on one of the low open strings is a popular guitar trick. Here we play power chords while the sixth string provides the drone. Allow the chords to ring for as long as possible. This will also work well with palm muting and a distorted amp setting.

LESSON 31

READING MUSIC FOR GUITAR

You have come a long way in playing guitar without having to read music other than tab notation. But understanding standard music notation will help you to progress as a guitarist and a musician. This lesson deals with the basics of reading music as it applies to the guitar.

Sight-reading on the guitar is not easy. It is much harder than learning to read chord diagrams or tab. It will take you some time and effort to master standard notation, but it is a skill that transfers to other instruments, and that will help you when you come to study music theory.

In standard musical notation, musical pitches (notes) are represented by symbols written on five horizontal lines known as a 'stave'. Each line, or gap between a line, represents a pitch. The higher the note on the stave, the higher the pitch. Notes can be written either on or between the lines, and they follow the musical alphabet, the notes A to G, as they ascend and descend. In the treble clef (which is used for the guitar) the notes on the lines, from lowest to highest, are often remembered by the words: Every Good Boy Deserves Favour. The notes in the spaces spell the word FACE.

Notes can be written above and below the stave by adding extra lines just long enough for them to sit on. These are called 'ledger lines'. The duration of a note is shown by the symbols you encountered on page 44. Rhythms are

A good first step to sight-reading on the guitar is to familiarize yourself with the positions of the open strings on the stave.

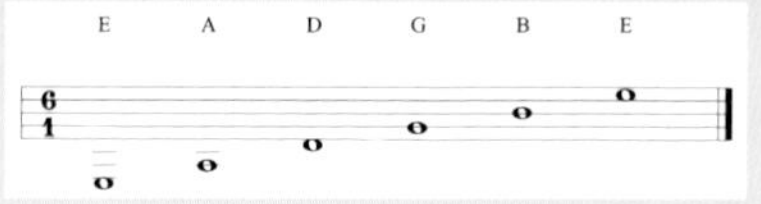

The stave and ledger lines for the treble clef

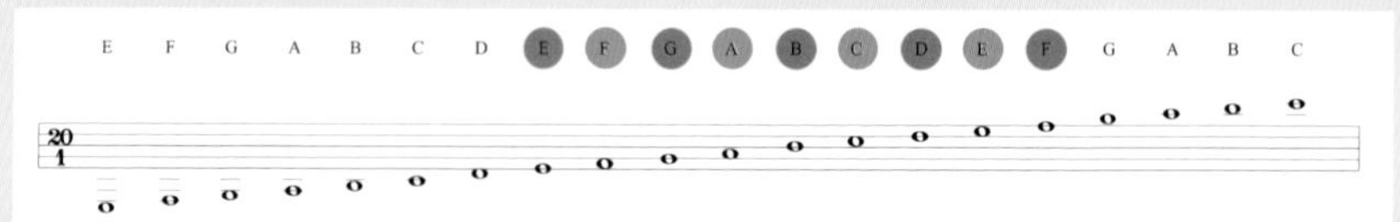

The notes that sit on the lines in the main part of the stave are highlighted in red; and the notes that fall between the lines are highlighted in blue.

measured by 'beats', the regular underlying pulse of the music. A beat can be any speed – that is to say, you can play a tune as fast or as slow as you wish. But once the length of a beat is established, these rhythmic divisions should be strictly adhered to: you cannot normally start playing faster or slower in the course of a single piece of music.

Each rhythmic symbol also has a corresponding symbol that represents a 'rest'. That is to say, it is telling you to be silent for a certain time, rather than play a note for a certain duration.

Some simple reading exercises

These exercise will get you used to reading the open strings of the guitar. Remember that the higher the note on the stave, the higher the pitch. Do this without looking a your right hand, and don't aim to memorize the tunes – the idea is to read the notes just as if you were reading a book.

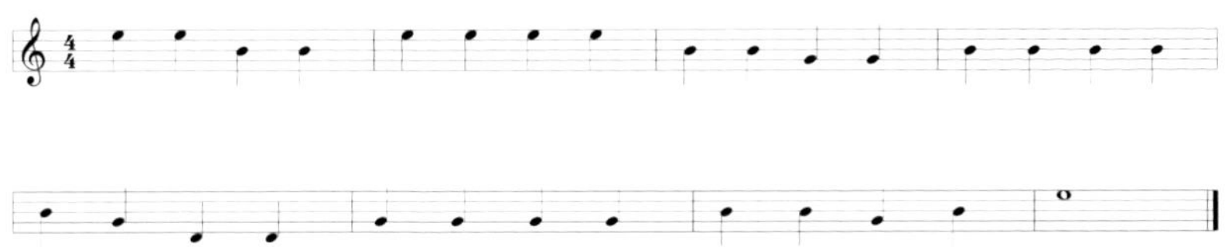

Open string exercise with crotchets (quarter notes) Try playing without looking at the strings. Your reading will improve more rapidly if you feel for the strings and keep your eyes fixed on the page.

Using different rhythms Keep a steady pulse and remember that there are four beats per bar. With the two beat notes (minims) it can help to tap your foot – once as you play the note, and again in the space after the note.

Playing quavers (eighth notes) The pairs of eighth-notes should be played using downstrokes and upstrokes. In the fourth bar count three beats for the dotted half-note.

NAVIGATING THE FINGERBOARD

You have learned to recognize the notes on the stave that correspond to the open strings on the fingerboard. Now the time has come to fill in the gaps so that you know all the notes of the scale in first position, that is, on the first four frets.

Thus far we have been able to manage without scales. But now you will learn the names of the notes you are playing.

The diagram below shows the scale from bottom E (the lowest note a guitar can play) to G on the third fret of the sixth string. When played in order, from the sixth string to the first, the notes will follow the musical alphabet over a little more than two octaves.

This scale does not include the sharps and flats. But, as we discussed in the section on bar chords (see pages 58–59) a sharp note (signified thus: ♯) is one fret or semitone higher than the normal note; while a flat (♭) is one semitone lower. These in-between notes are usually described in terms of the direction in which the music is moving through the scale: they are called sharps when it is ascending, flats when it is descending, so the note on the third string, third fret is described as A-sharp on the way up, and B-flat on the way down.

An overview of first-position notes

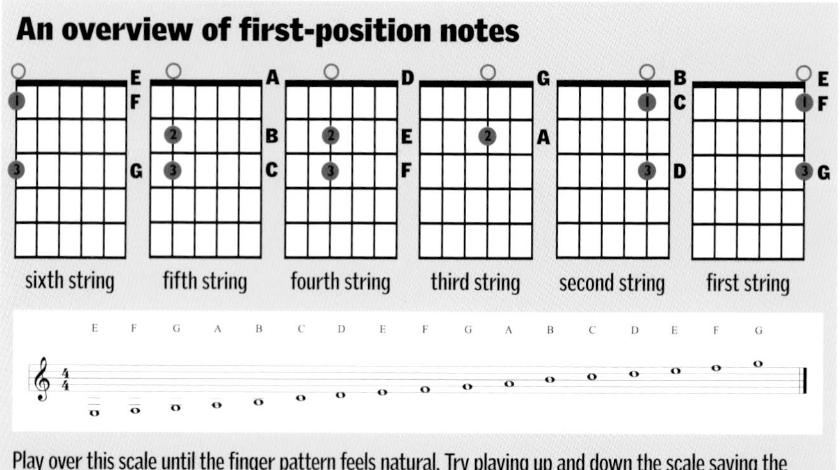

Play over this scale until the finger pattern feels natural. Try playing up and down the scale saying the letter name of each note out loud. You will almost certainly find going backwards much more challenging!

First-position exercises

Try the exercises below to familiarize yourself with the notes in first position. Refer back to the string guides as often as you need to in order to check the correct positions for the notes.

First and second strings.

First, second and third strings.

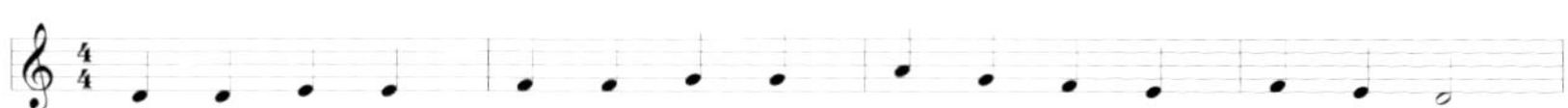

Third and fourth strings.

Third, fourth and fifth strings.

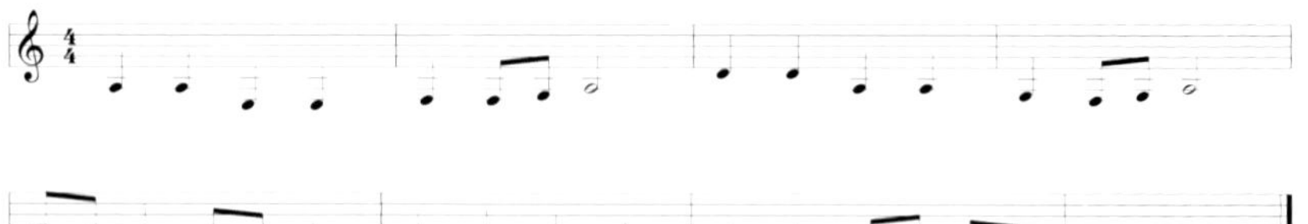

Fourth, fifth and sixth strings.

All six strings.

LESSON 33

ALTERED BASS NOTES

Chords with altered bass notes are standard shapes with an added low note. In notation, the name of the chord is given first, and the bass note is written after a slash. The examples of altered bass notes given here are all frequently used, but there are many others.

Chords with altered bass notes do not sound as solid as full standard chords. They are often used as passing chords in a progression.

When working out these chords, you should begin by making the standard chord shape then locate the additional note. The guide on page 92 will help.

Some of most common altered bass chords are given below, along with the best way to make the shape with your left hand. Usually, however, it is up to you to find a practical fingering solution. Missing out or blocking strings can help simplify things. For example, the D/F# can be played without the first string.

Some chords with altered bass notes

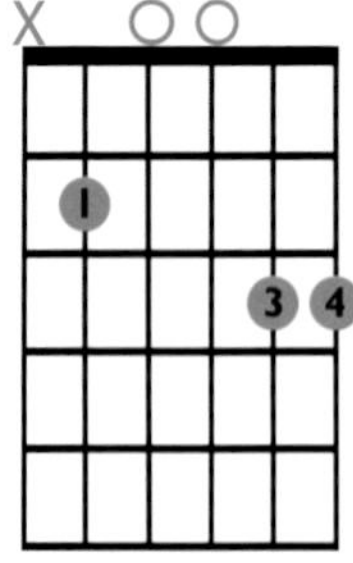

G/B This is an easy case. Play a standard G chord and take off the second finger. Miss out the sixth string when strumming, and the note at the base of the chord is a B.

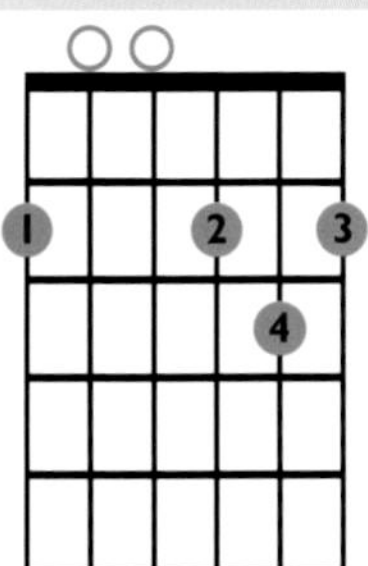

D/F# In this instance, the D chord needs to be played with the second, third and fourth fingers, leaving the first finger free to fret an F-sharp on the sixth string.

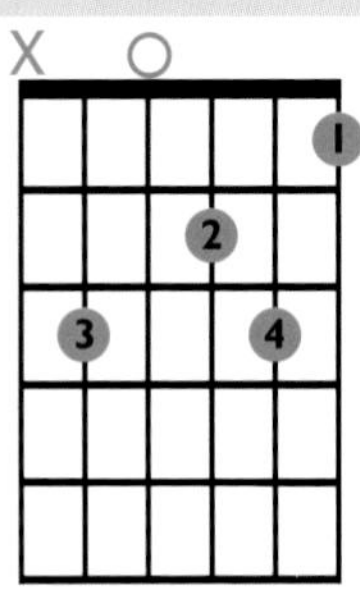

Dm/C Play a standard D minor and add the fourth finger on a C on the fifth string.

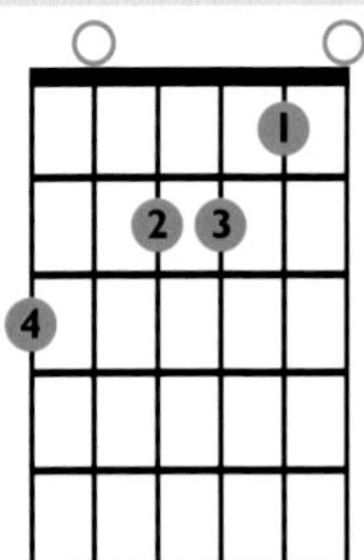

Am/G The A minor chord is played in full. Add the fourth finger at the sixth string, third fret and strum all the strings. This is a kind of Am7 chord, with a low G as the seventh note.

Altered bass note exercises

In the following exercises standard chord shapes are interspersed with altered bass note chords. Altered bass note chords have the effect of softening the changes between chords, and often only make sense as part of a longer sequence.

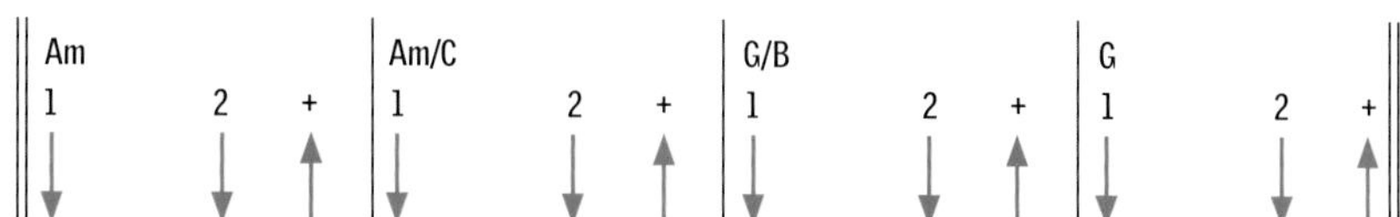

Exercise using the progression Am, Am/C, G/B, G For the Am/C chord, use the free fourth finger to press the fifth string at the third fret (a C note). This C bass note then falls one fret lower to the B in the bass of the following chord.

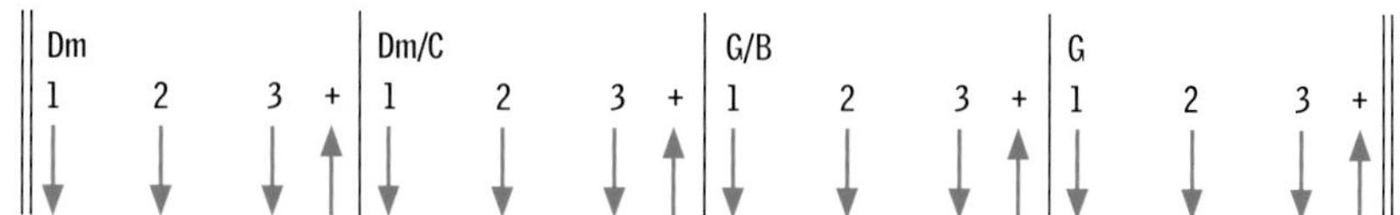

Exercise using the progression D, Dm/C, G/B, G Use the Dm/C chord shape shown on page 94. Using the fourth finger in the Dm chord instead of the third will help the smoothness of the change.

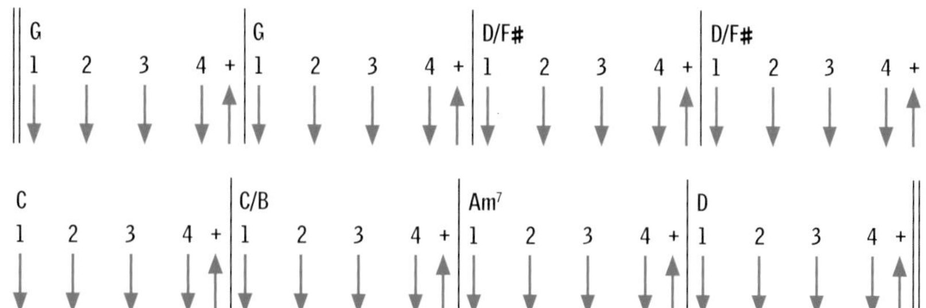

Exercise using the progression G, D/F#, C, C/B, Am7, D Use a fairly quick strumming speed for this exercise. The C/B chord is very much a 'passing' chord which does not sound good out of context. From the C chord, move the second finger down to a B on the fifth string and remove the third finger. Block the fourth string with the back of the second finger.

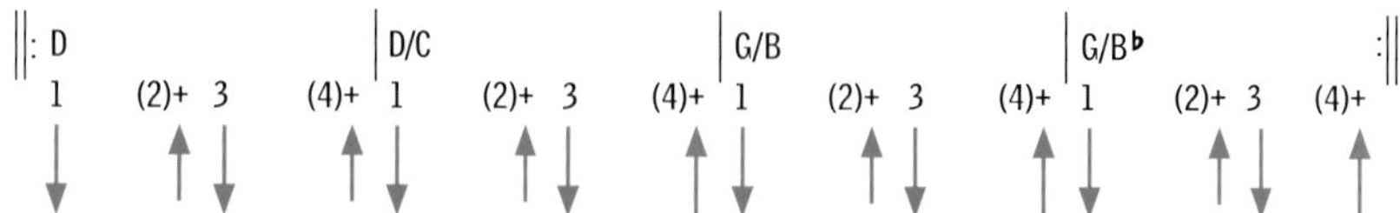

Exercise using the progression D, D/C, G/B, G/B♭ Keep the third finger rooted to the second string, third fret, throughout this exercise. When playing the D/C chord this means you will need to ignore the first string – play the C with the second finger. The B [flat] note of the final chord is in the first fret, fifth string.

DROP-D TUNING

There are a number of ways to tune your guitar so as to allow it to resonate better in certain keys or to make playing easier. The most common alternative tuning is known as the 'drop-D'. It involves changing only the sixth string, tuning it down a whole tone from E to D.

Detuning the sixth string naturally has an effect on fingering. For example, an F on the sixth string, usually in the first fret, will now be in the third fret; a G, normally in the third fret, will now be in the fifth fret, and so on.

D-family chords benefit from this tuning because the lower three strings can be played open much of the time.

Try alternating the open bass notes (the D on sixth or fourth strings, and the A on fifth string) while playing a melody above them. This is a great way of creating two-part music, because the open strings ring on and allow the instrument to resonate fully.

Try the exercises opposite to get a feel for the possibilities of this tuning.

Tuning guide for drop-D tuning

Only six-string chords and the chords of the D-family are affected by drop-D tuning. And the rest are fairly easily adapted, since only one string is different.

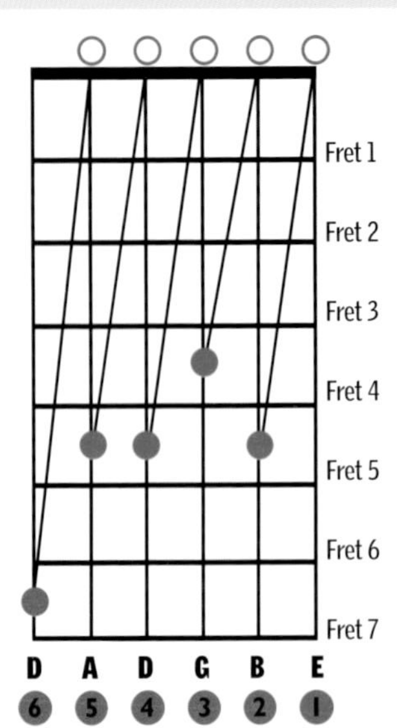

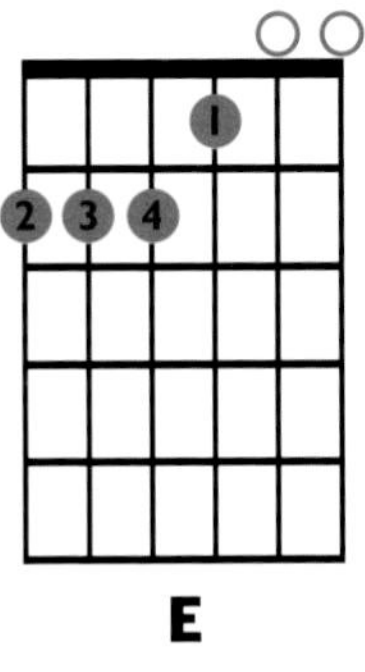

E

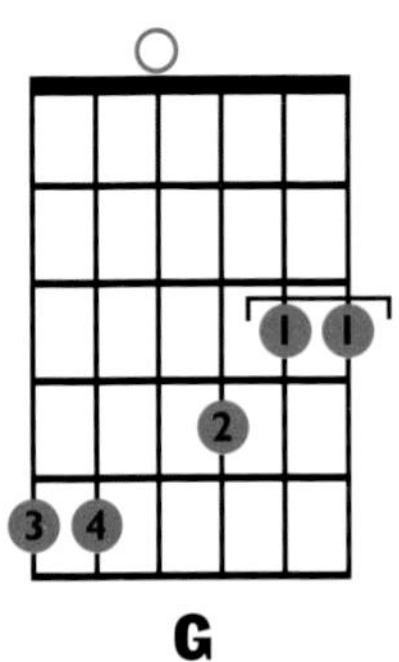

G

Here are two chords reworked for drop-D tuning: E major and G major. Both involve a change in the the fingering on the sixth string. You can use this principle to adapt all the six-string and D-family chords that you have learned so far.

Powerchords in drop-D tuning

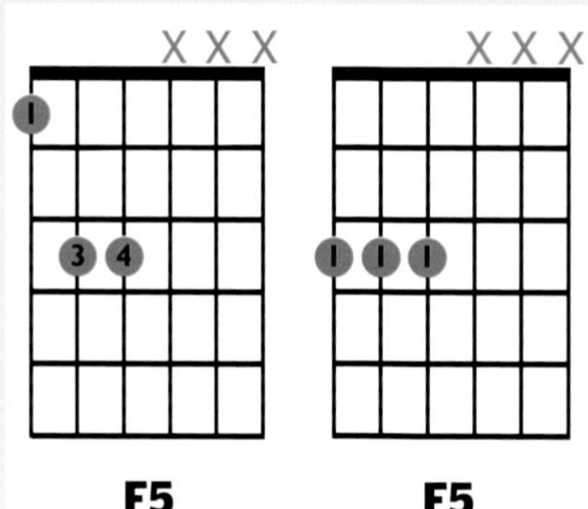

Power chords can also be easily adjusted to drop-D tuning.

Drop-D makes power chords very easy to play, as the sixth-string note has shifted up by two frets so that it is in line with the other two (see left). The best way to play this chord is to bar across all three notes with a flattened finger. Use this technique when you try the power chord exercise (below).

Left The same power chord in standard tuning (left) and its drop-D version (right).

Exercises using chords in drop-D

Have a go at these various exercises in drop-D. You will find that the deeper than usual bass note on the sixth string adds a kind of weighty feel to familiar chords fingered on the higher strings.

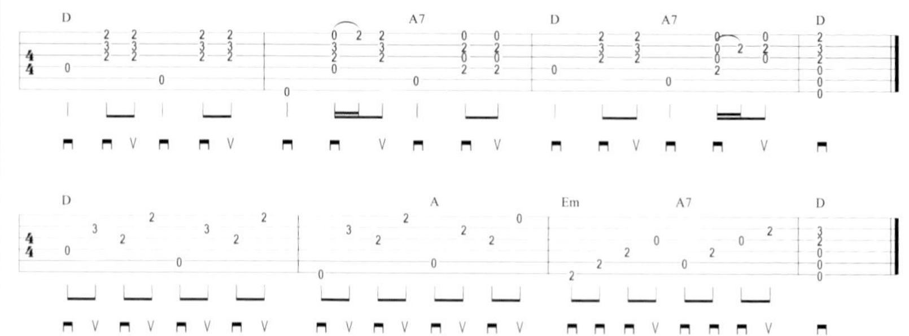

Strumming and picking These exercises in drop-D tuning are based around a D-chord shape and use alternating bass notes on the fourth, fifth and sixth strings.

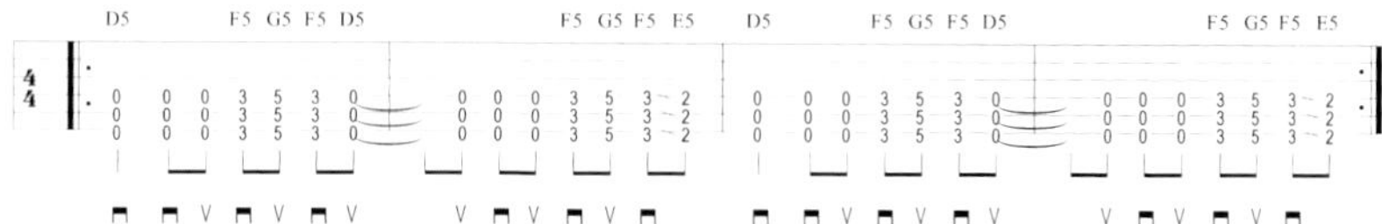

Flattened-finger power chords Use the first finger at the third fret and the third finger at the fifth fret. At the end of the second bar slide the first finger back one fret without plucking the second-fret chord.

FINGERPICKING

There are many styles of guitar playing, from classical to country, that use the right-hand fingers to pluck to strings. Using the fingers rather than a plectrum allows for a greater variety of textures – playing melody and accompaniment at the same time, for example.

In the next few lessons we will be concentrating on setting the right hand in a good position, with the thumb (labelled **p**) on the bass strings and the first three fingers (labelled **i**, **m** and **a**) on the third, second and first strings.

Remember to keep the following in mind while you are working through this next stage: hold the right-hand wrist away from the body of the guitar; pluck with the underside of the finger at the very tip – fingers should not get stuck in the strings; and try to pluck from the larger knuckle joint for maximum volume.

Concentrate on producing an even tone from each finger: play softly at first, keeping the hand as still as possible. All the work should be done with the fingers, not the wrist and arm.

Above This is the position of the right hand for fingerpicking. Notice how the thumb (**p**) sits outside the fingers from your point of view. This allows free movement of the fingers as they pluck in towards the palm of your hand. Notice also the arch of the wrist – don't let the wrist rest on the soundboard.

Fingerpicking exercises on open strings

The following exercises on open strings should help you establish a solid technique before introducing chords in the left hand.

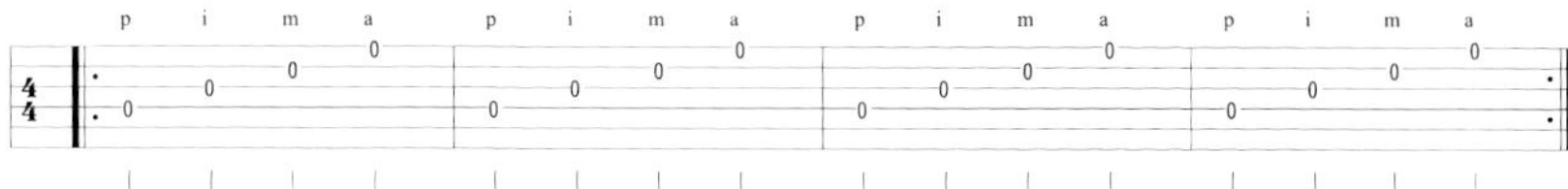

Place fingers on the strings to be played. Pluck one by one so that you finish up with all fingers in the air. Reset the fingers and begin again.

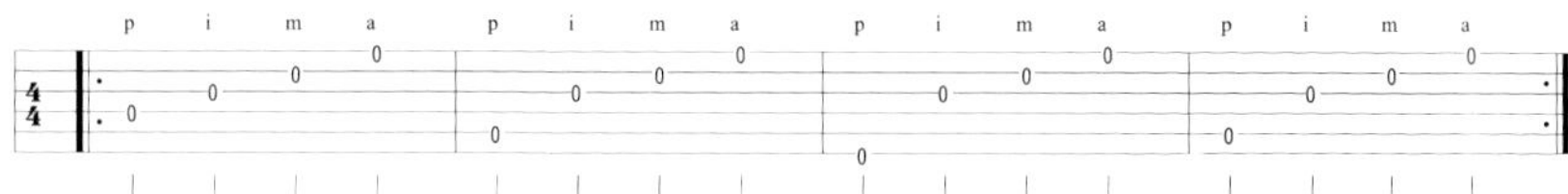

As above, but change the bass notes each time. Keep the hand as still as possible and feel the thumb stretch back towards the sixth string.

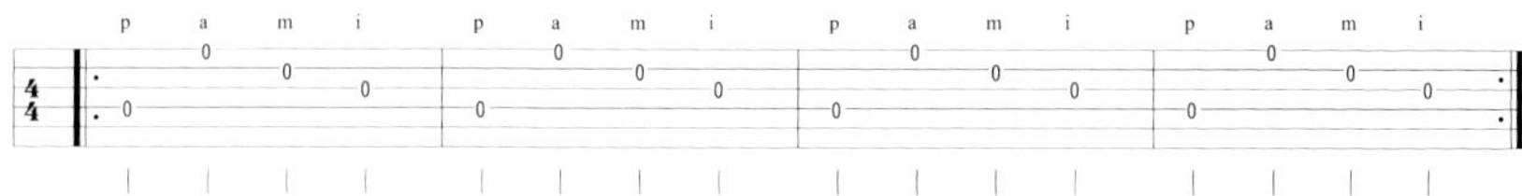

It is awkward to prepare the fingers to go in this direction, so try to set one finger at a time. Play **p** and place the **a** on the first string immediately; play **a** and place **m** on the string and so on.

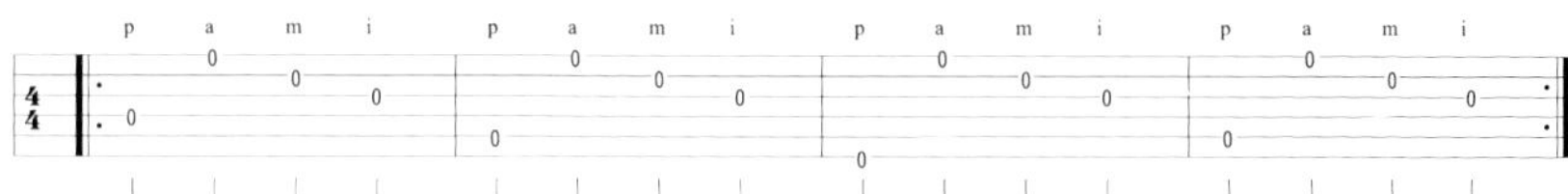

As above, but change the bass notes (like you did in the second exercise).

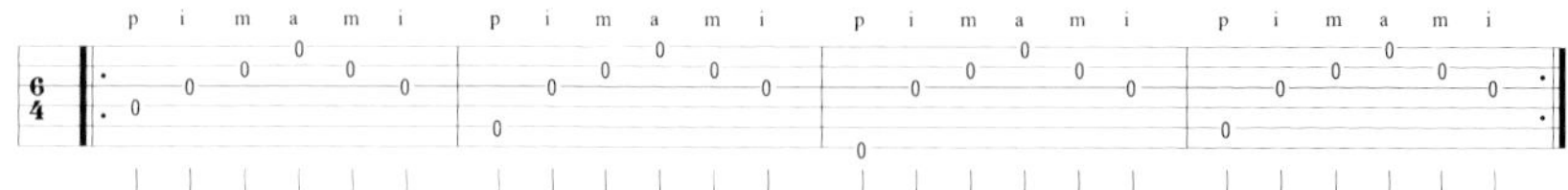

A combination of the exercises so far. Prepare fingers on the way up but not on the way down. Reset the right hand at the beginning of each bar. This is a widely used pattern.

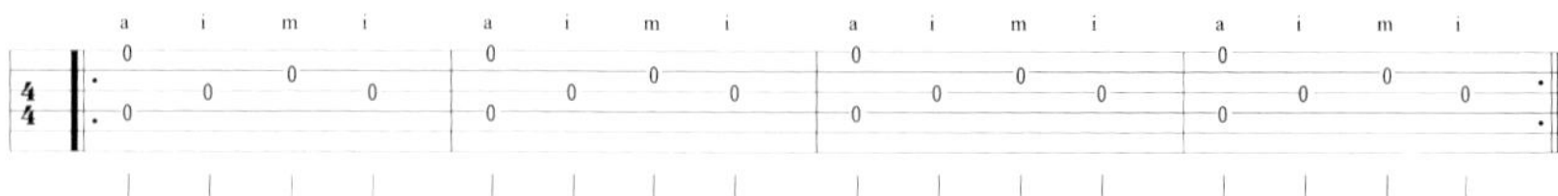

Pluck **p** and **a** together and the rest individually. Make sure **i** stays on the third string, **m** on the second and **a** on the first.

GETTING BETTER AT FINGERPICKING

As with many aspects of guitar playing, it is one thing to become proficient with one hand but quite another to sustain that proficiency when both hands are in action. In this lesson we look at fingerpicking with the left hand while the right hand selects and changes chords.

Fingerpicking while changing chords can cause coordination issues for many players at first. The right hand has to work hard, but in some ways this can take the pressure off the left hand. So, for example, if you spread out the notes of a chord rather than playing them as a block, then you can stagger the change and add the left-hand fingers one at a time, in the order they need to be played. This staggered approach can greatly improve the fluency of your playing. Keep this in mind when doing the exercises on these pages.

FOLK **GUITAR**

During the 1950s the folk-revival movement brought the steel-string acoustic guitar to the fore. Artists such as Woodie Guthrie, Lead Belly and Pete Seeger accompanied themselves using simple patterns on the guitar, faithfully collecting and interpreting traditional songs as well as composing their own. Later, in the 1960s and 1970s, artists such as Bob Dylan, Joni Mitchell, Joan Baez, Leonard Cohen, Neil Young and Paul Simon made further use of the acoustic guitar's folk connotations in their music. British folkies such as Davey Graham and Bert Jansch pioneered solo folk-guitar playing, drawing on traditional melodies, classical music and even African and Middle Eastern music to create unique styles. The acoustic guitar has also become an important instrument in traditional Celtic music, often as a solo instrument. Present-day folk guitarists make extensive use of fingerpicking, alternative tunings (see pages 96–97, 146–149) and capos (see pages 144–145) to introduce different textures and timbres to the sound of their instruments.

Tambourine man In his youth, Bob Dylan's songwriting and playing style were almost wilfully simple. It was as if he did not want any musicality to get in the way of the poetry and the protest.

Exercises combining fingerpicking with chords

These exercises begin with simple picked arpeggios, then get a little more challenging.

Using D major Make sure all the notes ring clearly.

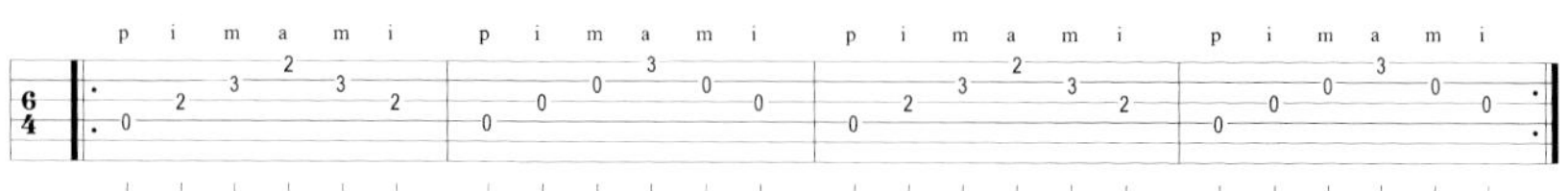

Using D and easy G The second chord here is an easy version of a G – the only note pressed is the first string, third fret. Remember to prepare the right-hand fingers as you go up the strings but not on the way down.

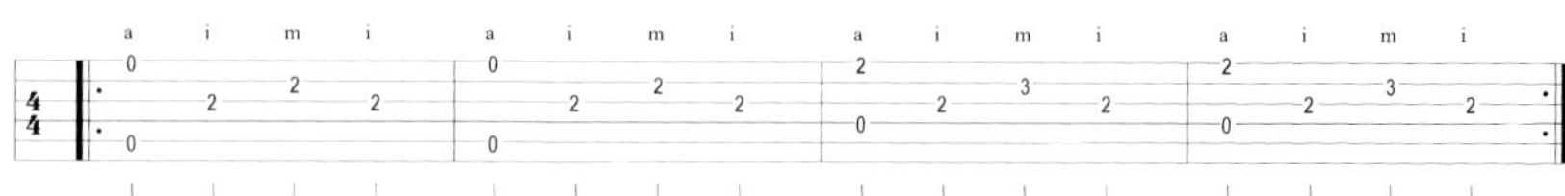

Using A and D Stagger the changes here. When changing to the D, play the open fourth string and first string, second fret, separately. Then add the first finger on the third string and finally add the third finger on the second string. This will help the continuity of the music. Think of adding one note at a time and holding them until you need to change.

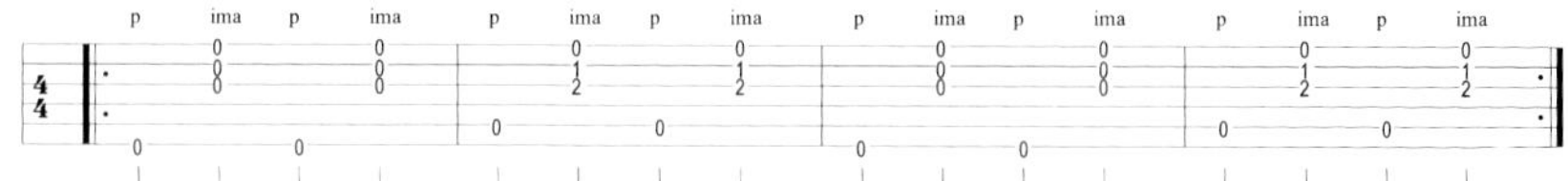

Using E minor and A minor The E minor is made really easy here. The fourth and fifth strings are not needed, so there is also no need to press the usual fingers down. Use only the open strings in the chord and get the A minor ready to go down.

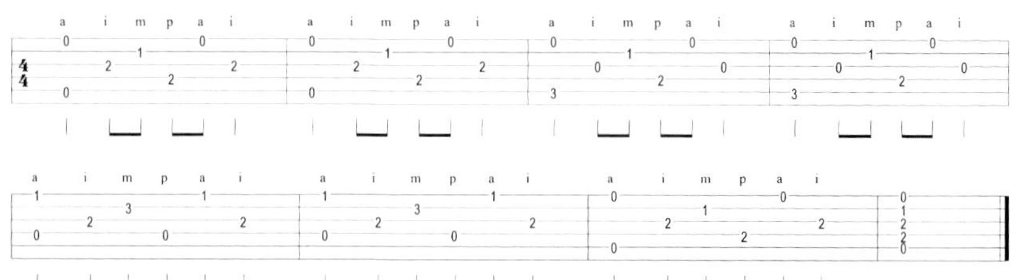

A longer exercise Stick to the string order – with **p** covering the three bass strings, **i** on the third string, **m** on the second and **a** on the first. Follow the chord shapes to be played and take note of the rhythm. A distinct bass line and treble part should emerge.

LESSON 37

PICKING AND STRUMMING

Now that your fingerpicking technique is established it is time to add some variety. It is possible to strum with the fingers at the same time as you pluck. This skill will add another texture to your playing. It is also a good way to strengthen the right hand fingers.

As a first experiment in picking and strumming, try the following: hold a D chord, then use your thumb to alternate playing the fourth and fifth strings – creating a simple bassline; next, use the index finger of the right hand to strum the third, second and first strings between the bass notes. Strum with the back of the index finger nail, as if flicking with your finger. A simple country-style line should emerge. This technique can be made more versatile by adding single finger upstrokes to the mix, which allows for more variation in the rhythm. These possibilities are explored in the exercises on the opposite page.

Above and right To combine fingerpicking and strumming, you should begin with your thumb on the bass notes and your index finger lightly brushing the strings. Keep your right-hand position constant, so that you can switch between the two techniques easily and accurately return your fingers to the fingerpicking shape (**p, i, m, a**) after strumming.

Exercises combining fingerpicking and strumming

Use these exercises as a starting point for experimentation. Many players have idiosyncratic ways of picking, or picking and strumming together. Get the feel of it, and go in search of your own style.

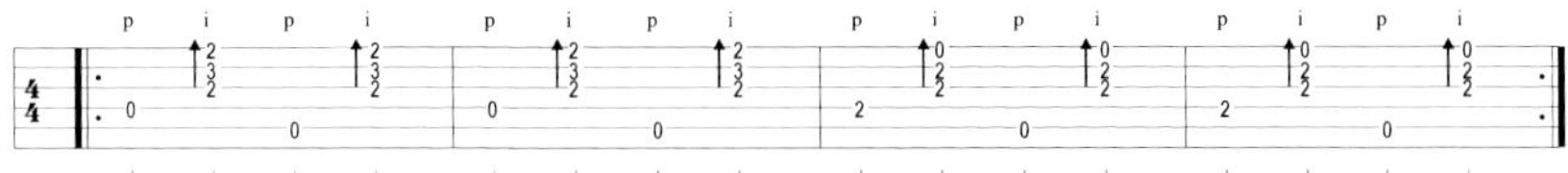

Alternating bass exercise with strummed chords This exercise uses simple D and A chords and **p** and **i** fingers with moving bass. Pluck all the bass notes with **p** and flick out the **i** finger in between to strum the chords.

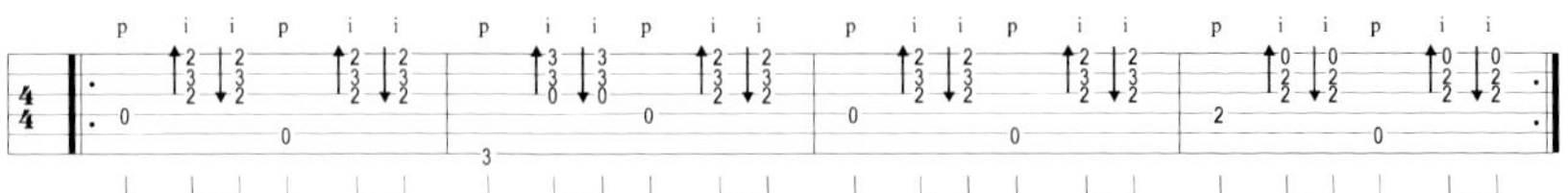

Exercise in index-finger upstrokes and downstrokes This uses a combination of **i** upstrokes and downstrokes. Strum downwards with the i finger as before then pluck up from the first string, aiming to catch the top three strings. Use a swing rhythm here. The chords are D, G and A.

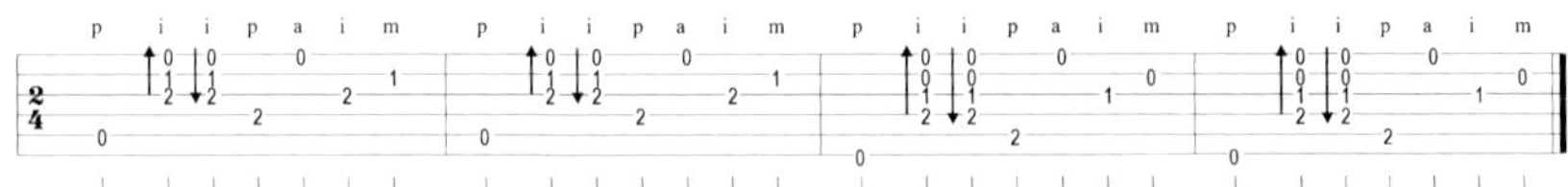

Combining a fingerpicking pattern and strumming In this exercise there is a mixture of strumming and plucking with the fingers. Practise very slowly at first, concentrating on keeping the strumming compact and finding the strings in the right hand without hesitation. Use a simple A minor to E minor progression.

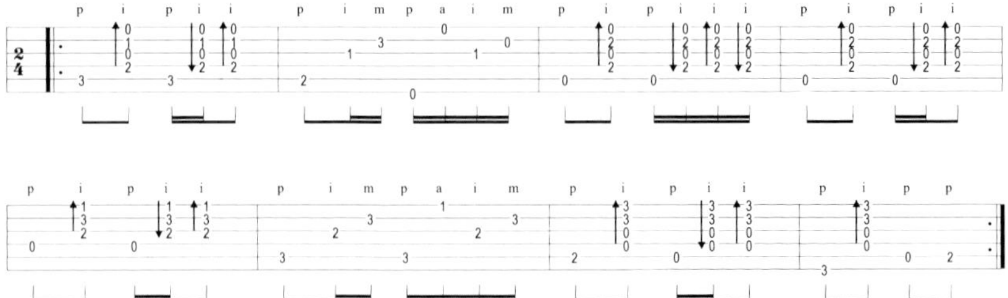

Advanced exercise with fingerpicking and strumming Here is a longer exercise to test out the right-hand fingerpicking technique. Follow all the finger markings and strumming directions closely. Hold a chord shape for each bar with the exception of the last two bars – here there is a walking bass line. In the sixth bar the chord shape is a D minor/C.

BASIC SCALES

Scales are an excellent way to improve your technique, and the aim of this lesson is to develop better finger control. If you practise scales regularly, you may well also find that you can play more quickly and that you expand your musical understanding, too.

All scales, major or minor, are made up of eight notes. Some of these notes are a whole tone apart, others are divided by a semitone. The placing and the size of these spaces determines the nature of the scale. When semitones fall after the third and the seventh notes, and all the other spaces are a whole tone, then the result is a major scale. When the semitones fall after the second and fifth notes, then you have a natural minor scale.

Plotting scales

The major scale is the most basic and familiar scale of all. It is the do-re-mi immortalized in the song that begins 'Doe, a deer, a female deer . . .' A major scale can be played in any key, but the simplest of them is C, because it contains no sharps or flats. In other words, if you were to play it on the piano, you would simply step up the white keys from C to C and never have to play a black note. In the diagram below, the key of C major is shown with the gaps between the notes. T stands for a whole tone, and S for a semitone.

T T S T T T S
C D E F G A B C

If the key were to change, the notes would be different but the pattern of Ts and Ss would remain the same. The same applies to a natural minor scale, the simplest of which is A minor.

T S T T S T T
A B C D E F G A

This scale, like C major, contains no sharps or flats, a fact that goes a long way to explaining why the change between the chords of C and A minor is so easy on the guitar, and why it sounds so right.

C major – a scale over one octave

First try to play this simple major scale by reading the notes or following the tab, then move on to the harder exercises opposite.

Exercises in major and minor scales

These exercises will help you to get familiar with some of the more commonly used scales, and they are a good practical workout for your left-hand too.

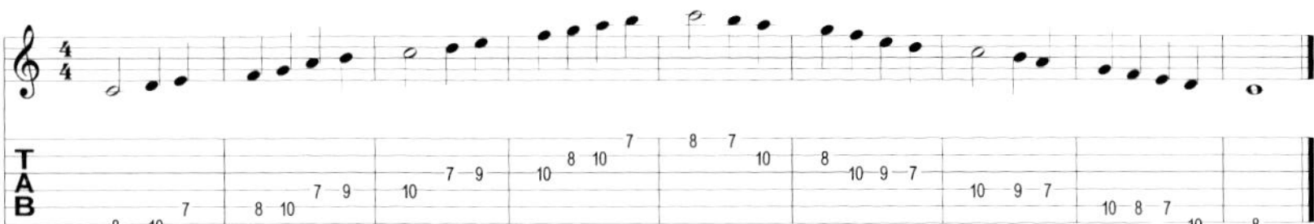

C major scale, two octaves over six strings This exercise is an extension of the C major scale that you have just attempted on the opposite page. Since this exercise is in C too, you have no sharps or flats to worry about.

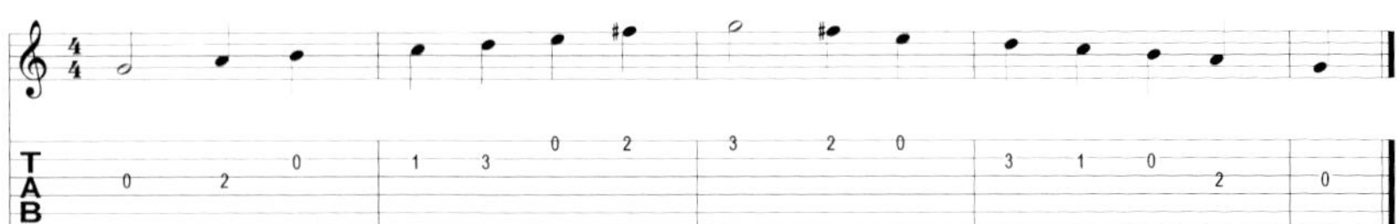

G major scale, one octave The G major scale requires an F-sharp note on the seventh degree of the scale to preserve the semitone step at the end.

A natural minor, two octaves over six strings The fingering given underneath in tab is the standard pattern, but there are many other ways. Try finding the notes in different areas of the fingerboard.

D natural minor, two octaves over five strings As with the A natural minor above, try finding the notes in different parts of the fingerboard, as this will give you more flexibility.

LESSON 39

OTHER SCALES

There are some more scale patterns that every guitarist should know and practise daily. In this lesson we are going to learn the harmonic and melodic scales (both forms of the minor scale) and we revisit the full thirteen notes of the chromatic scale.

The harmonic scale is altered by raising the seventh degree of the scale by a semitone (in the example below, which begins on A, to a G-sharp).

This creates a bigger leap of a tone and a half from the sixth to the seventh note and pushes the last two notes of the scale closer together, making a more emphatic finish. It also gives the scale a certain middle-eastern quality.

Melodic

The melodic minor scale raises the sixth and seventh degrees of the scale by a semitone on the way up, allowing for a smoother-sounding transition towards the top note.

When descending the scale, however, these notes are 'naturalized' to G and F natural, so that the descending half is the same as a natural minor scale.

Chromatic

A chromatic scale ascends and descends in semitones – playing every note available. We encountered the chromatic scale when we were first looking at tablature on pages 41–43. This time,we are thinking about how to read it from the stave and play it with four fingers. The scale below is in open first position, starting on E. It is an excellent workout for the left hand, and a good warm-up for the exercises on the opposite page.

Chromatic scale starting on E

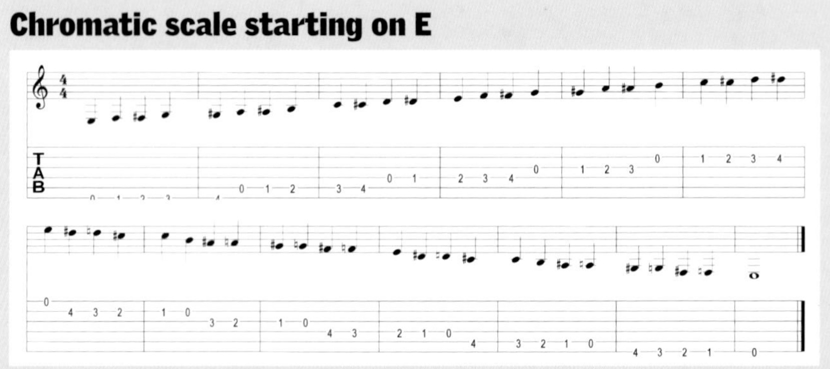

Simply keep one finger in each fret. You will see that there are only three frets to be played on the third string. Don't avoid using the little finger, and remember to use the open strings too.

Exercises in harmonic and melodic scales

Here are some examples of harmonic and melodic scales for you to practise.

A harmonic minor, two octaves over six strings The root of the scale is on the sixth string. Start in fifth position and use one finger in each fret. Shift up the fourth string into ninth position after reaching the first octave.

D harmonic minor, two octaves over five strings In this exercise the root of the scale is on the fifth string. Keep in fifth position until the final two notes of the scale. Slide up the first string with the second finger.

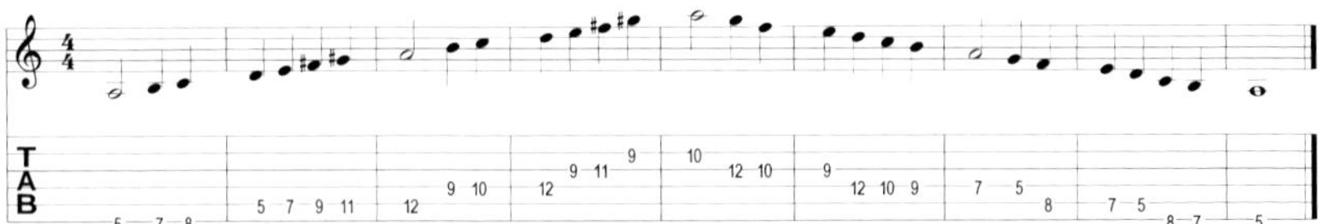

A melodic minor, two octaves over six strings Shift along the fifth string into ninth position as you ascend the scale. Descend by shifting back into fifth position on the fourth string. Remember that the melodic minor is different on the way down.

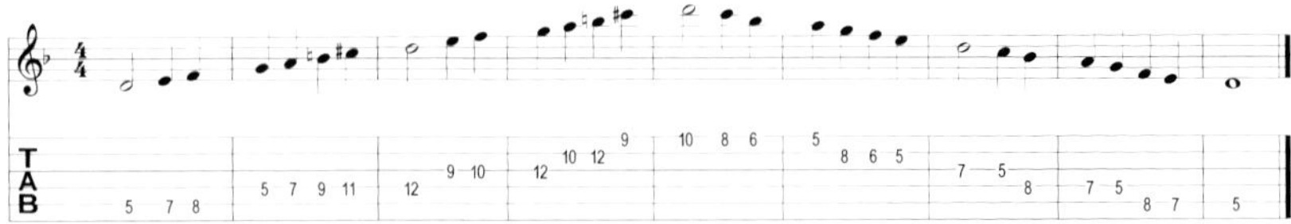

D melodic minor, two octaves over five strings Shift along the fourth string into ninth position as you ascend the scale. After playing the top note, D, shift immediately into fifth position with the fourth finger. Descend in fifth position.

LESSON 40

DOUBLE STOPPING AND INTERVALS

'Double stopping' means playing two notes together. It is a technique that is used to add body to melodic playing. Double stopping allows you to take a single-string melody and add a note to each note you play, one that harmonizes and moves in sympathy with the melody.

Playing two notes together creates an 'interval'. Intervals are measured by the distance between the two notes. For example, the distance between the open B string and the open E string is four notes, making a fourth, as in the diagram, right. There are also seconds, thirds, fourths, fifths, sixths, sevenths and octaves. Some intervals naturally harmonize while others, such as the fourth, can sound harsh.

B	C	D	E
1	2	3	4

The interval from B to E is a fourth. Always include the lowest note as you count up.

Thirds

On the guitar there are shapes, like chord shapes, to help you find the intervals easily. Let's begin with thirds. Intervals of a third can be either major or minor. Major thirds are four semitones apart, minor ones three semitones apart. The first example opposite shows a minor and a major interval on the first and second strings: D to F (three semitones, so minor), and D to F-sharp (four semitones, so major). You will notice that both these intervals are part of the basic D major and minor chords but without the second finger on the third string.

Exercise using a harmonized melody of thirds

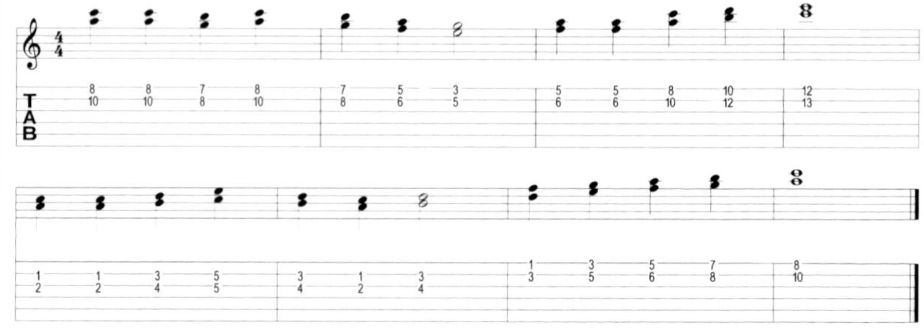

TAB (line 1):

String												
1	8	8	7	8	7	5	3	5	5	8	10	12
2	10	10	8	10	8	6	5	6	6	10	12	13

TAB (line 2):

String												
1								1	3	5	7	8
2	1	1	3	5	3	1	3	3	5	6	8	10
3	2	2	4	5	4	2	4					

Some third intervals

It is possible to play thirds on each pair of adjacent strings. In each of the pairs on this page, the minor third consists of an interval that is a semitone closer to the other note than a major chord, and so one fret closer on the fingerboard. On the second and third strings, the major third is on the same fret.

But don't worry too much about the theory for now. The finger positions are fairly consistent, and after a while will become as natural to you as the basic chord shapes.

First and second strings

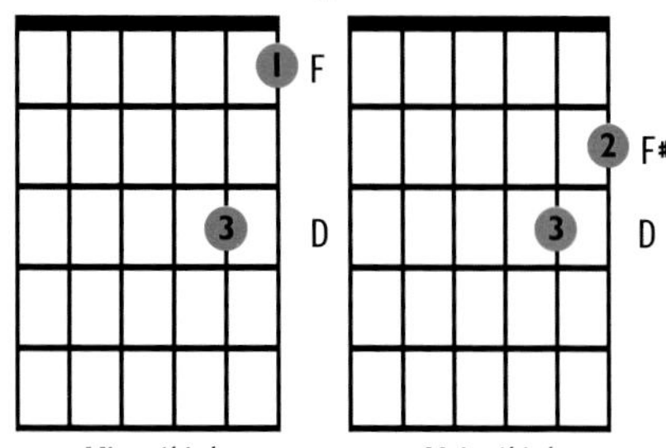

Use the second finger on all the third-string notes. Switch between the third and first fingers on the second string.

Second and third strings

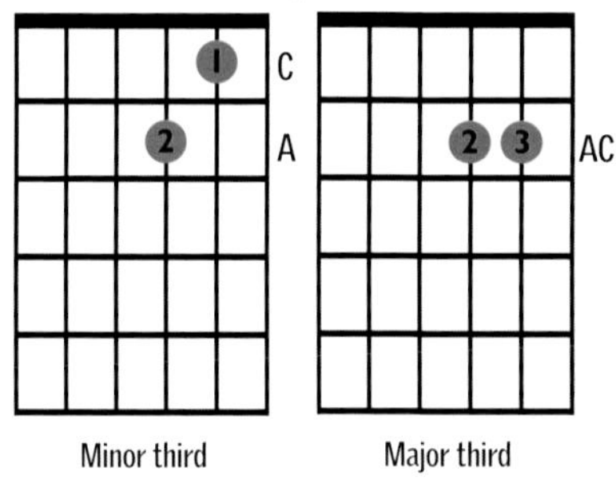

Use the second finger on all the third-string notes. Switch between the third and first fingers on the second string.

Third and fourth strings

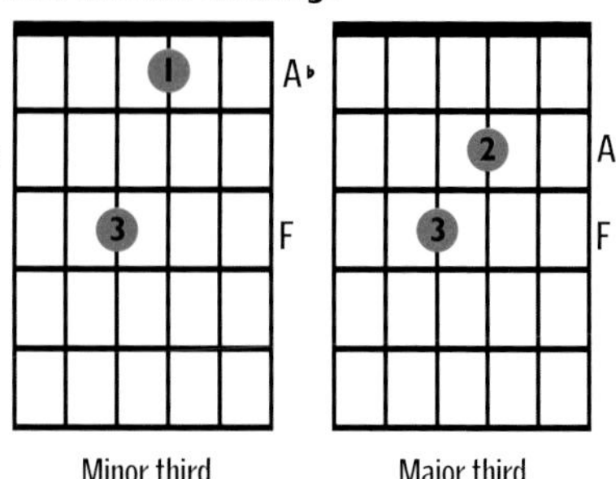

Use the third finger on all the fourth-string notes. Switch between the second and first fingers on the third string.

Fourth and fifth strings

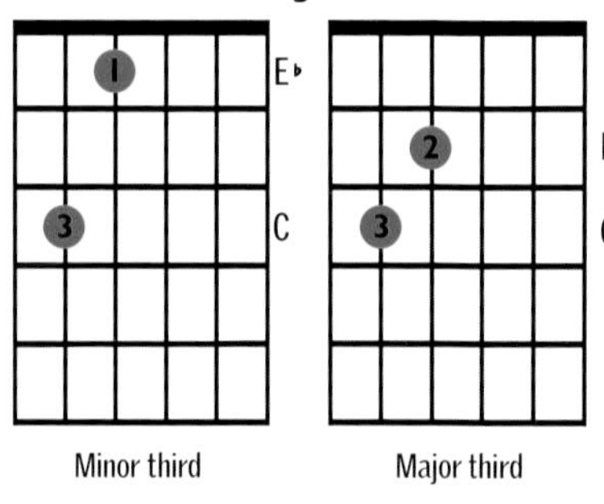

Use the third finger on all the fifth-string notes. Switch between the second and third fingers on the fourth string.

Fifth and sixth strings

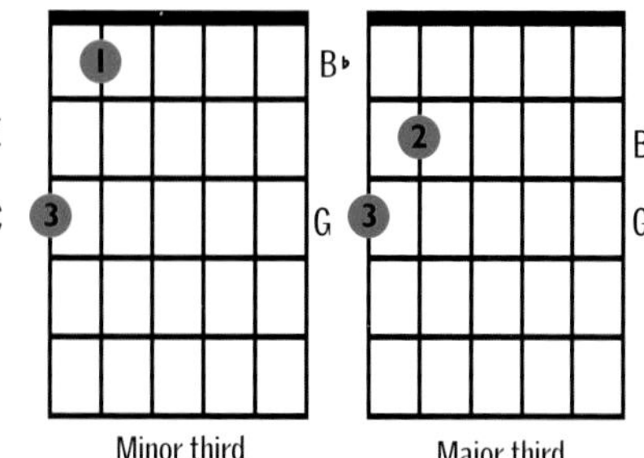

Use the third finger on all the sixth-string notes. Switch between the second and first fingers on the fifth string.

Sixths

Intervals of a sixth, like thirds, can be major or minor. Sixths can be plucked with two fingers or else they can be strummed. But they are not on adjacent strings, so care should be taken to block the string between the two fretted notes when strumming. To block the intervening string, play with your left-hand fingers slightly flat.

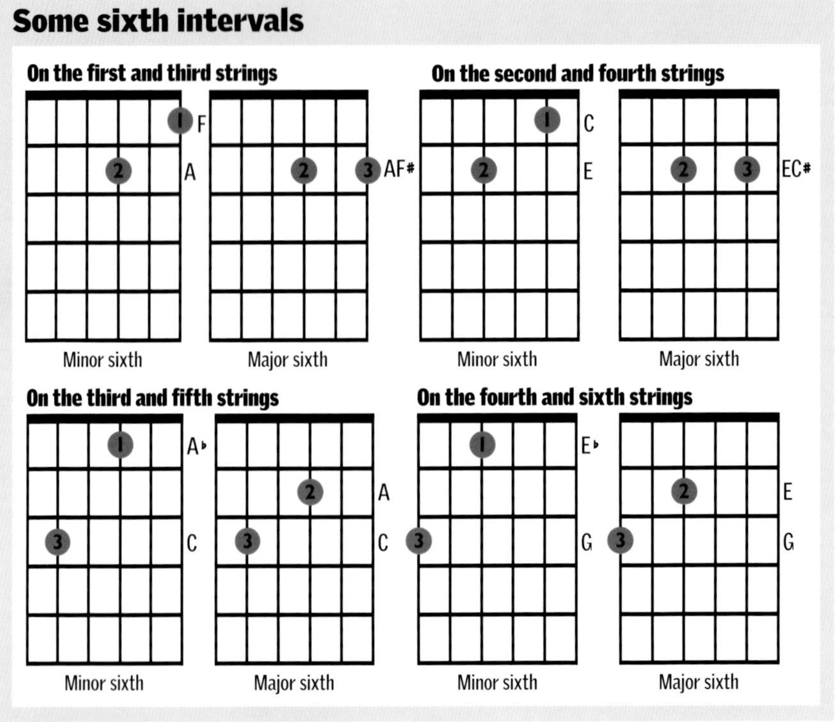

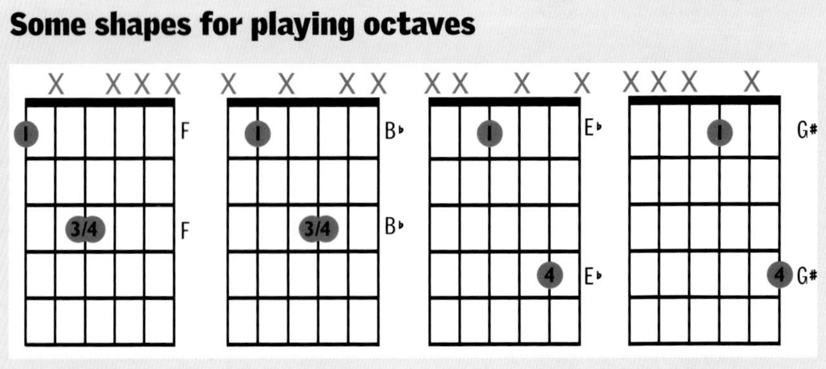

Octaves

Playing melodies in octaves can have a powerful effect. This method doubles up the melody note being played and, with some damping in the left hand, allows the performer to strum fully and play with a big sound. Of course, it can be used more subtly. Jazz guitarist Wes Montgomery often improvised in octaves, which gives his guitar a wonderfully warm tone.

Exercise using sixths

Playing in sixths is a great way of boosting a melody. The second finger will play the lower notes and connect the shapes as you move around the neck. All other notes will be played with the first or third fingers.

Exercise using octaves

Most players will play octave shapes with the first and fourth fingers of the left hand. This helps with the stretch, and makes it easier to damp the unwanted strings.

GOING ELECTRIC

You may have been playing electric from the start; or you may have been playing acoustic, and now feel ready to try a different kind of guitar. On these pages we look at the many interesting effects you can achieve when your guitar is wired for sound.

If you can play an acoustic guitar, then you can play an electric, and vice versa. They are the same instrument; the difference lies only in the way that the sound is amplified. But they feel very different: if you have only ever played acoustic, the thin body of an electric takes some getting used to, as do the various switches and knobs.

Pickups

On an electric, the job of the soundhole is done by the pickups. These are devices that 'pick up' the vibrations of the strings and transmit them to the amplifier. Most electric guitars have two or three pickups; some have only one, or as many as four.

The number of pickups and their arrangement on the body are two factors that affect the sound of the guitar. More crucial, however, is the type of pickup. The two main types are single-coil and humbuckers. Humbuckers were invented to counter a problematic humming noise with the older, single-coil variety. They are generally held to have a warmer and more powerful sound. Both types are still current: many guitars have a combination of single-coil and humbuckers, so as to maximize the range of the instrument.

On the electric guitar some of the work of altering the timbre is done by the use of the pickup-selector switch. This switch, sometimes marked 'rhythm' and 'lead', selects one or more of the available pickups. Depending on the make and model of the guitar and the number of pickups fitted, there will be between three and five possible positions.

Above and right Humbuckers (above) are normally square, often all chrome. Single coils (right) are smaller, with individual magnets for each string.

Tone and volume

The number of tone and volume knobs also varies from model to model. Simpler designs such as the Fender Telecaster can have just one of each, and the sound from all the pickups will be governed by a single knob. Other guitars – the Gibson Les Paul, for example – have volume and tone controls for two separate pickups, which allows you to preset contrasting sounds.

The tone control varies the brightness and 'attack' of the sound. The best way to judge its effect is to play around with it, and with all the other variables on your guitar. But bear in mind that the control knobs are not a substitute for technique. It is the job of your right hand to provide colour, whatever guitar you are playing.

Amplifiers

To play electric you need an amplifier. A 20-watt amp is quite loud and powerful enough for practising at home. Amplifiers come as a single unit (a 'combination' amp), or in two parts consisting of a 'head' and a separate speaker. The guitar's sound is controlled by a preamplifier, which may incorporate electronic effects such as distortion and reverb.

Until the 1970s, amplifiers used vacuum tubes known as 'valves'. These days, solid-state transistor technology is more common, but there are still amps that use valves, or a combination of both technologies. Some players feel that valve amps give a warmer, more natural sound than solid-state amps.

Basic amplifier settings

Whatever kind of amplifier you go for, knowing how to get some good basic sounds is essential. The basic settings (below) can be adapted to most amplifier configurations and should be used as a starting point from which you can experiment.

CLEAN

Gain: 0 Bass: 4 Mid: 4 Treble: 8 Reverb: 2

Use your amplifier's 'clean channel', if it has one. If not, use a low amount of gain and turn the master volume up to compensate.

CRUNCH

Gain: 2 Bass: 5 Mid: 5 Treble: 7 Reverb: 1

This setting should give you a subtle distortion when you are playing chords, and also more sustain when you are playing solo lines.

BLUES AND ROCK

Gain: 5 Bass: 8 Mid: 5 Treble: 6 Reverb: 4

This setting will give you a rounded distortion which is ideal for big blues solos and bending strings. The reverb setting is optional, but it can add more depth to the sound.

METAL

Gain: 10 Bass: 10 Mid: 8 Treble: 8 Reverb: 0

The high bass and gain will make for a smoothly distorted sound, ideal for power chords and bass riffs. Reduce bass for a harsher thrash-metal sound. Beware of feedback – unless that's what you want!

PEDALS AND ELECTRIC EFFECTS

Most professional electric-guitar players use an array of foot-operated effects in addition to the controls on the amp and on the guitar itself. These 'pedals' create yet more musical possibilities, and they allow a performer to radically change the sound of the instrument mid-song.

All of the classic devices discussed on these pages work by intercepting the signal on its way down the lead from the guitar to the amplifier and then modifying it in some way. Each pedal affects the sound differently. You can now buy digital pedals that contain most of the classic effects in a single unit. These can be programmed, sequenced and edited to create an almost infinite range of acoustic possibilities.

Distortion

The effect known as 'distortion' was first heard as a symptom of a weak or damaged amplifier. Early rock guitarists found that they liked the fuzzy noise and sought to engineer it deliberately by playing amplifiers at high volume and 'overdriving' (that is, overloading) the valves. Basic distortion pedals seek to recreate this sound, while others go beyond natural distortion levels for more extreme effects.

Left A distortion pedal.

Tremolo

Tremolo was one of the first effects to be built into guitar amplifiers. The Fender Twin Reverb, a vintage 1960s guitar, featured tremolo – though on that model it was misnamed 'vibrato'. Tremolo is a volume-based effect in which a bell-like sound is created by a rapid variation in volume for the length of a single note. The speed and depth of the tremolo can be controlled by the player.

Delay

A delay pedal works by reproducing the sound of the guitar after a preset time. It can take the form of a 'slap' delay, which is a single repetition of the sound, or there can be multiple repetitions – an echo. The player controls the length, depth and rate of these repetitions. Some delay pedals also have a 'loop' function: at the press of a switch the pedal records

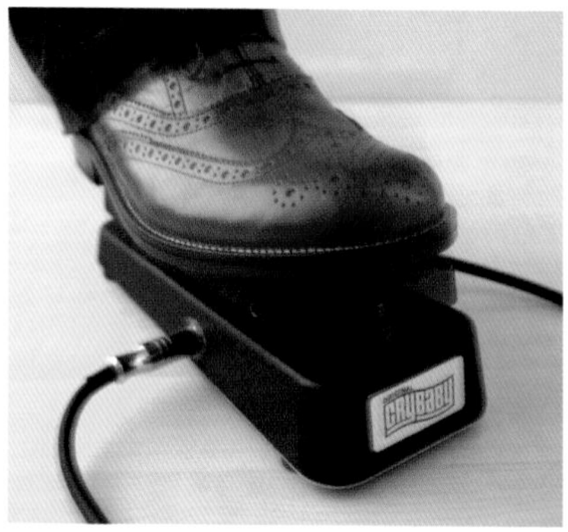

Above A wah-wah pedal.

Above The EBow.

a short musical phrase that can then be repeated while the guitarists plays something else over the top.

Wah-wah

A wah-wah pedal is different from other gadgets in that it has to be played by the guitarist, note by note. The top of the pedal rocks back and forth and works by allowing low or high frequencies to pass through according to the position of the pedal. It is the variance in frequency that creates the distinctive 'wow' sound. The effect was very popular in the late 1960s and 1970s, when it was a trademark of guitarists such as Eric Clapton and Jimi Hendrix.

Other devices

There are many other devices that work by adding layers to the texture of the music. A chorus pedal, for example, creates a sound with a warm, shimmering quality, as if there were more than one guitar playing. The effect is created by splitting the sound signal in two, modulating the pitch of one signal, then mixing it back into the original. An octaver pedal generates a synthetic signal one or two octaves above or below the original. This can be used to fill out the bass register or to create an edgier sound when soloing. Harmonizer pedals work in the same way, but can be set to different intervals to create automatic harmonies.

EBow

The EBow is not a pedal but a rather strange hand-held electromagnetic gadget that is used to 'bow' the strings electronically instead of striking them with the fingers or a plectrum. The electromagnets in the device cause the strings to vibrate, creating a sustained drone that can be made to sound variously like a bowed violin or cello, a harmonica or even bagpipes.

Tuning pedal

Not the most glamorous device, a tuning pedal is used to bypass the amplifier so that a guitarist can tune up quietly, without disturbing the rest of the band.

BEING CREATIVE

The third and final section of the book focuses on expanding your repertoire of playing techniques. The goal is to get you thinking about your development not just as a guitarist, but as a musician. Composing your own pieces is a good route to fine musicianship, and it is a practical, creative way of learning about music theory. The step-by-step method in this chapter will get you started as a writer of music. You will also be learning to play some jazz chords, and getting to know specialized techniques such as open tunings and slide guitar. While exploring these skills, you should continue to polish your technique with the daily exercise routine (see pages 168–173).

MODIFYING BAR CHORDS

Full bar chords use either five or six strings to get a rich sound from the guitar, but they can be very tiring for the left hand to play. Here we learn how to cut down each shape, so as to make simple accompaniments less demanding.

As a rule, you do not want to exert more effort than you have to when playing the guitar. Bar chords are hard work, and there is no point in barring unless you are playing the whole chord. So it is worth learning shapes that do the same job as bar chords when you are playing only the top three, four or five strings.

Reducing the bar

Take the E-shape, for example. If you are playing on five strings, then the first finger need only cover the top two strings at the first fret (see photograph, below).

When you play an E-shape in this manner, the wrist can be straighter than before, and the left-hand thumb can even edge over the neck to damp down the now open sixth string. Many players find that they prefer to make an E-shaped bar chord this way when they are playing standing up.

Below A five-string E-shape bar chord at the fifth fret.

If you want an even lighter sound, it is a simple matter to reduce the chord to four strings by removing the third finger from the third fret, fifth string.

Remember that this shape is still moveable, that is, it can be placed anywhere on the neck. Keep the full shape in mind, as the original root note (the sixth string) still determines the chord you are playing. Remember, too, that having cut down the number of strings in the left hand you will need to avoid playing those strings with the right.

This pared-down bar-chord technique also works for the A-shape, the Em-shape and the Am-shape. Overleaf you will find a gallery of these common bar shapes in both their full and their reduced forms. You will also find the full forms of the A7-shape and the E7-shape. Practise making these chords in all their forms, then do the exercises below.

Reduced bar-chord exercises

Do these exercises once you have learned the reduced bar-chord shapes, overleaf.

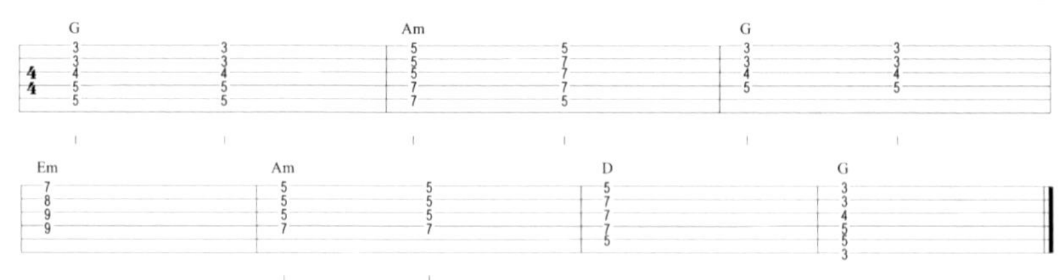

Some modified bar chords This is a simple progression using bar chords with reduced strings. Treat this as a very slow and freely played piece. Don't rush the changes, and concentrate on making a good sound on each chord. Slide fingers along the string where possible – the third and fourth fingers from the G to A minor in the first bar, for example.

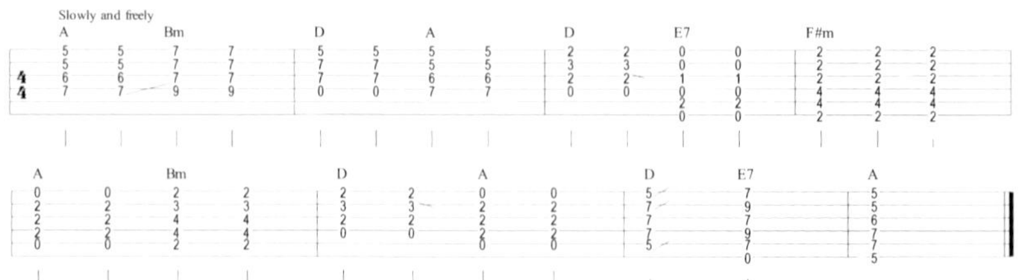

Combining modified bar chords and standard chords This is a challenging piece, as it mixes six-, five- and four-string chords with seventh chords and standard chord shapes. Follow the slide marks to connect the chords more easily. These guide fingers will help you get around the neck, and give your fingers a path to follow. Treat the rhythm loosely here. Play as if it were improvised, and focus on moving around neatly. Relax the left hand between shapes by releasing the pressure on the fretboard of your guitar.

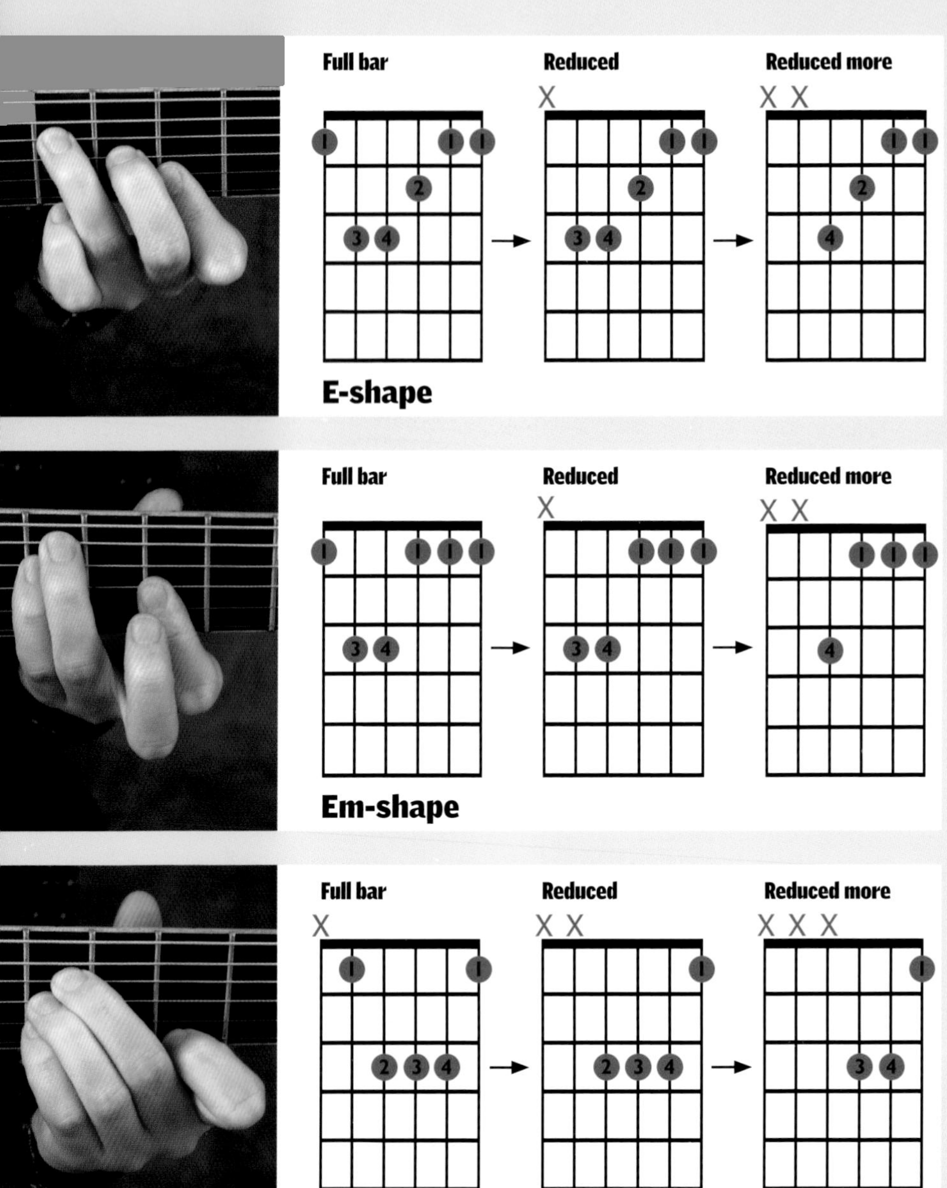
Full bar
Reduced
Reduced more
X
X X
1 1 1
1 1 1
1 1 1
2 2 2
3 4
3 4
4
E-shape
Full bar
Reduced
Reduced more
X
X X
1 1 1 1
1 1 1
1 1 1
3 4
3 4
4
Em-shape
Full bar
Reduced
Reduced more
X
X X
X X X
1 1
1
1
2 3 4
2 3 4
3 4
A-shape

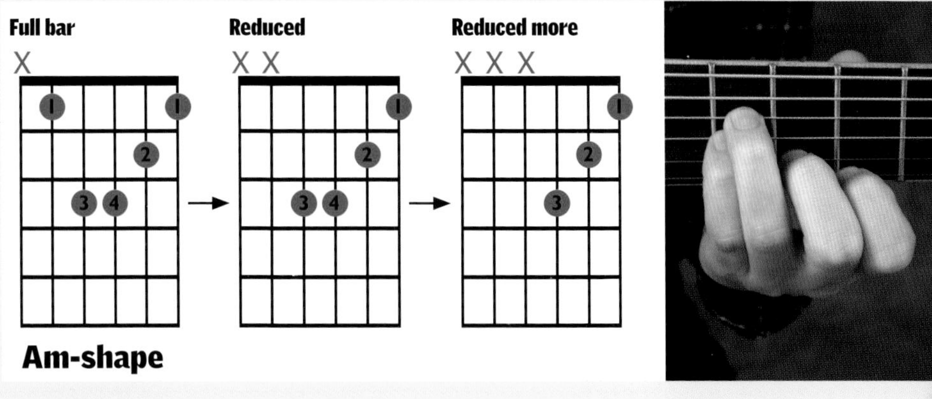

Seventh chords

We have learned how to turn standard chord shapes into bar chords; it follows that we can do the same with seventh chords. Study the E7 and A7-shapes and try the exercise on page 119 that combines the modified chords with standard chords.

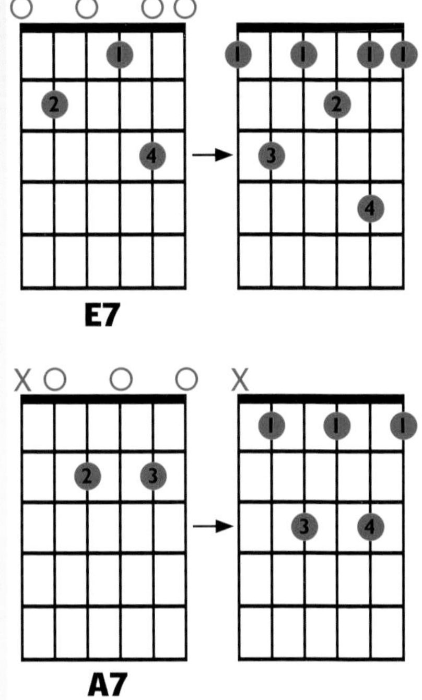

The E7-shape is easy to bar, and to move up and down the neck.

WRITING A SONG

In this section we get really creative. We will be using basic chord shapes along with your knowledge of the notes in first position to compose a simple melody with accompaniment. With the help of the five-point method described here, you can begin writing your own songs.

In this extended lesson you will be constructing a song from the bottom up. You will first choose a key, then a chord progression, which will serve as the foundation and the outline of your song. To this bare structure you will be asked to apply a style of accompaniment. When these elements are in place you will build a melody around the chords. At the final stage you can refine the tune, and even add some words if you want.

1. Pick a key

The first task is to pick a key. Let's go for C major: this is the 'home chord', the one that the song will most likely begin and end on. Now look at the scale below. If you take each note and add in the third and the fifth note above it in the scale, you will generate the chords shown. Do this in any major key, and the second, third and sixth chords will always be minor, the fourth and fifth major.

These chords are your harmonic palette, the colours you will use in your song. The three major chords are the strongest ones in the list, and these will be used most often. Very many songs use only these three chords (see 'three-chord tricks' on pages 36–37).

SETTING WORDS TO MUSIC

The starting point for your song might be a poem that means something to you. There is a long and venerable tradition of setting poetry to music, but not all poetry lends itself to a musical treatment. For your first experiments, pick something with a regular form and a strong, simple metre.

C major scale with chords

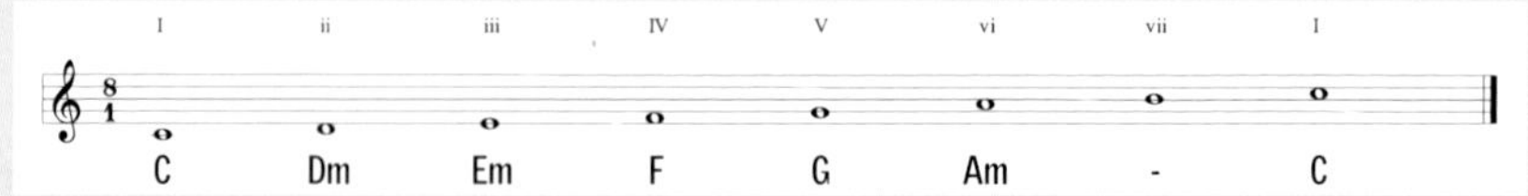

Each note of the scale represents a different chord shape, and these are numbered with roman numerals. You can see that the major-chord numerals are written in upper case Roman numerals (I, IV, V) and the minor chords in lower case (ii, iii, vi). These are all basic shapes with the exception of chord vii, which will not be used at this stage. So your chord palette in this key consists of C, Dm, Em, F, G and Am, that is, chords I–vi. You can pick any of these and be sure that they will sound good together.

2. Choose your chords

You are now ready to experiment with the chords in the key of C major to create a progression. This will be the roadmap of your song; it will dictate the directions in which the melody can go. A good way to start is to set out two rows of four bars on a piece of paper (1. below). Place the home chord, C major, in the first, fifth and last bars. They will provide solid points of reference – a beginning, an ending and a 'pitstop' for your song.

Next, fill in the vacant bars with chords from the list. The examples below (2. and 3.) should give you some ideas, but don't be limited by them. Play around until you find a progression that you like. Be sure to use one or two minor chords; you want something more adventurous than a major three-chord trick, after all. But be aware that too many minor chords can overcomplicate the sound. They are best deployed to add depth and richness to the music, so use them sparingly.

Building a chord structure for your song

Progressions two and three represent different ways of fleshing out the first, unfinished progression.

C I	–	–	–
C I	–	–	C I

1. An unfinished chord progression in C

C I	F IV	C I	G V
C I	Am vi	G V	C I

2. A completed progression in C

C I	Am vi	G V	F IV
C I	Am vi	F IV	C I

3. An alternative progression in C

3. The accompaniment

You have a chord structure for the song; next you have to decide how you want the guitar accompaniment to sound.

Adding a strumming or fingerpicking pattern at this stage will help the song to take shape. You can play the chords any way you want, and to any beat that appeals to you. If you are stuck for inspiration, look back through this book and choose a pattern at random. But opt for something you find easy to play. You can always add complexity later on.

Below are two suggestions for an accompaniment. One is a strumming pattern, the other is a fingerpicking scheme. Both options are based on the alternative finished chord progression – No.3 – that is given on page 123. This is the progression that we will proceed to mould into a song.

4. Add a melody

Now that the accompaniment is fixed, it is time to write an instrumental or vocal melody to go with it. We are about to construct a tune based on the chords in our progression. Standard chords are composed of a set of three notes known as a 'triad'. Aspiring guitarists sometimes

A sample strumming pattern

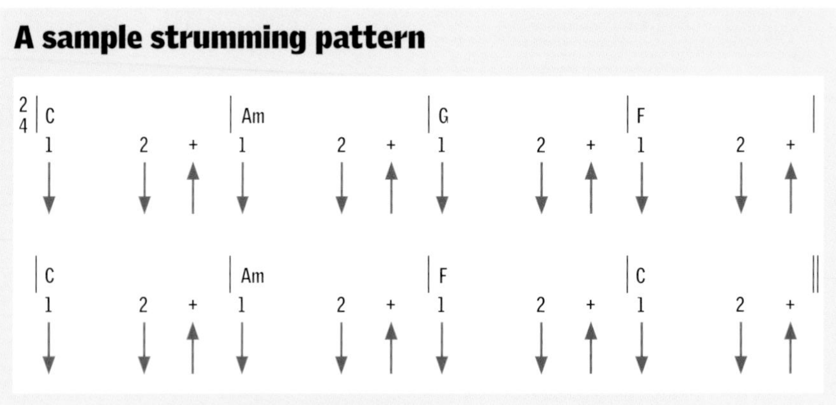

A sample fingerpicking pattern

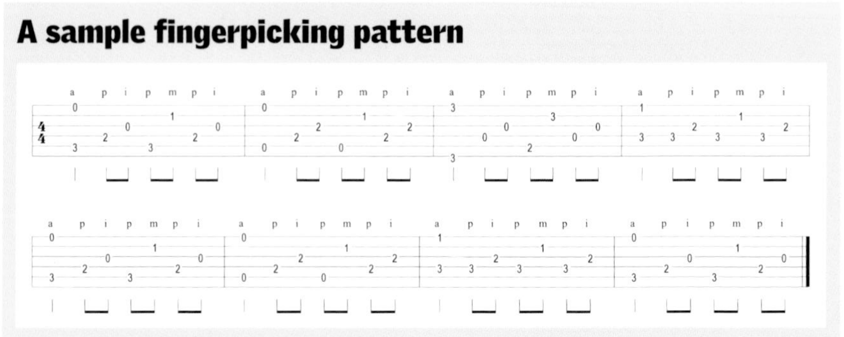

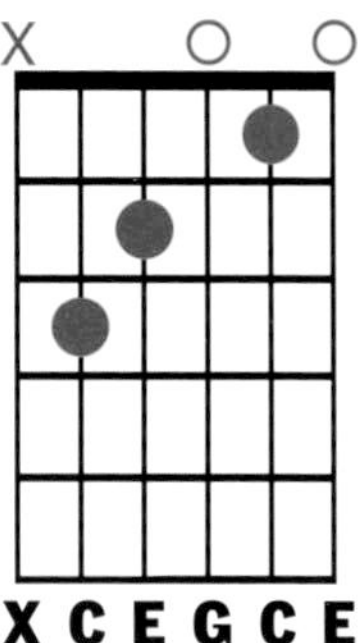

Left A C major chord played on five strings contains only three notes: it is called a triad. There is a single G on an open string, while the C and E occur twice, an octave apart.

find this fact confusing, since in most guitar chords there are five or six strings to be played. But if you look at any basic chord shape, you will see that there are only three different notes. The other strings merely duplicate notes already in the triad. C major, for example consists of only of C, E and G, as the chord diagram (right) illustrates.

We can make use of the triads to build our melody. Choose one note from each chord in the progression (the possibilities are spelled out in the chord scale below). Any note in the triad will work as a melody note, but try various ideas and possibilities. Now return to the chord progression you noted down earlier, and write in your chosen note above each chord. The example at the foot of this page is just one possibility; feel free to create your own tune.

Try playing the melody on the guitar at first, then see if you can hum the tune while you play the chord progression. Leave out the strumming for now if this confuses matters.

Triads in the scale of C major

The scale of C major, showing the triads and chord names. (Note that chord vii is a dissonant chord – diminished – and will not be used at this stage.)

I	ii	iii	IV	V	vi	vii	I
C	Dm	Em	F	G	Am	—	C
(CEG)	(DFA)	(EGB)	(FAC)	(GBD)	(ACE)		(CEG)

Melody with chord progression

Chord:	C	Am	G	F
(Melody:)	(E)	(E)	(D)	(C)

C	Am	F	C
(E)	(E)	(F)	(E)

5. Finishing touches

If you are happy with the framework of your melody, reintroduce the strumming or fingerpicking pattern and practise playing and singing the melody together.

This is the point when you might like to add some words (unless you have been working with words in mind from the start). You could write a few lines of your own, or else you could borrow some lyrics from another song or from a poem. Try to fit the words to your tune. In the process you will find that the melody naturally changes as it shapes itself to the rhythms inherent in language.

At this stage you might also choose to introduce some 'passing notes'. These are intermediate notes that connect the main melody notes. They do not necessarily have to be part of the chord triad.

You now have a song, complete with melody, passing notes, a lyric, perhaps, and a chord accompaniment. You could call it a finished piece and leave it there, but you might like to continue the creative process and embellish your chord progression and melody still further. Don't be afraid to rewrite if you think you can improve on your work.

The method described here should be used as a jumping-off point. Be flexible with the process: you might decide to change the chords or melody once you have your words, or you might abandon your strumming pattern halfway through. The point of this exercise – indeed of any songwriting method – is to open the floodgates of your own creativity, and let the music flow out.

Songsmith Noel Gallagher's melodies are often built around clever progressions. The four-chord opening riff of 'Wonderwall' is a prime example.

The finished song

This melancholy melody, with its lilting picked guitar line, is a result of the 5-step songwriting method.

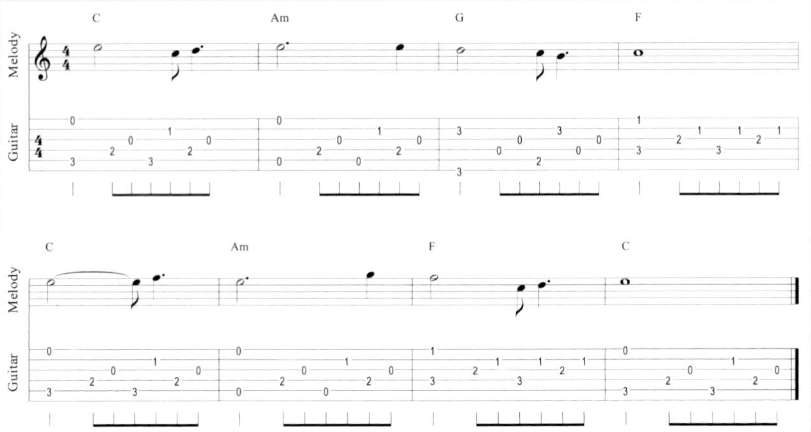

Melody / Guitar

C Am G F

C Am F C

MORE ON SONGWRITING

You have now written a song, but there are still things you need to know about the art of composition. This lesson contains some additional guidance on structuring your musical ideas. It also deals with the theory and practice of writing in other keys – both major and minor.

There is more to most songs than the brief melodic line that you have so far learned to write. It is a good thing if somewhere in the mix there is a 'hook', a catchy musical phrase that sticks in the mind and makes people want to hear that song again. It takes experience and real musicianship to come up with a good hook: they are very elusive.

Compositional tricks

Songs – popular songs, at least – tend to consist of an alternating series of verses and choruses. Verses can be as simple as two repeated chords, while choruses should contain more interest. Most songs also have a 'middle eight' or 'bridge', a musical digression that contrasts with the melody of the verse, and is sometimes in a different key, but usually resolves by leading back into the verse.

You can use the composing method for all these elements of your songs. You might use a different strumming or fingerpicking pattern for each section, or you could experiment with the order to create a structure that flows well.

Think, too, about your use of chords. Seventh chords are most commonly found on chord V, and are very effective and emphatic when followed by I, the home chord. Try going from G7 to C in the key of C major, or from E7 to A minor in the key of A minor. Alternatively, go for the unexpected by juxtaposing two chords that are not in the same key. D major and B-flat major, for example, do not naturally belong side by side, but the ear can get used to such strange combinations. Fit a melody around the notes of unrelated chords for some interesting results.

Making notes If you are serious about songwriting, you should jot down ideas for lyrics and melodies as they occur to you. Keep a pencil and paper handy.

Different keys

You can use the method outlined on pages 122–127 to write in any key. But in keys other than C major you will have to use accidentals (sharps and flats) in order to keep the correct pattern of intervals in the major scale.

The circle of fifths

It is always helpful to know how many accidentals you are letting yourself in for in any given key since, generally speaking, the more accidentals there are, the harder a piece is to play. Understanding keys requires a little musical theory. Look at the diagram below, on which the keys are arranged like the numbers on a clock face. C is at 12 o'clock; it is the neutral key with no sharps or flats. A fifth above C is G (at one o'clock), which has one sharp. A fifth above G is D, which has two sharps, and so on round to F-sharp, with its six sharps, at six o'clock. At the base of the circle there is an overlap: the key of D-flat, for example, has five flats or seven sharps, depending on how you look at it. You won't be surprised to learn that there are few guitar pieces with seven sharps.

Overleaf is a table of common major scales with their chords. This fulfils the same function for the other keys as the 'Triads in C major' diagram you used on page 125. It shows you at a glance where the accidentals fall. Use it to help you choose a good key for your compositions, and remember that chords I, IV and V will always be major and chords and ii, iii and vi will always be minor, no matter what key you decide to use.

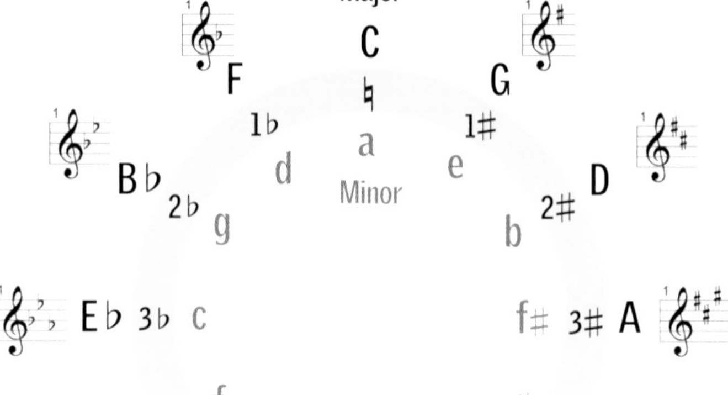

Left The circle of fifths tells you that F-sharp is the same key as G-flat, which has six flats. On the left-hand side, each key has one less flat with every jump up to the next fifth. D-flat at seven o'clock has 5 flats; F, at 11 o'clock, has one. The next step is back to C.

The major keys with their chords

Here are some of the commonly used major keys, along with the chords available to you.

I	ii	iii	IV	V	vi	vii	I
G	Am	Bm	C	D	Em	—	G
(GBD)	(ACE)	(BDF#)	(CEG)	(DF#A)	(EGB)		(GBD)

G major

I	ii	iii	IV	V	vi	vii	I
D	Em	F#m	G	A	Bm	—	D
(DF#A)	(EGB)	(F#AC#)	(GBD)	(AC#E)	(BDF#)		(DF#A)

D major

I	ii	iii	IV	V	vi	vii	I
A	Bm	C#m	D	E	F#m	—	A
(AC#E)	(BDF#)	(C#EG#)	(DF#A)	(EG#B)	(F#AC#)		(AC#E)

A major

I	ii	iii	IV	V	vi	vii	I
E	F#m	G#m	A	B	C#m	—	E
(EG#B)	(F#AC#)	(G#BD#)	(AC#E)	(BD#F#)	(C#EG#)		(EG#B)

E major

I	ii	iii	IV	V	vi	vii	I
F	Gm	Am	B♭	C	Dm	—	F
(FAC)	(GB♭D)	(ACE)	(B♭DF)	(CEG)	(DFA)		(FAC)

F major

I	ii	iii	IV	V	vi	vii	I
B♭	Cm	Dm	E♭	F	Gm	—	B♭
(B♭DF)	(CE♭G)	(DFA)	(E♭GB♭)	(FAC)	(GB♭D)		(B♭DF)

B-flat major

Composing in minor keys

Every minor key shares a key signature with a major key. That is to say, there is always a minor key that has the same number of sharps or flats as a major key. Look again at the circle of fifths on page 129. The inner circle shows the relative minor keys. We can see that E minor is related to G, Am to C, and so on.

In the harmonic-minor scale the seventh degree of the scale is raised by a semitone. In the melodic minor, both the sixth and seventh degrees of the scale are raised by a semitone. The scale patterns affect chords IV and V, as you can use the raised sixth and seventh notes in these chords. This subtly alters the composition method you have learned because it means that the raised sixth and seventh notes are available to you as well as the natural notes.

Look at the example below in A minor, where the sixth and seventh notes are F and G. Try the sample chord progression and listen to the different effects created by using the alternative chords IV and V.

TIP

When composing in minor keys bear in mind that the most commonly used chords will still be I, IV and V. Other chords are used to add colour. Chord V will typically become a major chord when moving to chord I, as this makes a more satisfying resolution.

Example in A minor

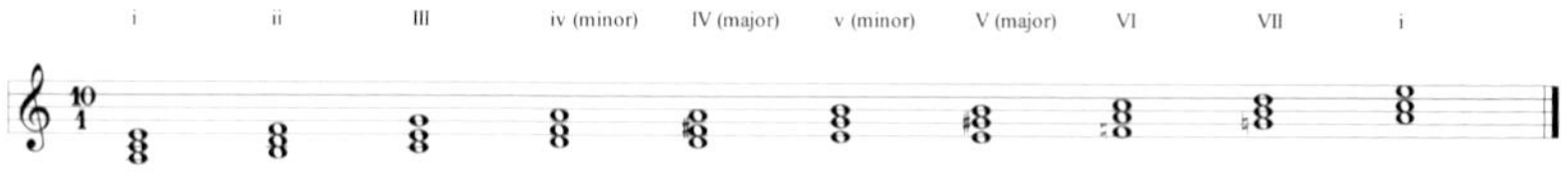

i	ii	III	iv (minor)	IV (major)	v (minor)	V (major)	VI	VII	i
Am	—	C	Dm	D	Em	E	F	G	Am
(ACE)		(CEG)	(DFA)	(DF#A)	(EGB)	(EG#B)	(FAC)	(GBD)	(ACE)

In the key of A minor, chords IV (D) and V (E) can be minor if no accidentals are added, or major if the F and G notes are raised. In effect, this gives you two options when picking your chords – both major and minor will sound good here. Note: chord ii is a dissonant chord (diminished), and it will not be used.

An A-minor progression

Am i	Em v	Dm iv	Am i
Am i	D IV	E V	Am i

Try playing the following examples using both major and minor versions of chords IV and V.

TIME SIGNATURES

Time signatures are another compositional element that can bring interest and complexity to your songwriting. Most rock and pop music uses the standard four beats in a bar, but there are many other signatures to try – and you can even change time mid-song.

In musical notation, time signatures are always given at the beginning of a piece of music, right after the clef sign. The signature is indicated by two numbers stacked on top of each other like a fraction. The upper number represents the number of beats in each bar; the lower number represents the note value to be used as one beat – quarter, half, eighth, and so on. So, a 3/4 time signature means three crotchets (quarter-note beats) in each bar – which is waltz time. A 2/2 time signature means two minims (half-note beats) in each bar.

Types of signature

There are two types of time signature, simple and compound. The term 'simple' is used for the most common signatures, for example, 4/4, 3/4 and 2/4. In the rarer 'compound' time signatures – 6/8, 9/8 or 12/8 – the beats are divided into smaller groups. In 6/8, for example, there are six quavers (eighth notes) in each bar. These are usually divided into two groups of three, which means that the listener will hear two main stresses in the bar. In 9/8, you would find three groups of quavers, and in 12/8 there are four. Compound time signatures make great use of the dotted crochet (dotted quarter note) as this is equal to a group of three quavers (one and a half beats).

That is the theory. In the exercises on the opposite page we are more concerned with the business of strumming to various time signatures, and using this practical knowledge to lend an interesting rhythmic feel to your compositions.

Tempo

You should bear in mind that the time signature of a piece of music is not the same thing as its 'tempo'. The term tempo refers to the speed at which a piece should be played. This is a matter of performance, and is largely up to the player to decide – although it is true that a slow 6/8 can sound very similar to a fast 3/4. As for your music, the main thing is to choose a signature that best describes the character of the music, and makes it clear to read on the page.

SONGS IN UNUSUAL SIGNATURES

'Blackened' – Metallica
'Take Five' – Dave Brubeck
Theme from *Mission: Impossible*
'Paranoid Android' – Radiohead
'Money' – Pink Floyd

Time signature exercises

Here are some exercises to try in various time signatures. Count the main beats as you play and follow the strumming patterns very precisely. Remember that main beats are usually downstrokes, and offbeats are usually upstrokes. Repeat each exercise many times until the rhythms are internalized. You can practise these exercises on open strings at first, or damp the strings with the left hand, and then try adding chord shapes afterwards.

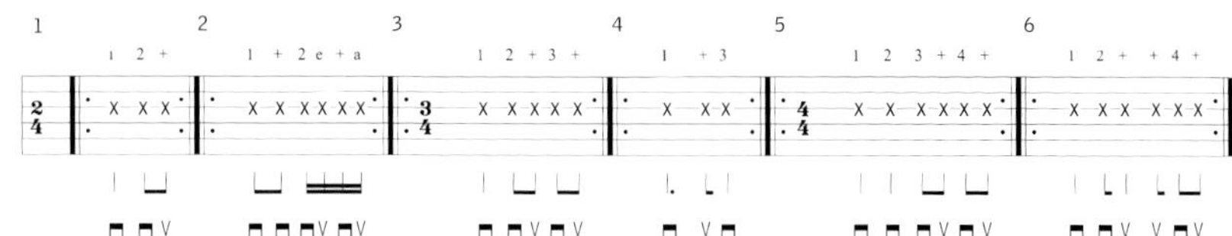

Accent the first beat of each bar Repeat each exercise so that a continuous strumming pattern is created. Be sure to 'feel' the missing numbered beats so that the upstrokes fall on the plus signs.

These exercises are divided into groups of three quavers Accent the first strum of each group and follow the right hand directions very closely.

Most time signatures are there to give order to the music. The signature usually divides the beat into two, three, or four beats, making it easy for the listener to follow. There are, however, time signatures that are deliberately used to unbalance the music. These often use odd numbers of beats and subdivide into unequal groups.

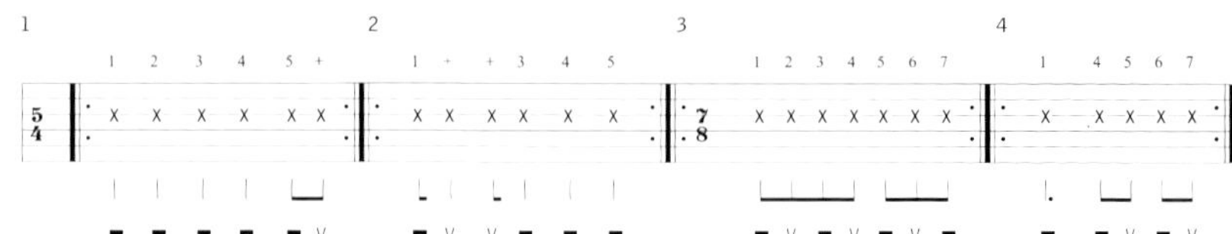

Unusual time signatures The first exercise in 5/4 subdivides into a 3 + 2 grouping, and the second is a 2 + 3. Try to reflect this by accenting the first of each group. The two 7/8 bars divide into 4 + 3 quavers, and then 3 + 4.

EXTENDED CHORDS

It is time to introduce you to some complex chords. You already know some of the sevenths (see pages 82–83). On the following pages you will get to know the rest of the seventh family, and you will also tackle ninths, elevenths, thirteenths, sixths and suspended chords.

Extended chords are standard chords to which an extra note has been added. This fourth note can radically change the character of the harmony. You already know that the sevenths (more properly termed 'dominant sevenths') have a jazzy feel. Sixths, to take another example, can sound otherworldy and ethereal in the right context. Ninths are also somehow spacy, while diminished sevenths jangle in an unsettling way.

Try these and other extended chords in various juxtapostions. You will be amazed at the unexpected effects you can achieve.

As for the numbers in the names of the chords, these tell you whereabouts in the scale the extra note falls. A sixth is a chord consisting of the usual triad – the first, third and fifth notes – plus the sixth note of the scale. Chords with numbers higher than seven contain notes in the next octave up. An eleventh, for example, contains the note that comes three steps above the octave: eight plus three.

As more notes are added to a chord, the shapes can become difficult to reach. It is sometimes necessary to leave notes out altogether in order to make the chords playable. Some notes are more important in defining the sound of a chord than others. The fifth is the most expendable. Most extended chords will sound effective as long as the root is there along with the third (which determines major or minor) and the extended note (9, 11 or 13).

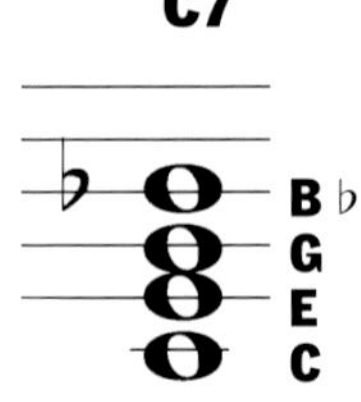

Left Using C7 as an example, you have the notes C, E, G and B-flat.

You should be comfortable with all the chords and bar shapes that you have already learned before you go on to these new categories. All the chord diagrams on the following pages are accompanied by an example of a stave showing that chord in C. This diagram, because it contains the notes of each chord in the simplest key, will help you to understand their structure. We begin our exploration of extended chords with the widely used and multifaceted sevenths.

Major sevenths (major 7/maj7)

Major-seventh chords consist of a major triad plus a major seventh on top. To find the major seventh from the root note, think of the major scale and count up to the seventh degree. Alternatively, think a semitone below the root note and transpose up an octave.

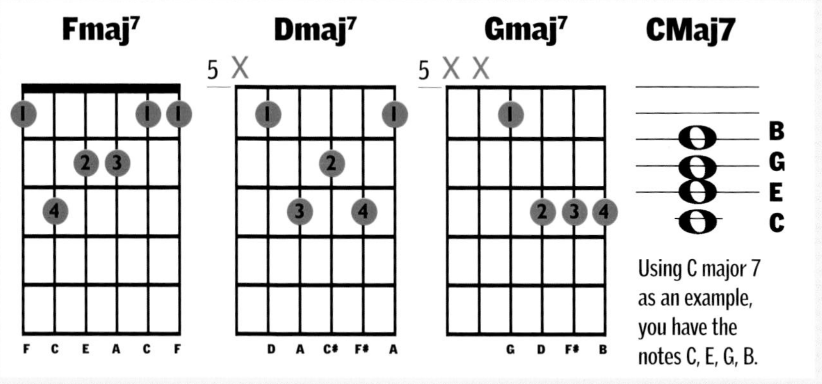

Using C major 7 as an example, you have the notes C, E, G, B.

Diminished sevenths (diminished 7/dim7)

The notes of a diminished triad are equally spaced with an interval of a minor third between each note. On a root note of A this would read A, C, and E-flat. The diminished-seventh chord adds a minor-third interval on top of that, so the full chords consists of A, C, E-flat and G-flat.

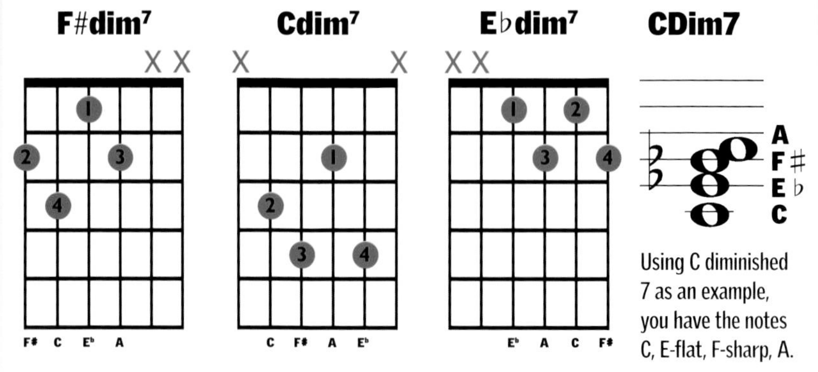

Using C diminished 7 as an example, you have the notes C, E-flat, F-sharp, A.

LESSON 47

Ninths (9)

The ninth chord is essentially a dominant seventh chord with an extra note added. This chord has the four notes of the dominant seventh plus a major ninth (an octave plus one tone).

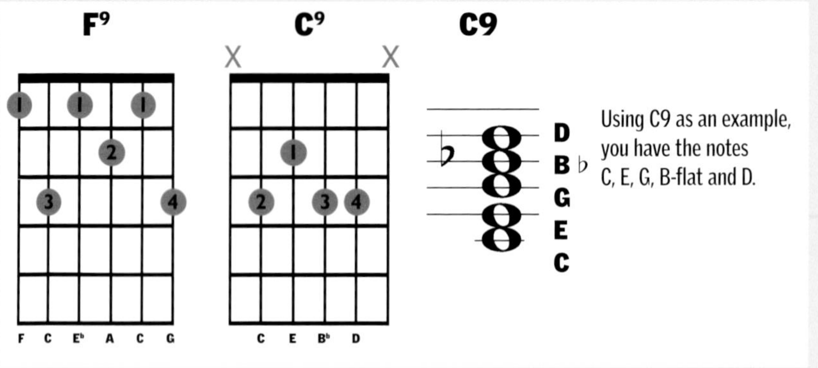

Using C9 as an example, you have the notes C, E, G, B-flat and D.

Major ninth (major 9/maj9)

The major ninth has the same notes as a major seventh plus a major ninth above.

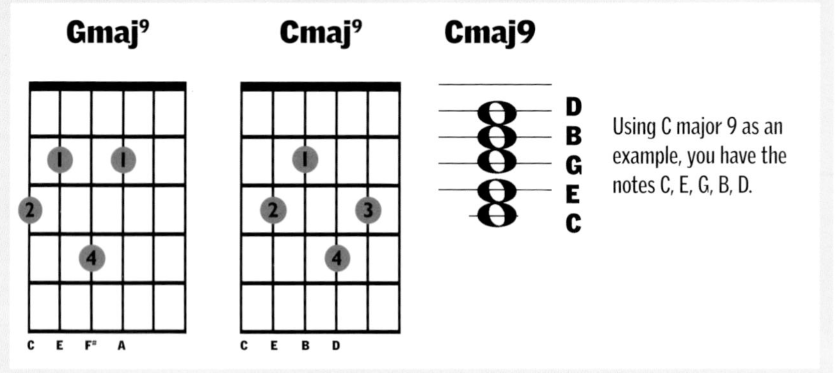

Using C major 9 as an example, you have the notes C, E, G, B, D.

Minor ninth (minor 9/m9)

A minor ninth has the four notes of a minor seventh plus a major ninth on top.

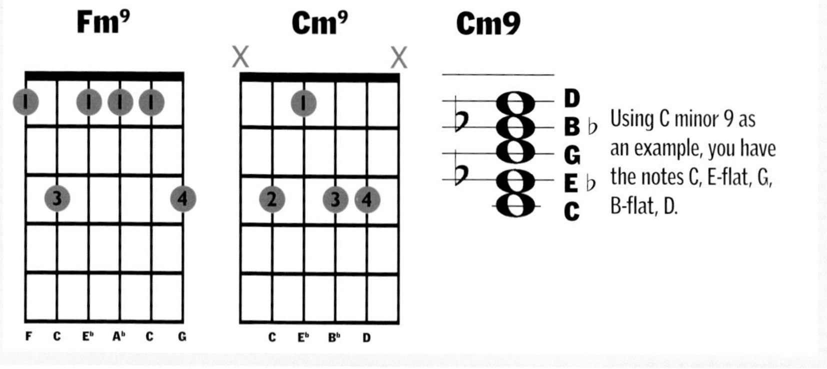

Eleventh and thirteenth chords (11, 13)

The eleventh chord includes the eleventh above the root note. The thirteenth chord adds another note (a major sixth plus an octave) making seven notes in all. It is usual to omit the fifth, ninth or eleventh notes.

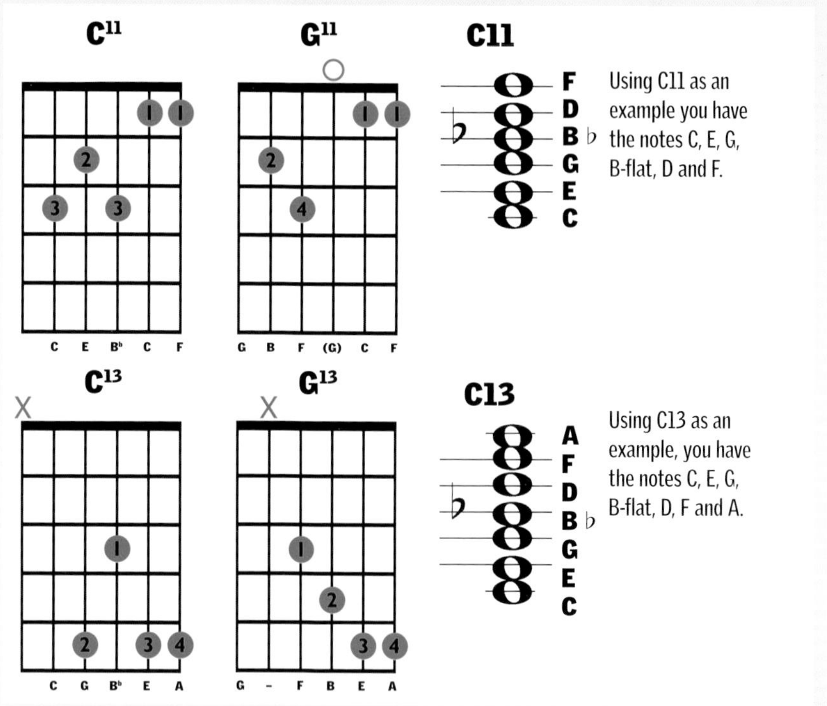

Suspended chords (suspended 4/sus4)

Suspended chords replace the third of the chord with a fourth – you will quite often see these written as a 'sus4'. This creates an unstable chord that usually resolves to a standard major or minor chord by allowing the fourth to fall back to the third.

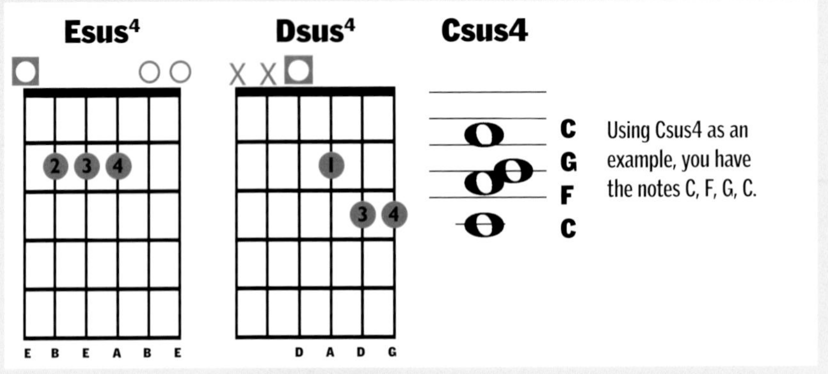

Sixth chords (6, minor 6/min6)

Sixth chords are formed by adding a major sixth above the root. This additional note works in both major and minor chord triads.

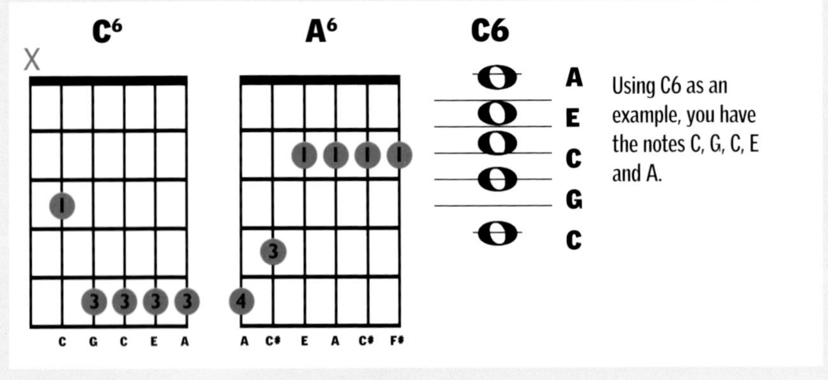

Extended-chord exercises

The most important shapes to commit to memory are the adapted open-chord shapes (first position) and the moveable shapes. Practise the exercises below to put these shapes into context. Using the chord-building formulas you've learned you will also be able to devise your own shapes and different voicings.

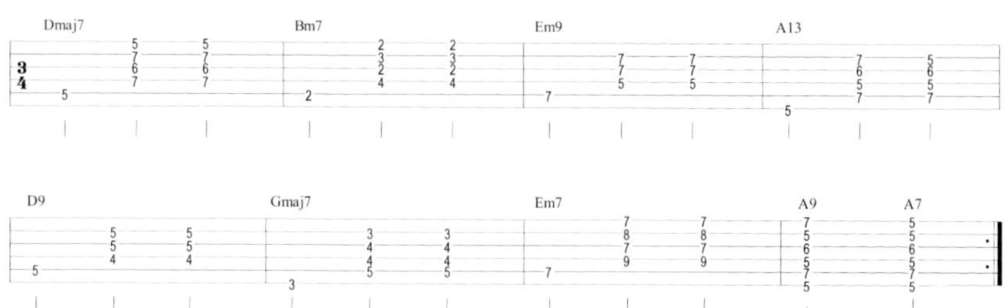

This piece is in 3/4 time. The bass note (root) of each chord is played at the beginning of each bar, which should give you a little more time to find the shapes. Keep an even beat and build up the speed gradually.

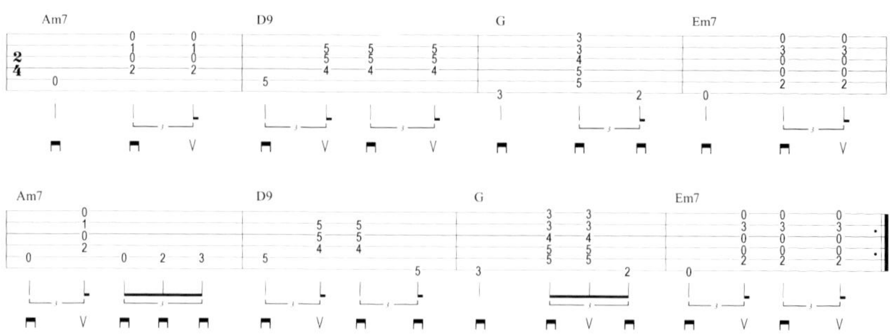

Use a swing rhythm for this exercise and follow the strumming directions carefully. This is a very common jazz progression – chords ii, V, I, vi repeated. To make this more challenging, there are some added bass runs between the chords.

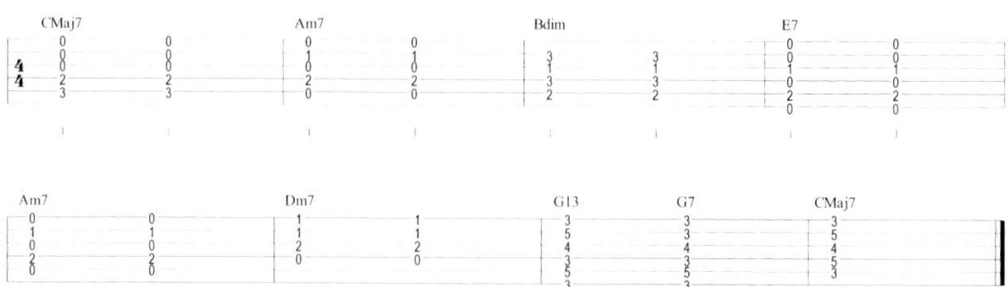

This exercise mainly uses chords adapted from the basic shapes. Follow the tab carefully at the end and use bar chords for the last three shapes. Keep the tempo slow and strum the chords gently.

EXTENDED SOLOING

You can now build on your knowledge of the pentatonic scale by introducing some new notes – 'blue notes' – into the mix. In this lesson you will also be learning a few new techniques that involve playing two strings at once as part of your solo.

There is an elaboration of the pentatonic known as the 'blues scale'. It works best when you are improvising to a blues or rock accompaniment in a major key.

The scale contains extra so-called 'blue' notes that clash with the key of the accompaniment. So, a standard blues progression in A would contain a chord consisting of the notes A, C-sharp and E. The A scale shown below, however, also contains a C natural and an E-flat, which jar and jangle against the chord. In a blues context these 'wrong' notes lend a tense air or bittersweet flavour to the music.

Blues scale in A

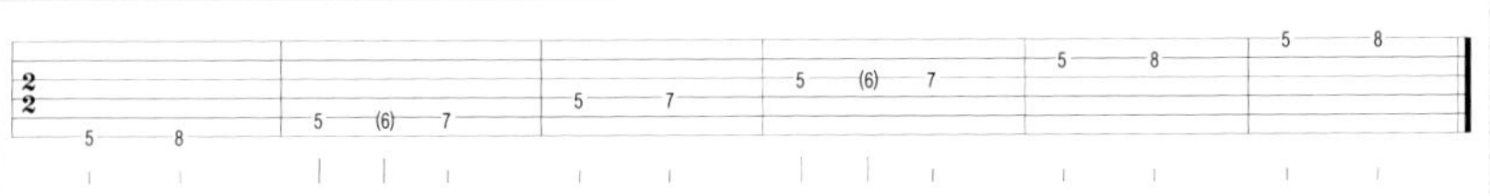

This example of a blues scale is the minor pentatonic scale in A, but with added notes in brackets. The added fifth string, sixth fret, can be used as a brief passing note. The sixth-fret note on the third string can be held to coincide with the key chord (A in the key of A, for example). The clash of the first- and second-finger notes on the third string plays with the major–minor sound found in blues music.

Some blues licks in A

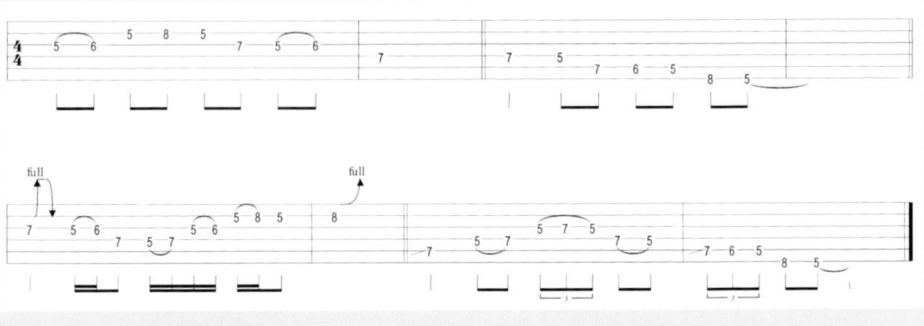

Double stopping

The double stop involves flattening the fingers of the left-hand over two strings rather than placing the fingertips 'correctly' on the strings. Aim to bar the left-hand fingers over two strings and squeeze the strings against the frets to draw out the sound. Here (below) are some licks using double-stopped notes.

Exercise in double-stopped soloing

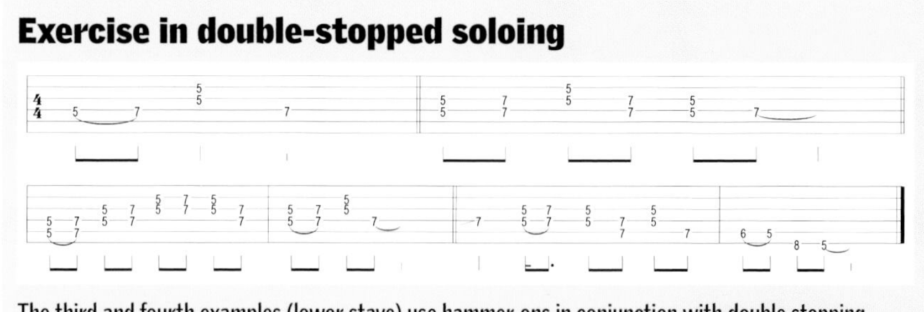

The third and fourth examples (lower stave) use hammer-ons in conjunction with double stopping.

Unison bend

A unison bend is made when the third or fourth fingers of the left hand are used to bend the string while the first finger holds the note one string above. The result is a doubled note being played over two strings. As the lower note is gradually bent upwards the notes clash, then resolve.

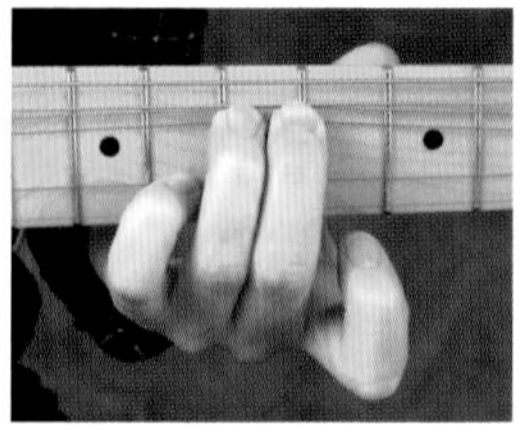

Fixed-string bend

A fixed-string bend works in a similar way to the unison bend, but is a little more difficult to execute. The third finger bends the third string, say, while the fourth finger remains stationary on the second string. You can also bend the second string up to a fixed first string.

Examples of third- and second-string bends

Start by placing both fingers on the string. Keeping the higher note fixed, separate and bend the lower string up a whole tone. At the top of the bend, play the higher note and listen to the sound of the notes working together. Finally, try plucking both notes together and executing the bend in one movement.

Exploring the pentatonic

The five notes of the pentatonic scale can be found at many points on the neck of the guitar. Once you have learned to seek them out, you can use that knowledge to improvise soaring and diving solos all over the fretboard.

Look at the exercises below. Position one represents the standard scale shape. In this example, it is given at the fifth fret, in the key of A, but it could be anywhere on the fretboard: on the open strings in the key of E, on the third fret in the key of G, or on the seventh in the key of C.

The five positions

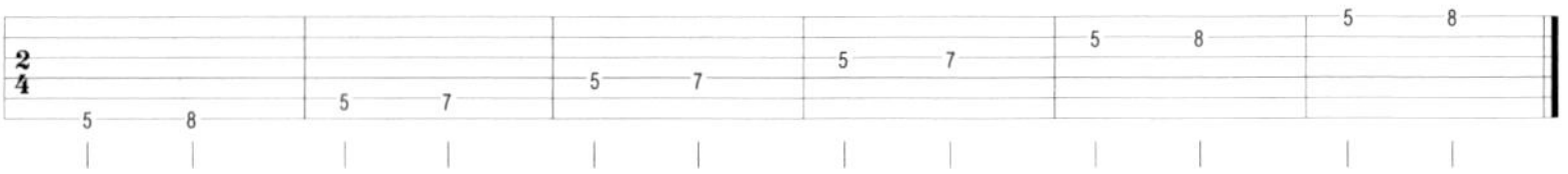

```
2/4
e|---------|---------|---------|---------|---------|--5---8--||
B|---------|---------|---------|---------|--5---8--|---------||
G|---------|---------|---------|--5---7--|---------|---------||
D|---------|---------|--5---7--|---------|---------|---------||
A|---------|--5---7--|---------|---------|---------|---------||
E|--5---8--|---------|---------|---------|---------|---------||
```

Position one This is the standard position that you learned in Lesson 22.

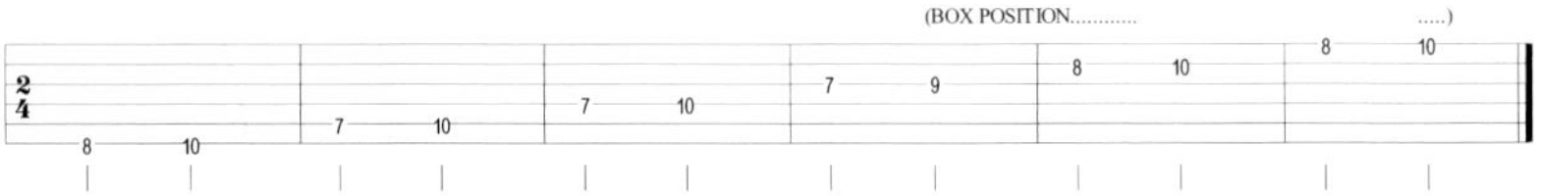

```
                                         (BOX POSITION.................)
2/4
e|---------|---------|---------|---------|---------|--8--10--||
B|---------|---------|---------|---------|--8--10--|---------||
G|---------|---------|---------|--7---9--|---------|---------||
D|---------|---------|--7--10--|---------|---------|---------||
A|---------|--7--10--|---------|---------|---------|---------||
E|--8--10--|---------|---------|---------|---------|---------||
```

Position two The higher portion of this pattern is often called a 'box', where the notes fit a nice symmetrical shape. These notes fit the left hand very well and are commonly used as a partial extension from position one.

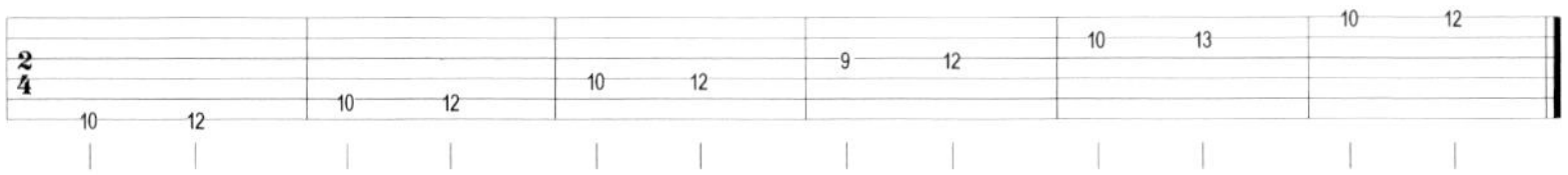

```
2/4
e|---------|---------|---------|---------|---------|-10--12--||
B|---------|---------|---------|---------|-10--13--|---------||
G|---------|---------|---------|--9--12--|---------|---------||
D|---------|---------|-10--12--|---------|---------|---------||
A|---------|-10--12--|---------|---------|---------|---------||
E|-10--12--|---------|---------|---------|---------|---------||
```

Position three The last three bars require some stretching in the left hand.

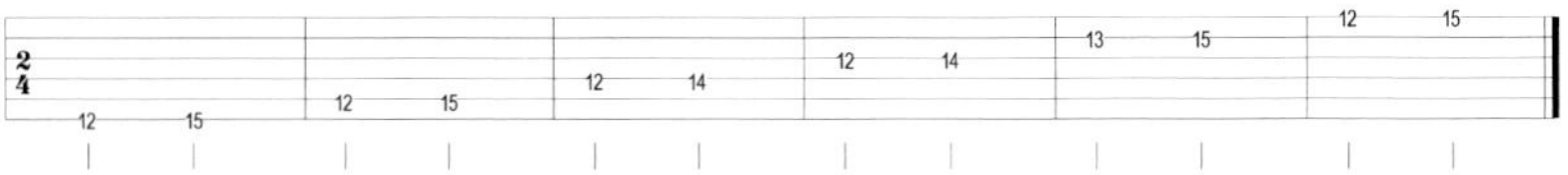

```
2/4
e|---------|---------|---------|---------|---------|-12--15--||
B|---------|---------|---------|---------|-13--15--|---------||
G|---------|---------|---------|-12--14--|---------|---------||
D|---------|---------|-12--14--|---------|---------|---------||
A|---------|-12--15--|---------|---------|---------|---------||
E|-12--15--|---------|---------|---------|---------|---------||
```

Position four The left hand can maintain a constant position here, with the first finger anchored firmly at the twelfth fret.

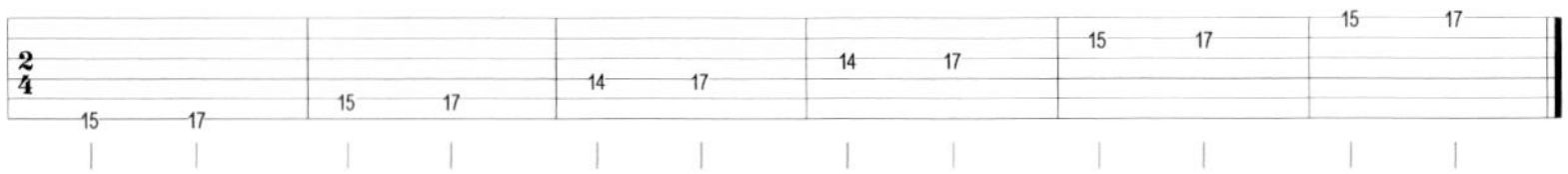

```
2/4
e|---------|---------|---------|---------|---------|-15--17--||
B|---------|---------|---------|---------|-15--17--|---------||
G|---------|---------|---------|-14--17--|---------|---------||
D|---------|---------|-14--17--|---------|---------|---------||
A|---------|-15--17--|---------|---------|---------|---------||
E|-15--17--|---------|---------|---------|---------|---------||
```

Position five The third finger of the left hand plays all the notes at the seventeenth fret. The first finger has to shift up and down by one fret to reach all the other notes. This pattern can also be played in the same position but one octave lower. The guitar neck can accommodate certain keys better than others, so if playing at the highest frets feels awkward, look for a lower version of the same pattern.

From the starting point on the fifth fret, you can begin to explore the five positions of the pentatonic scale. The exercises will guide you through them. Each of the positions has a different finger pattern that should be practised thoroughly before proceeding to the next. Remember that in this case the five notes in the scale are A (the root note), then C, D, E and G.

As you explore the upper reaches of the neck, you should continue to practise the various solo techniques that you have learned so that you can add spectacular splashes of colour to your solo playing. The exercise below will test your mastery of the pentatonic scale and your familiarity with the fingerboard. It also makes use of some of the techniques you have learned in recent lessons: added notes, double-stopping and the various ways of bending notes while playing two strings at once.

REACHING THE TOP NOTES

The shape of an acoustic guitar's body can make it hard to reach the high frets. Some guitars are 'cut away' to give the left hand access to this part of the neck. On a good guitar, a cutaway will not impair the sound.

Extended-solo exercise

The position changes have been marked in the score. This piece is written for a traditional twelve-bar blues in A major, and in 4/4 time.

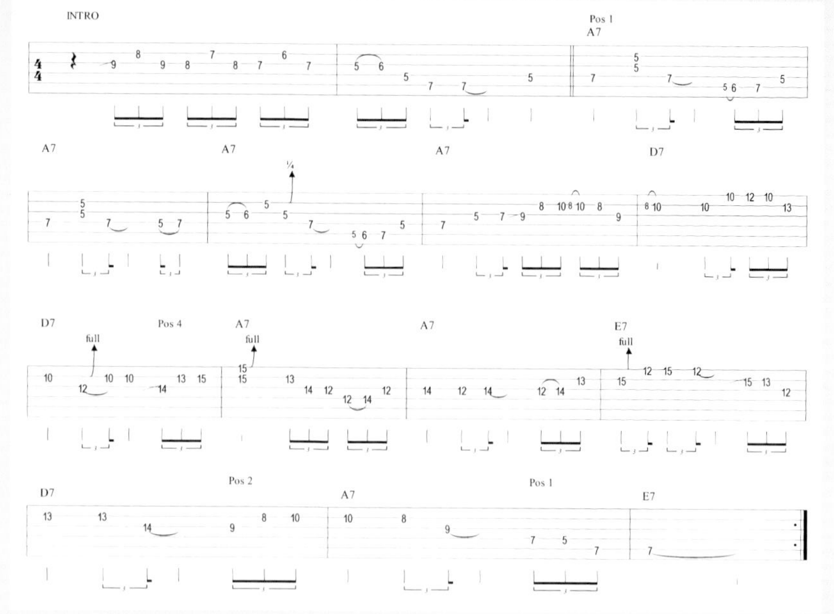

USING A CAPO

A capo is a device that is clamped to the guitar neck to shorten the string length, so raising the pitch of the open strings. It can be positioned at any fret and covers all six strings, allowing you to play in higher keys without altering all the chord shapes.

Above The chord of B major played by making a G-shape with a capo on the fourth fret. A G-shaped B chord would be very difficult to make without a capo.

It is common practice in music to transpose a melody, that is, to shift the key up or down. Singers routinely transpose songs to make them fit the range of their own voice, but this can be awkward for accompanying musicians, who might then have to play in a key that is difficult on their instrument.

A capo makes it easy to transpose on a guitar. In effect, it creates an alternative nut position and a higher pitch for the instrument.The player can then stick to the chord shapes that the music calls for. You could, of course, achieve the same effect using bar chords, but a capo makes a transposed song more comfortable to play, and the notes will resonate better.

Moreover, some guitarists like the sound quality that a capo gives when placed higher up the neck, and use one for that reason alone. An example is the Beatles' 'Here Comes the Sun'. It is in A, but is played with a D-shaped chord and a capo on the seventh fret, which gives a fresher, brighter tone than a standard A.

Types of capo

Your choice of capo will depend on how often you plan to use it, how quickly you need to be able to put it on and remove it, and the kind of guitar you play. For occasional use on a steel-string guitar, there are light, simply designed capos that consist of a bar and a nylon band. There are capos designed specifically for electric, steel-string acoustic and classical

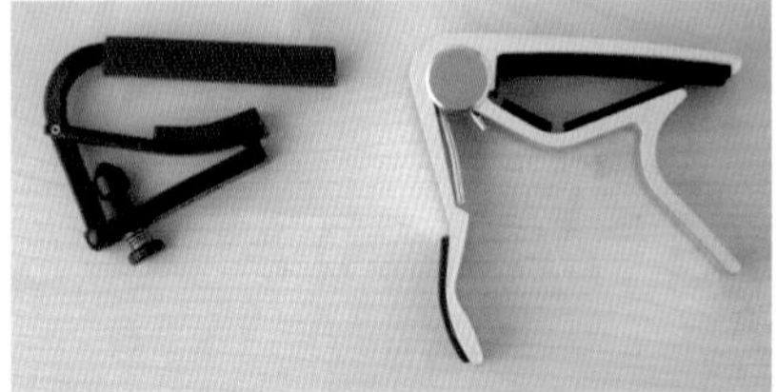

Above A spring capo and an adjustable capo – just two of the available designs. Be sure that you get the type that best suits your playing needs.

guitars, since classical-guitar fingerboards are always flat, while other guitars usually have slightly cambered fingerboards.

If you are going to be changing the capo position frequently while playing (if you will be using it in performance, say), go for a spring-loaded capo, which grips the neck like a vice and can be moved around easily. The best capos for precise tuning have adjustable screws so that the pressure on the strings is set just right, but these are not so quick to attach.

Transposition guide

Use the guide below to help you transpose to different keys. There are different options for each chord. For example, a C could be played as an A-shape with the capo at the third fret or else as a G-shape with the capo at the fifth fret.

Chord Shape	Fret Position and transposed chord at pitch											
	1	**2**	**3**	**4**	**5**	**6**	**7**	**8**	**9**	**10**	**11**	**12**
C	C#	D	D#	E	F	F#	G	G#	A	A#	B	C
G	G#	A	A#	B	C	C#	D	D#	E	F	F#	G
D	D#	E	F	F#	G	G#	A	A#	B	C	C#	D
Dm	D#m	Em	Fm	F#m	Gm	G#m	Am	A#m	Bm	Cm	C#m	Dm
A	A#	B	C	C#	D	D#	E	F	F#	G	G#	A
Am	A#m	Bm	Cm	C#m	Dm	D#m	Em	Fm	F#m	Gm	G#m	Am
E	F	F#	G	G#	A	A#	B	C	C#	D	D#	E
Em	Fm	F#m	Gm	G#m	Am	A#m	Bm	Cm	C#m	Dm	D#m	Em
F	F	G	G#	A	A#	B	C	C#	D	D#	E	F

Sharps have been used for ease of reading, but remember that flats can be found one fret below the main notes. Therefore B-flat is the same as A-sharp, D-flat is the same as C-sharp, and so on.

A major transposed to E-flat major Here is an example that shows how to transpose a chord progression from the key of A major to the key of E-flat major.

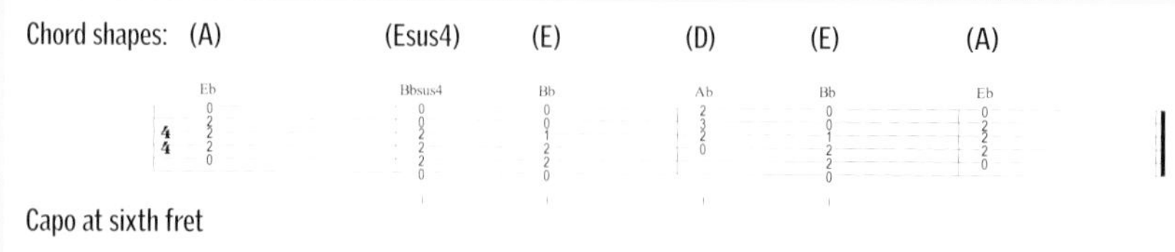

The chord progression in the transposed example would be hard using bar chords in E-flat. With the capo at the sixth fret and using the original chord shapes, the fingering is easier and the sound more resonant. (It is usual to show the chord shapes in brackets above the actual pitch of the chords.)

ALTERNATIVE TUNINGS

We have already looked at Drop-D, one of the alternatives to standard tuning. Now we are going to explore other tuning options. They all have a more limited scope than the versatile EADGBE, but each can add something magical to the guitar's sound.

Many players of steel-string acoustic guitars make use of alternative tunings. Altered tuning makes for different chord voicings, meaning that familiar chords sound strangely new on the ear when made up of unexpected patterns of notes.

The use of alternative tunings is common among folk guitarists. Most folk music is written in guitar-friendly keys such as D, G, or C. Some alternative tunings involve tuning the open strings to these chords. They are discussed overleaf.

DADGAD tuning

One of the most widely used alternative tunings is known as DADGAD. The letters DADGAD spell out the pitches of the strings from the sixth to the first. This tuning lends itself well to combinations of chords and melody, and for this reason is a particular favourite of folk musicians. It has been used extensively by guitarists such as Bert Jansch, Nick Drake, Neil Young and Richard Thompson. It is not exclusively a folk technique, however. Jimmy Page used it in Led Zeppelin's 'Kashmir', which gets its distinctive sound from DADGAD tuning.

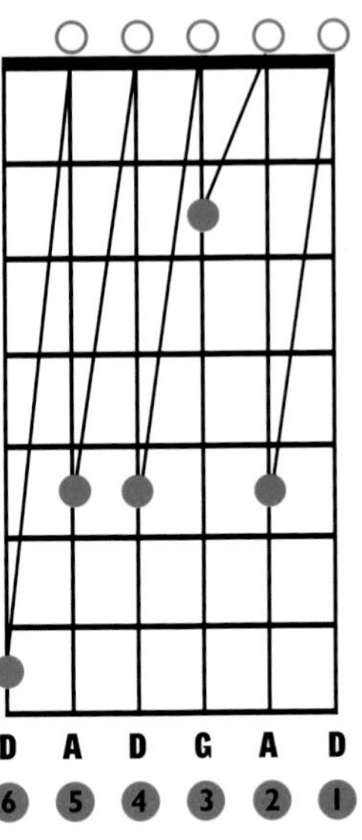

Above These are the relative tunings for DADGAD, First you should lower the sixth, second and first strings by one whole tone from their standard-tuning notes.

Most guitarists like to make use of drone notes when playing in DADGAD. The exercise opposite uses the open first and second strings to lend a pleasant hum to the chord sequence. To get the most out of the DADGAD sound, try fretting parts of these chords while allowing open strings to ring underneath.

Chords in DADGAD

This is not an exhaustive list, since there are many ways to play the same chords in DADGAD, particulary ones in the D-family. The major and minor shapes can be moved around the neck.

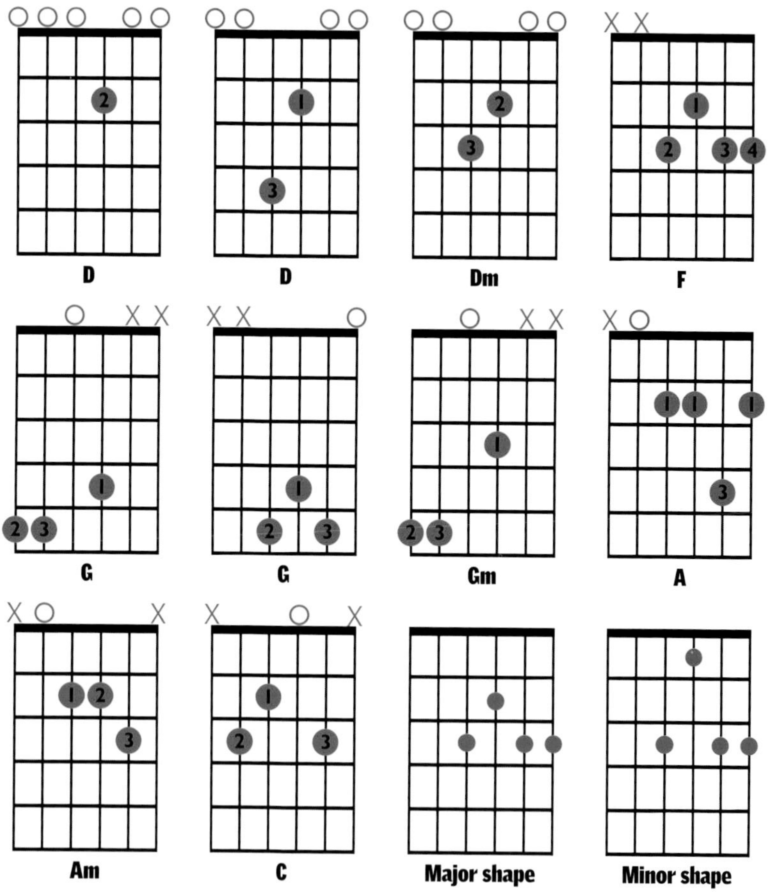

D

D

Dm

F

G

G

Gm

A

Am

C

Major shape

Minor shape

DADGAD exercise in D major

The chords used in this strumming exercise are variations on standard chords. The drone strings (first and second) alter the make-up of each chord, adding suspended notes and dissonances.

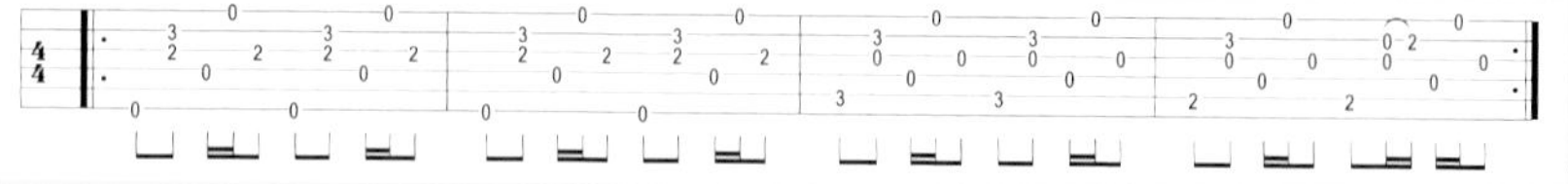

Open tunings

An open tuning is one where all six strings have been tuned to the notes of a chord. The most commonly used are open D, G and C.

The diagrams below show you how to make these tunings. In open tunings it is really easy to play chords just by barring across the six strings with the first finger at the required fret. It is handy to bear in mind that chords IV and V will be in the fifth and seventh frets respectively, which makes it a simple matter to play that most common of chord progressions. But the real attraction of open tuning is that you can use them to create interesting chord voicings and cross-string melodies with drone notes.

A guide for open tunings

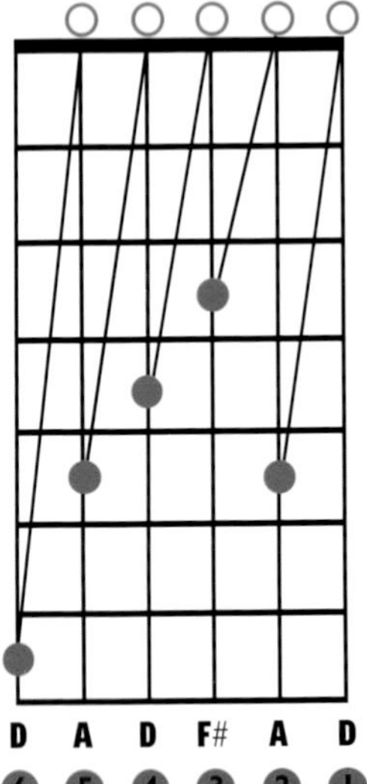

Open D This tuning is nearly the same as DADGAD except that the third string is tuned down a semitone from G to F-sharp. This is an excellent tuning to use when you are playing slide guitar (see pages 150–151, overleaf).

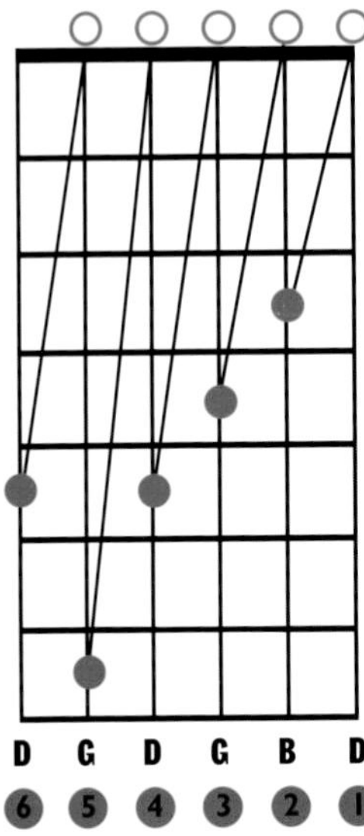

Open G This deeply resonant tuning is good for folk and blues. Drop the sixth string to D, then use the guide to tune. In open G, you can use the open fifth and sixth strings (G and D) as the root notes of chords I and V in G major.

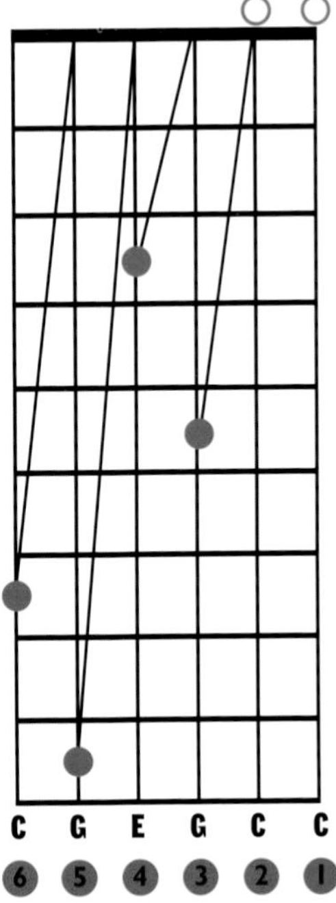

Open C This experimental tuning has a sitar-like sound, because the first and second strings are tuned to the same note.

It is better for your guitar to use tunings that require slacker strings rather than tighter ones. Be careful with open-C tuning for this reason: the fourth string is raised a tone, which puts strain on it, so tune it in gradually.

Players who make regular use of these alternative tunings tend to choose heavier strings as they hold pitch better.

ONE TUNING AT A TIME

By all means try out all the different tunings on these pages, but pick one and explore its possibilities before moving on to the next. You are sure to get confused if you attempt to learn chords in several tunings at once.

Exercises in open tuning

These exercises make good use of the drone string and chord voicings inherent in each tuning.

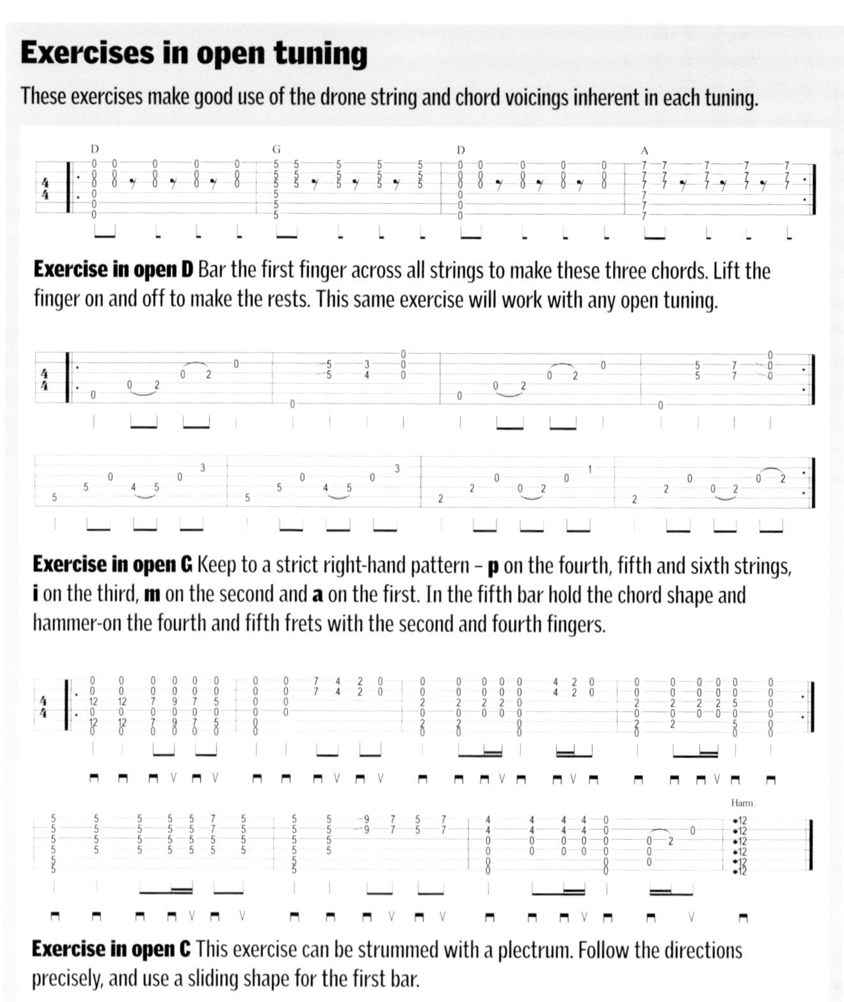

Exercise in open D Bar the first finger across all strings to make these three chords. Lift the finger on and off to make the rests. This same exercise will work with any open tuning.

Exercise in open G Keep to a strict right-hand pattern – **p** on the fourth, fifth and sixth strings, **i** on the third, **m** on the second and **a** on the first. In the fifth bar hold the chord shape and hammer-on the fourth and fifth frets with the second and fourth fingers.

Exercise in open C This exercise can be strummed with a plectrum. Follow the directions precisely, and use a sliding shape for the first bar.

SLIDE GUITAR

Slide guitar involves using a hard hollow cylinder rather than your fingertips to select the notes on the fingerboard. The use of a slide creates striking effects, like a sigh or a cry or the yowl of a cat. It is a technique that is particularly associated with the blues.

Guitar slides are cheap to buy. They come in various materials, such as glass, metal or ceramic, and a variety of sizes is available. The slide should fit over the third or fourth finger of your left hand, whichever feels more comfortable for you when you play.

Using a slide

You can play slide in standard tuning, but the slide limits what the left hand can do, so many slide players opt for open tunings (see pages 148–149). These tunings let you play chords with the slide or flattened fingers; the fifth fret in open G, for example, will give you a C major, the seventh fret a D major, and so on. Drop-D, open D, and open E are also commonly used.

Slide works well whether you are fingerpicking or playing with a plectrum. But whichever right-hand technique you are using, it is important that the slide only touches the strings lightly, gliding over them without pressing down. If you can hear the slide sounding the individual frets then you are pressing too hard. The note position is not 'in the fret', as when playing with fingers, but directly over the fret wire. The positioning has to be precise

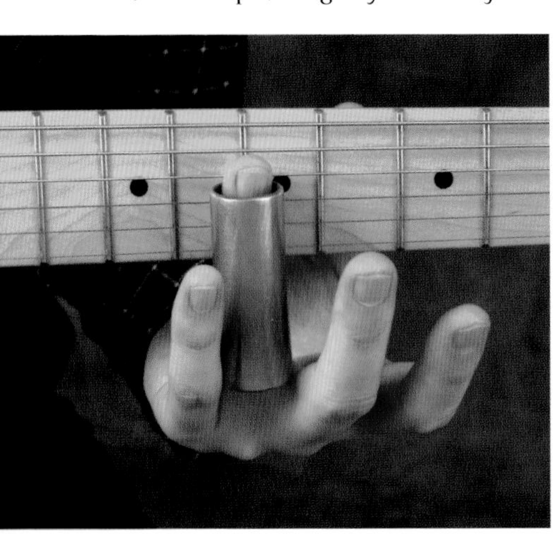

Above Keep the slide parallel with the fret bars.

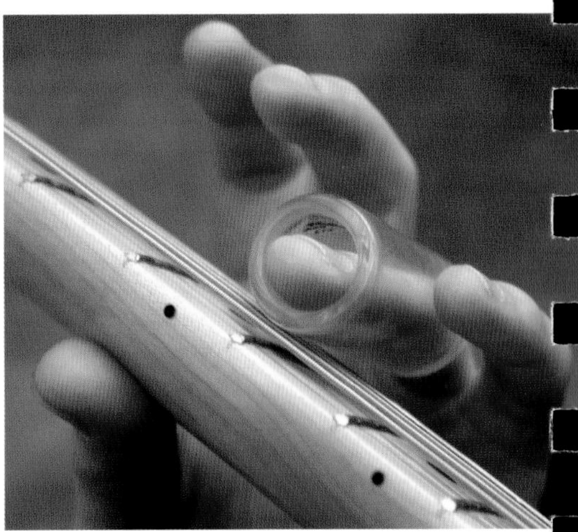

Above Balance the slide on the strings without depressing the string to the fret. Do not press down, as you would when making a bar chord.

or the note will be out of tune – a little vibrato can help to blur the edges here.

The slide makes a lot of noise as it moves around the neck, so you may need to mute strings in order to play single-line melodies cleanly. You can do this with the right hand or with the first two fingers of the left hand on the nut side of the slide.

Some exercises in slide guitar

Don't worry if the sound is not good at first: there is a knack to a slide, and it comes with practice.

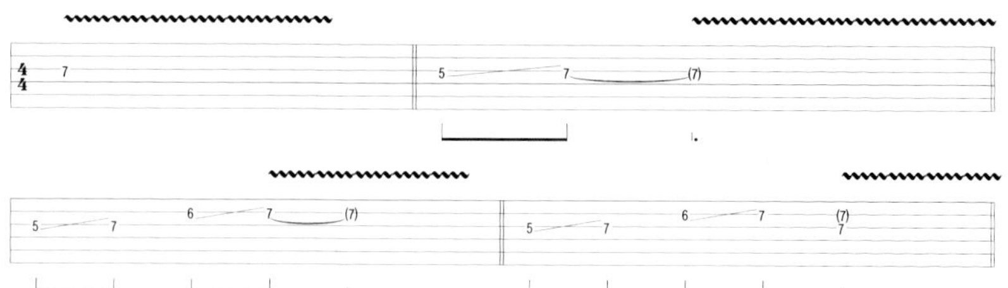

Slide exercise in standard tuning Start by making a good sound on the third string, seventh fret and trying a little vibrato (moving from side to side). When sliding along the string use your right hand to mute any unwanted noises caused by the slide. Lift the slide a little when changing strings to cut the sound and maintain a single line. When playing a chord with the slide, make sure that it is positioned exactly parallel to the frets for accurate tuning.

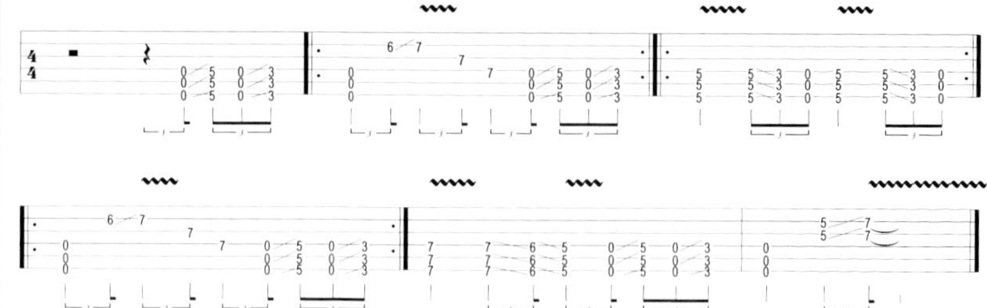

Blues exercise in drop-D tuning The mark '/' before a chord means you start the chord one or two frets below, then sliding up to the fret indicated in the tab. Notice how chords are made on the bottom three strings (power-chord sound) and also on the second, third and fourth strings (major chord).

A rhythmic exercise using open-g tuning Pick with the right hand, using your thumb on the bass strings and fingers on the higher notes. Lift the slide when playing the open strings in the second bar.

FINGER-TAPPING

Finger-tapping is a technique that takes hammer-ons and pull-offs to a higher level. Although it can be done on any stringed instrument, it is generally regarded as an electric-guitar technique. It is often used by metal guitarists to allow them to play solos at blistering speed.

Finger-tapping ('tapping' for short) involves using both the left and right hands on the fingerboard. You sound the strings by tapping in the frets with both hands. This sounds most effective on electric guitars with a low action. You also need to use lots of amp distortion and sound compression to even out the notes.

You can tap with the first finger (**p**) or the second finger (**i**) of the right hand. There is an advantage in using the second finger, in that this allows the player to keep hold of a plectrum in its normal place, between the thumb and the first finger.

The secret to developing speed is to practise slowly and evenly at first. Begin with the finger-tapping exercises on the opposite page, focusing on getting a solid, even sound from the fingertips. Once all the notes are sounding clear, you will be able to increase the pace of your playing, little by little.

Left With practice, finger-tapping makes it possible for you to play extremely fast solo riffs; the technique also allows you to play arpeggios with intervals that would be impossible to fret with the left-hand alone.

EXTREME **GUITAR**

In the 1970s and 1980s a number of guitarists began to develop a flamboyant brand of rock music characterized by pyrotechnical guitar solos. Artists such as Eddie Van Halen, Joe Satriani, Steve Vai and Yngwie Malmsteen pioneered a style that focused on speed, complex handwork and showmanship. The guitar in their hands was not so much an accompaniment to a vocal or part of a backing band, but a virtuoso solo instrument. Finger-tapping was one of the core techniques for this style of playing; others included the related technique known as 'sweep picking', as well as dive bombing (extreme use of the tremolo arm), and modifications to the design of the guitar itself such as 'scalloped fretting', which facilitates extremely fast playing.

Some tapping exercises

Try these tapping exercises. A letter 'T' signifies a right-hand tap.

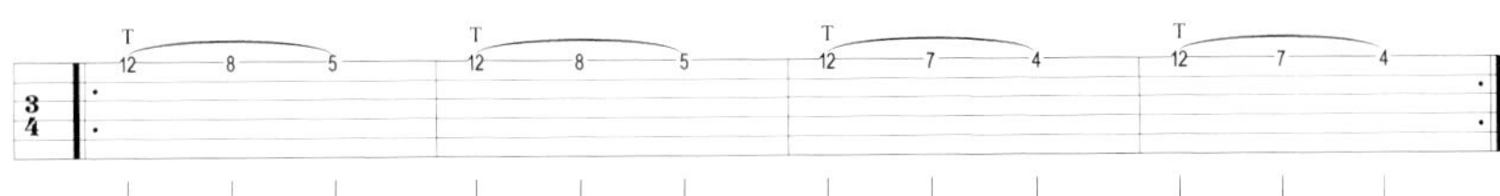

On the sixth string Start by positioning the left hand in fifth position with the first finger at the fifth fret and the fourth finger at the eighth fret. Tap the twelfth fret on the first string with the **m** finger (right hand) then pull-off so that the eighth fret sounds. Next, pull-off the fourth finger so that the fifth fret sounds. Repeat this process keeping an even speed. In the third and fourth bars the left hand slides back one fret so that it is in fourth position. Once the first four bars are flowing well, try the faster version, making sure that the rhythm is even throughout.

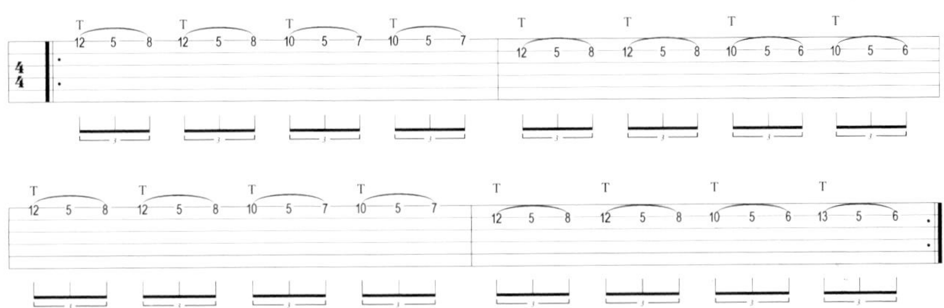

On two strings Here is an exercise that involves string crossing, that is, moving the right hand back and forth across the strings. Start very slowly and gradually increase the speed. Every note should be even and clear. Watch for the fret changes – the first finger stays anchored to the fifth fret.

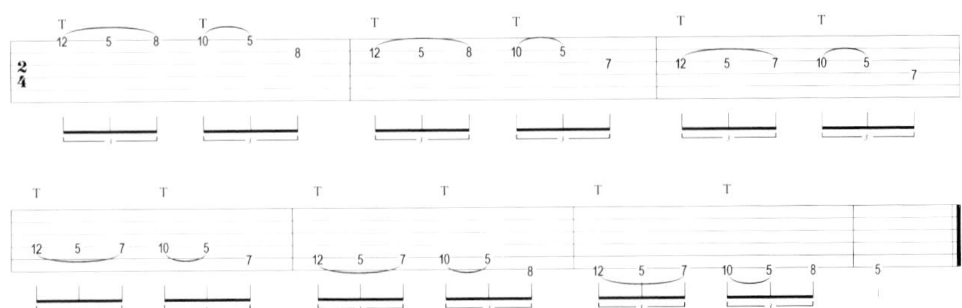

On all the strings This example in A is based on the standard pentatonic-scale shape. The left hand traces the shape of the scale, while the right hand moves between the tenth and twelfth frets. The last note of each bar is sounded by a left-hand hammer-on. This is a good pattern to learn, as it can be moved around the neck to fit with different keys.

HARMONICS

At certain points on the neck you can use a particular technique to amplify the overtones present in a normal note. These 'harmonic' notes have a very particular timbre, and the highest of them extend the range of the guitar beyond the fingerboard.

Every musical note is made up of a 'fundamental' frequency and a series of overtones, known as the 'harmonic series'. As listeners we only perceive a single note when, in fact, there are many.

Natural harmonics

So-called 'natural harmonics' can be played by lightly touching the string with the left hand at specific frets, namely the twelfth, seventh, fifth, fourth and ninth on each string. There are other harmonics in the series, but these are the strongest, and so the most usable when playing.

To play a harmonic note, use the third finger to lightly touch any string precisely over the wire of the twelfth fret. Pluck the string with the right hand. As the note sounds, take the left-hand finger off the string, allowing the note to ring free. You should hear a clear, bell-like tone. Use this same method on the seventh and fifth frets: you will get a different note. Then try it on other strings.

Above A natural harmonic on the first string at the twelfth fret. A harmonic played down at the fifth fret yields a note an octave higher than one played at the twelfth.

Now try getting a harmonic from all six strings at once using your finger as a bar. This is particularly effective when done in conjunction with open tunings.

Artificial harmonics

Other harmonic notes can be generated by fretting a string with the left hand and playing the harmonic the same number of frets higher up the neck. For example, if you are pressing the second fret, play the harmonic at the fourteenth, ninth, seventh, sixth, and so on.

This requires a bit more skill because you have to both touch the string and pluck it with the right hand. There are various ways to do this. You can use the **i** finger of the right hand to touch the string at the harmonic position (over the fret wire) while the **a** finger plucks the string; or you can touch the harmonic position on the string with your thumb and pluck with the **i** finger. The second and third exercises on the opposite page will help you to practise artificial harmonics.

Pinch harmonics

The technique known as 'pinch harmonics' is specific to the electric guitar. The harmonic spot is to be found above the pickups. Hold the plectrum with just the tip showing. Pluck the string and immediately stop the sound with a light brush of the tip of your thumb on the string. If it is in the right spot you should get a squealing sound. Move along the string to find different harmonic positions while fretting notes with the left hand.

Above Pinch harmonics work best with powerful pickups, heavy strings, and lots of distortion.

Harmonic exercises

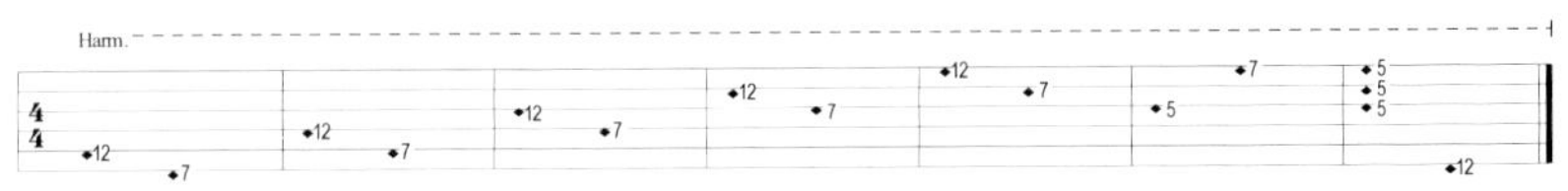

Natural harmonics Here you will use natural harmonics to create a scale. Use the fourth finger to play all the harmonics at the twelfth fret and the first finger to play at the seventh fret. The left-hand thumb can maintain a position around the ninth fret to steady the hand. Use a flattened first finger to cover the chord at the fifth fret in the final bar. Be careful not to press too hard.

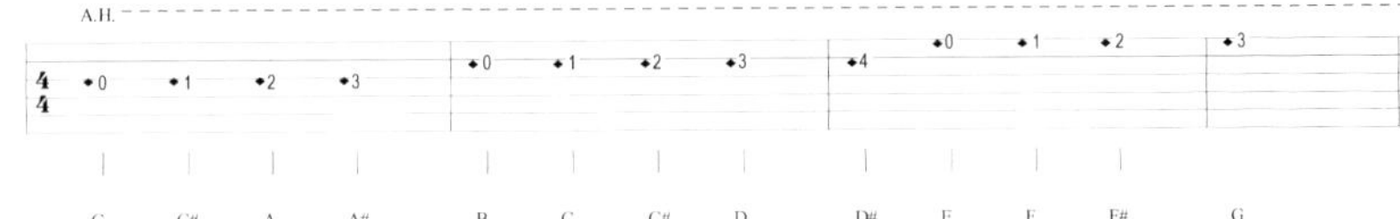

Artificial harmonics Starting with the right hand over the twelfth fret and no fingers pressing in the left hand, gradually move up the string one fret at a time. The left hand plays a simple chromatic pattern (0-1-2-3-4) while the index finger of the right hand moves from the twelfth to sixteenth frets, playing a harmonic at each.

Scale of G major Copy the movement of the left-hand notes with the right-hand harmonics. Memorize the scale, and make sure that you look only at your right hand. Concentrate on touching the string directly over the fret wires.

GOING CLASSICAL

Classical guitar differs from other styles in that it uses the nails of the right hand to aid tone production. It requires fabulous dexterity in the fingers, so a basic grounding in classical techniques will provide you with skills that are transferable to any style of guitar playing.

Classical guitar is a style that has given rise to some fabulous music down the centuries. Many fine composers have written for the guitar, and the works of many others who never did – notably Johann Sebastian Bach – have been adapted so that guitarists can play them.

The aim of this section is not necessarily to turn you into a classical guitarist, however. Mastering classical techniques on the guitar – as on any orchestral instrument – requires years of tuition and dedication. The more modest goal of this part of the book is to use classical

CLASSICAL **GUITAR**

The classical guitar has its roots in older guitar-like instruments such as the lute and the vihuela. The modern instrument came about in the 19th century, and acquired its familiar shape through the work of a Spanish luthier (guitar-maker) named Antonio Torres. Today's classical guitarists call on a repertoire which reflects the instrument's long history. There are pieces adapted from works written for the lute that date back to the Renaissance. Then there are transcriptions of works by the great Baroque composers, as well as Spanish classics influenced by flamenco and a wealth of contemporary music in all styles. Among the most notable classical players are Francisco Tarrega, Miguel Llobet, Andres Segovia, Julian Bream, John Williams, Manuel Barrueco, David Russell, and Ana Vidovic.

Past master Andres Segovia helped to establish the guitar as a concert instrument. Many modern composers wrote performance pieces especially for him.

techniques as a means of turning the spotlight on the right hand. This brief excursion into apoyando and tirando, rasgueado and tremolando, is intended to bring about improvement in aspects of your playing such as tone production and finger control.

After all, most guitarists tend to focus on the left hand when learning, with the result that this aspect of their playing tends to develop more quickly. Yet it is the right hand that is largely responsible for the quality of the sound that your guitar produces; its function is just as demanding and important. The exercises overleaf are designed to help you move beyond familiar fingerpicking patterns, and so raise your guitar-playing and your musicianship to the next level.

Apoyando and tirando

In classical guitar there are two main plucking techniques, known by the Spanish terms 'apoyando' (rest stroke) and 'tirando' (free stroke). In apoyando, the finger plucks through the string and comes to rest on the string below. This method makes for a full, strong sound, which is perfect for playing single-line melodies.

In tirando, on the other hand, the fingers pluck from the big knuckle joint towards the palm of the hand. The player angles the wrist and must take care to miss the strings below. This stroke is used when the music requires the strings to overlap, as in arpeggio playing.

Using nails

To play classical guitar, the nails of the right hand need to be shaped in such a way that they play through the strings without too much resistance. When you are plucking the string, it is the fingertip that makes contact first. Then, as pressure is applied, the string will pass on to and over the nail edge in one fluid movement. The string should travel from the left of the tip to the right. Many people think that classical guitarists have very long nails; this is not the case, as long nails create a brittle sound and actually make playing harder. However, the nails do have to be trimmed in a particular way – see the box below.

Nail shape

In the photo, near left, you can see that the nail slopes upwards from left to right. The correct angle of the nail in relation to the strings is important: it must be such that the string travels up the slope before exiting on the right side of the nail. A good way to gauge the correct length of the nail is to look at the finger from the back (far left): you should just be able to see the line of the nail above the fingertip.

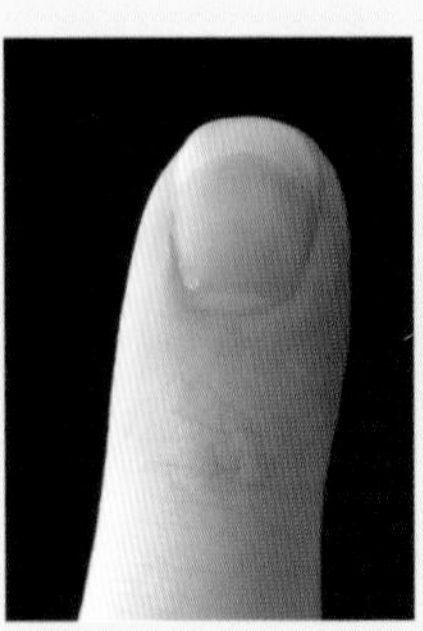

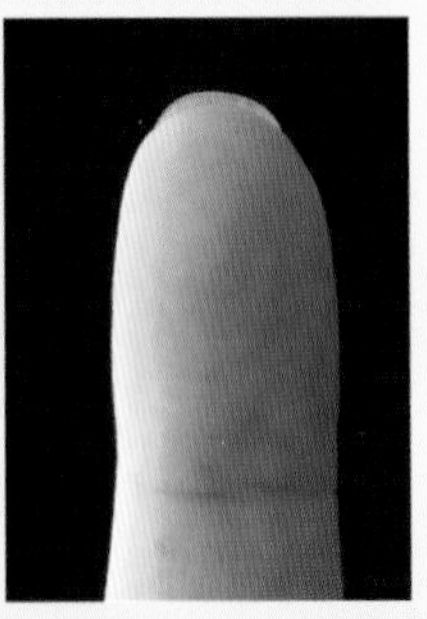

Walking fingers

Walking fingers means using the **i** and **m** fingers alternately when playing scales. Switching back and forth between fingers in this way lets you play faster; it is like using downstrokes and upstrokes with a plectrum. This is the skill that you will be practising in the exercises below. As usual, you should start slowly and gradually build up speed. Stay relaxed and focus only on the muscles in your fingers. Be aware of involuntary tensing in the arm and shoulders. Follow the right-hand fingerings closely. The fingers should alternate throughout.

Walking-finger exercises

Try your hand at these exercises on the first, second and third strings.

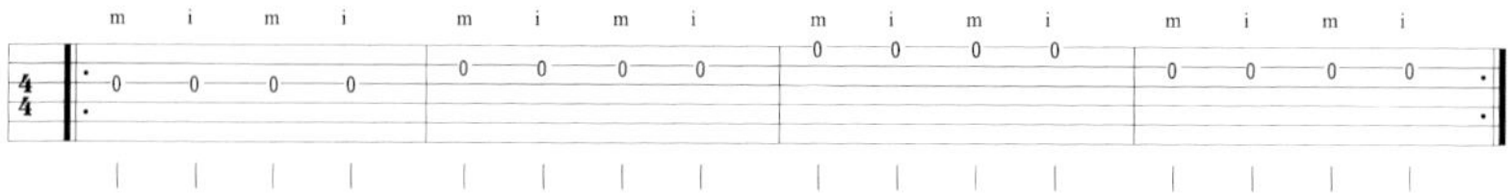

Walking on open strings Stretch out with the **m** finger when crossing strings, pulling your hand into a slightly new position each time.

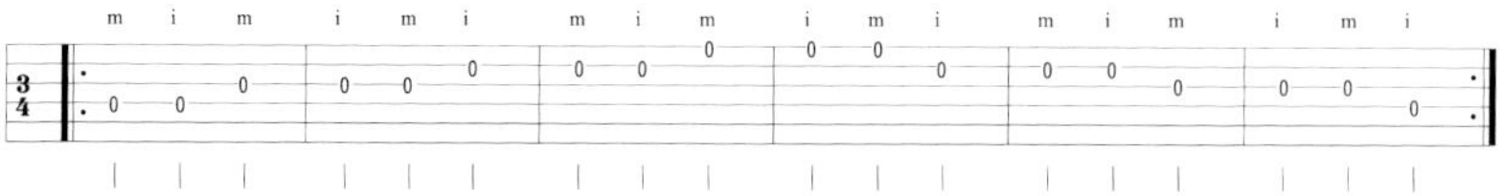

String-crossing Concentrate an alternating your **i** and **m** fingers, exactly as shown. The string crossings are awkward at times, but avoid repeating the same finger all the same.

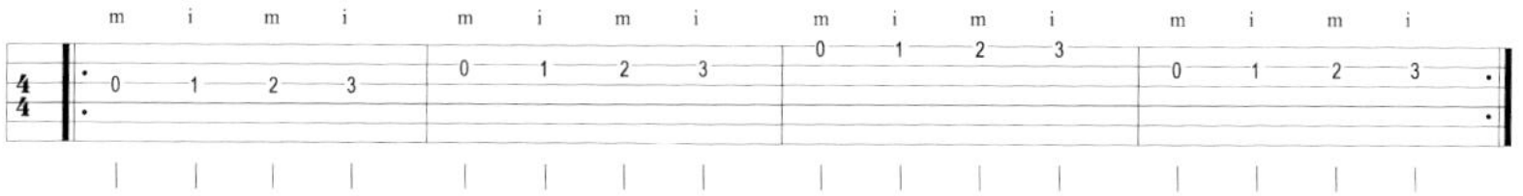

Chromatic scale and walking fingers Study this coordination exercise until the walking fingers in the right hand feels 'automatic'.

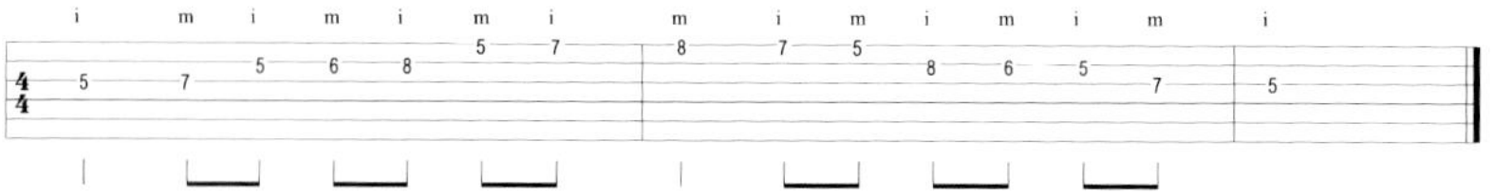

C major in fifth position This is a simple major scale over three strings. Start and finish on the **i** finger. Aim for an even tone on each note.

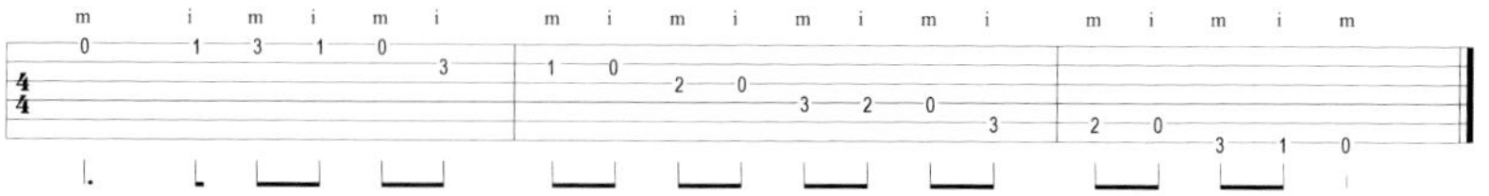

Scale crossing all six strings This descending scale has a Spanish flavour. Treat the rhythm as a guide only – see if you can gradually speed up towards the lower end of the scale and finish with a flourish.

Fingers and thumb

The guitar, along with instruments such as harp and the piano, is capable of playing more than one line of music at a time.

This overlap of melodies is known by the term 'counterpoint'. On the guitar, it is quite a difficult skill to master. The thumb and the fingers of the right hand need to develop independence of each other in order to control the separate parts. The left hand also needs to be well ordered, so that each voice sounds smooth and complete.

Some guitar music contains as many as three or four voices. Professional classical players will spend a lot of time working out the best fingering in both hands so that each line maintains its integrity.

The simplest kind of counterpoint, however, consists just of a melody accompanied by a bass line. On the guitar, playing a simple contrapuntal piece involves plucking the bass line with the thumb, while walking the **i** and **m** fingers on the melody. The **a** finger is sometimes used to help with string crossings.

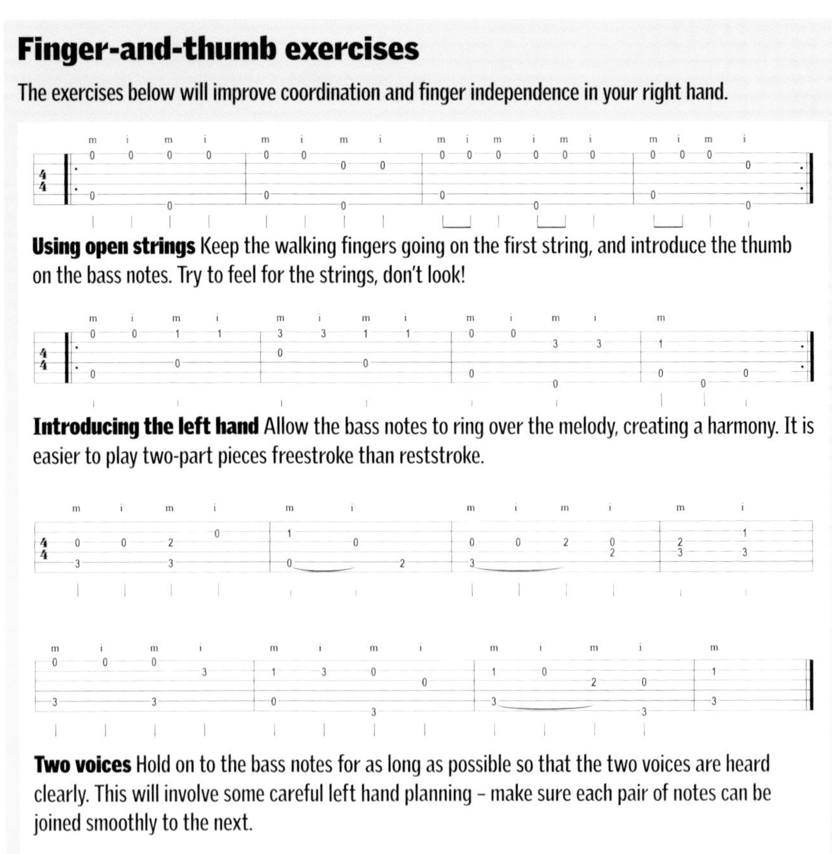

Finger-and-thumb exercises

The exercises below will improve coordination and finger independence in your right hand.

Using open strings Keep the walking fingers going on the first string, and introduce the thumb on the bass notes. Try to feel for the strings, don't look!

Introducing the left hand Allow the bass notes to ring over the melody, creating a harmony. It is easier to play two-part pieces freestroke than reststroke.

Two voices Hold on to the bass notes for as long as possible so that the two voices are heard clearly. This will involve some careful left hand planning – make sure each pair of notes can be joined smoothly to the next.

Classical tricks

There are more right-hand techniques you can borrow from the classical-guitar repertoire. When you get on to the exercises over the next four pages, practise carefully and repeatedly to strengthen your right hand.

Arpeggio technique

Basic arpeggio technique, as discussed on pages 52–53, uses **p** on the lower three strings and **i**, **m** and **a** on the third, second and first strings respectively. This approach is fine for most fingerpicking patterns, but classical playing demands far more flexibility. The **p**, **i**, **m**, **a** stance, with each finger assigned to a string, must be ready to be positioned on any group of four strings and should be easily adaptable.

Try the exercises below, paying close attention to the right hand fingering.

Exercises in classical arpeggios

You have played arpeggios before (pages 52-53). Now try these exercises in the classical style.

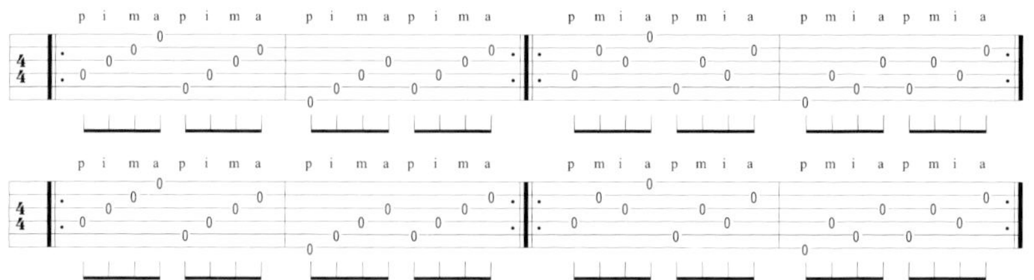

On open strings This is a good starter exercise, as the left hand has nothing to do.

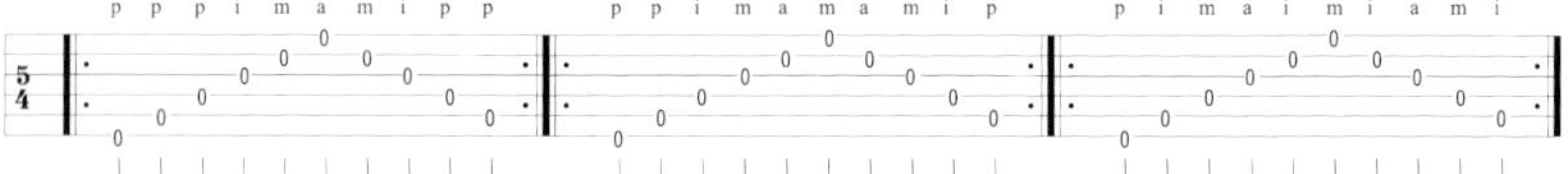

Using p, i, m, a over six strings There are three separate exercises here. The **p**, **i**, **m**, **a** shape moves to a new position in each one.

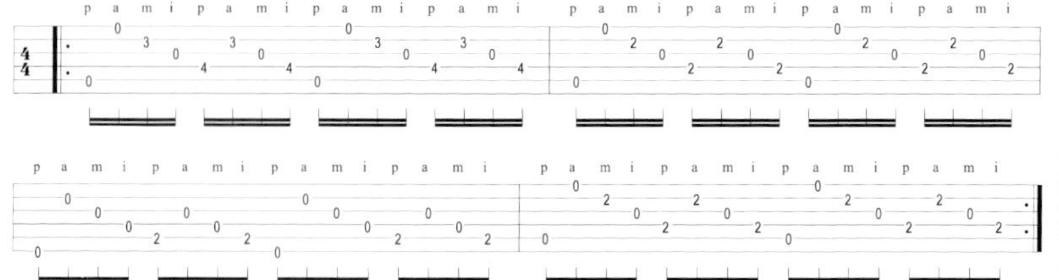

More right-hand exercises Practise the three underlying chord shapes before putting in the right-hand patterns. Hold one chord shape for each bar.

Repeated patterns

Repeated patterns in the right hand are often used in classical playing to add texture to the music. Rapid and precise movements of the right-hand fingers are needed to produce this 'tremolando' effect, which is a sustained shimmering sound.

The key skill here is 'planting', which means preparing the fingers on the strings before plucking. This improves control by having constant contact with the strings. The simplest example of this is a 'spread', or 'rolled', chord (see the exercise below), where the notes of a block chord are separated, from low to high, with a roll of the fingers.

Triplet figures

In triplet figures, the player uses only three fingers in the right hand: **p**, **i** and **m**. Start with all three on the relevant strings then pluck in ascending order. As **m** plucks the first string, **p** plants on the bass note. As **p** plucks the bass note **i** and **m** plant on the third and first strings. In the exercise overleaf the thumb will need to change strings according to the melody, while **i** and **m** return to the same strings.

Tremolo

Classical tremolo can sound stunning when played well. Here the thumb controls all the bass notes while the **a**, **m** and **i** fingers play on one string. When played up to speed this gives the illusion of a sustained melody.

For practice purposes, plant each finger in turn: as **p** plays, **a** is prepared; as **a** plays, **m** is prepared; as **m** plays, **i** is prepared; as **i** plays, **p** is prepared on the next bass note; and so on.

Tremolando exercises

Have a go at this rapid, rolling technique, which is fundamental to classical guitar-playing.

'Rolled' chords To play the rolled chord directional, begin by placing **p**, **i**, **m** and **a** on the strings in advance then releasing the fingers in ascending order. This feels like peeling the fingers from the string one by one and should be performed in one fluid movement. Practise this example so that the notes come out evenly, and then gradually increase the speed. Reset, or 'plant', the chord each time.

A repeated pattern A slightly different technique: start as above with all the fingers plucking in ascending order. As the finger **a** plucks the first string, **p** resets itself on the bass note ready to play. As **p** plucks the fourth string, **i**, **m** and **a** plant on the third, second and first strings. The pattern can then pick up speed. The right hand is always in contact with at least one string.

Triplet exercise

Keep the second finger of the left hand on the second fret of the third string throughout. The melody is in the bass here and is played by the thumb.

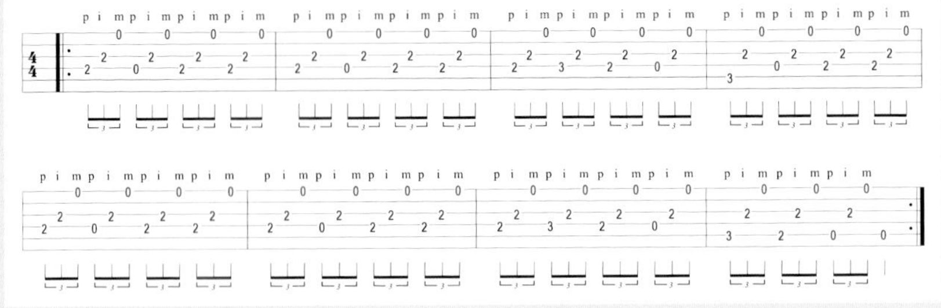

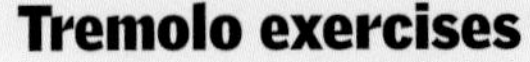

Tremolo exercises

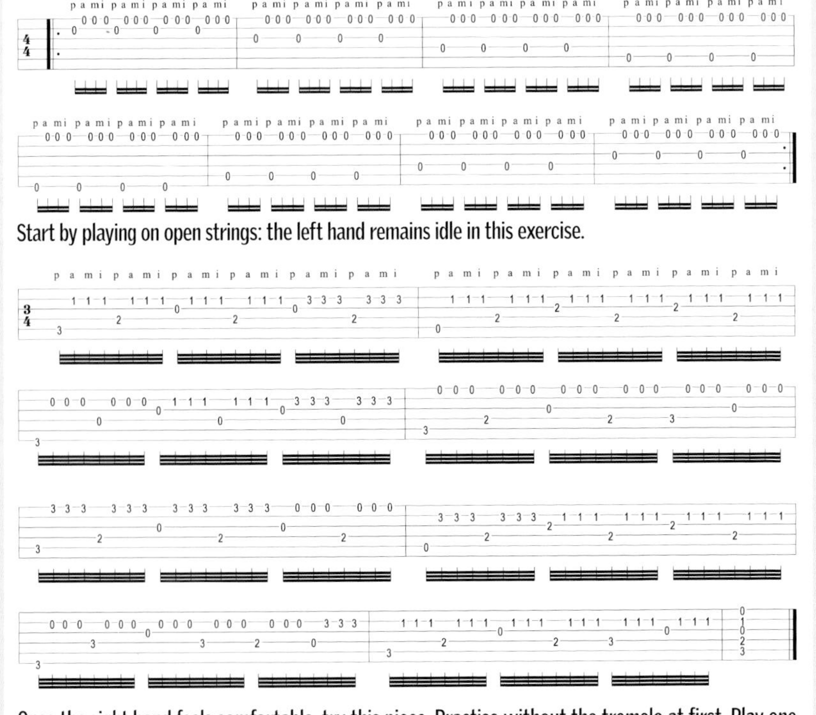

Start by playing on open strings: the left hand remains idle in this exercise.

Once the right hand feels comfortable, try this piece. Practise without the tremolo at first. Play one note instead of three to get a feel for the fingering. Each bar holds a chord shape while the tremolo melody moves between the first and second strings.

Rasgueado

Rasgueado is a flamenco-guitar technique that entails striking the strings with the backs of the nails.

Rasgueados involve percussive, rhythmic strumming patterns that can use all of the fingers of the right hand. They are an excellent way to strengthen the weaker fingers of the right hand, especially the little finger **c**. To perform the rasgueado roll, start by fixing your thumb on the sixth string. Next, dig your fingers into the palm of your hand as if making a fist. Strike down through the strings with your **c** finger, followed by **a**, then **m** and finally **i**, which provides a strong finish. The rasgueado should be played at speed, but practise slowly at first, concentrating on getting good separation between the fingers.

Above The rasgueado, finger by finger: **c**, **a**, **m** then **i**.

Rasgueado exercise

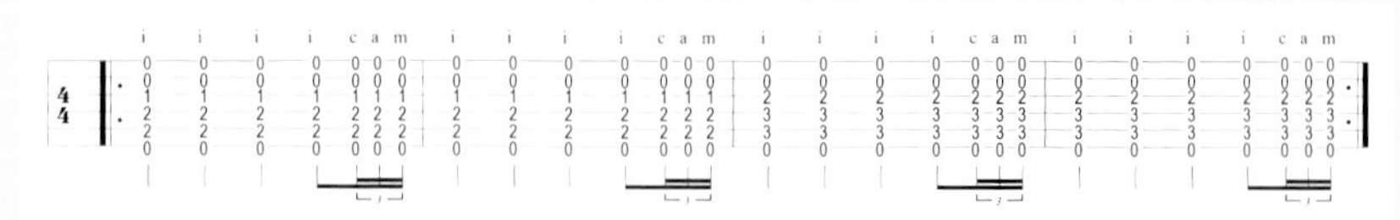

Play all the block chords with the back of the **i** fingernail and intersperse these main beats with the rasgueado roll. The chords played are very simple – a plain E major slides up one fret to create an altered F chord.

TECHNICAL DEVELOPMENT

A commitment to music involves a certain perfectionism. Good instrumentalists are always looking to refine their playing. These technical exercises are a vital part of that process, a surefire way to ensure that you constantly and steadily make progress as a guitarist.

A little focused work each day can make the world of difference to your playing. One approach is to divide your practice time between learning new pieces and technical study. But don't practise so much that your technique becomes lifeless and mechanical: the aim is to help you to play music better.

Left-hand strength

The left-hand fingers are not equal. The first and second fingers are strong, and the third and fourth fingers can feel sluggish by comparison. Some guitarists try to avoid using the weaker fingers, but this is a mistake: strengthening these fingers can be done. The exercise below is one of the best for boosting the strength and independence of the left-hand fingers. Concentrate solely on the left hand; there is no need to pluck with the right.

Pull-offs

The pull-off is demanding, because the left hand must be perfectly positioned to pluck downwards with the fingertips. The key to making pull-offs feel easy is to keep the third and fourth fingers close

Walking exercise for left-hand strength

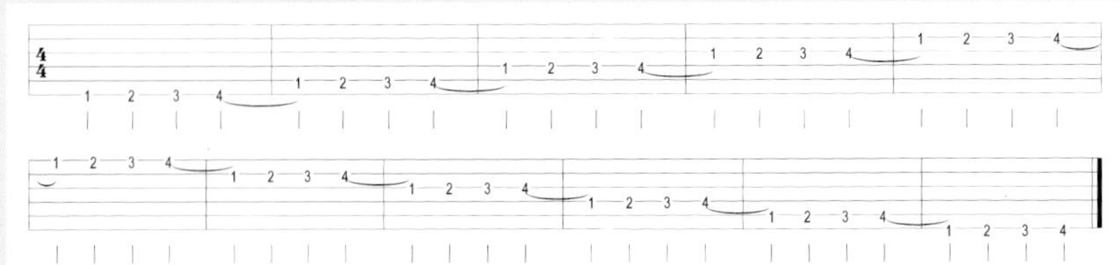

Start with your fingers in fifth position with one finger in each fret. Press all the fingers down at once on the sixth string and hold. Lift the first finger and place on the fifth string and hold. All other fingers stay rooted to the sixth string. Lift the second finger and place on the fifth string and hold. Lift the third finger and place on the fifth string and hold (don't let the fourth finger lift from the sixth string). Lift the fourth finger and place on the fifth string and hold. Continue in the same manner moving up one string at a time. Only lift one finger at a time and maintain the left-hand shape described.

to the strings, accurately poised on their fingertips. The exercise below will help.

Left-hand mobility

The mobility exercise below is an excellent way of improving the movement of the left hand and arm as you move around the neck. Try to be especially focused on maintaining the horizontal position of the left-hand fingers in relation to the strings. The left-hand thumb should travel with the hand, and it should remain behind the second finger at all times.

Exercise for pull-off drills

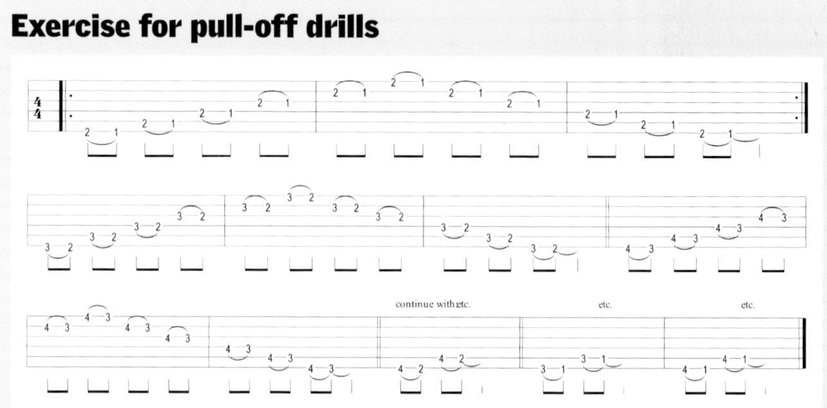

Make sure both fingers are in position on the string before executing the pull-off. Aim for a clearly defined snap to the sound. Relax the fingers and move lightly between pull-offs. This exercise can be played anywhere on the neck – the numbers here refer to fingers rather than frets. Choose a higher position at first, where the frets are closer together; this will cause less strain on the hands.

Exercise for left-hand mobility

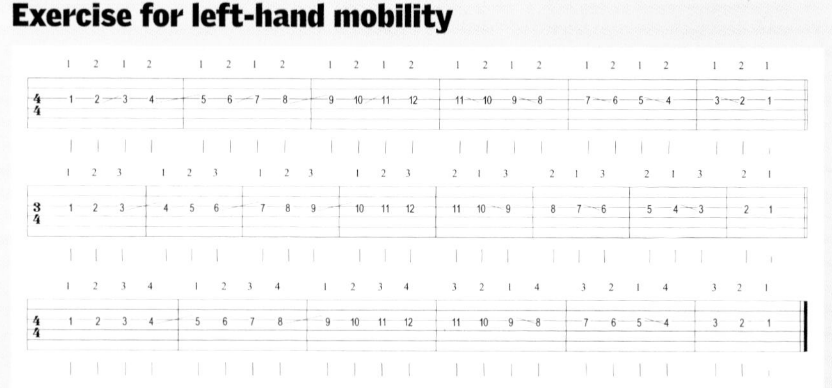

To shift positions accurately, use a guide finger where possible to make the changes smooth. The left-hand fingers are marked above the score.

LESSON 55

Coordination

The coordination exercises below can be practised with either a plectrum or with alternating **i** and **m** fingers. Start slowly and gradually increase the speed. The aim here is to improve control rather than speed, so make sure every note sounds clear and is fretted correctly.

Sweep picking

Sweep picking is a plectrum technique that involves playing multiple strings at speed. Drag the plectrum across the strings in a series of rest strokes. This should come to feel like a continuous movement. Special attention should be given to coordinating the movements of the left and right hands. Practise using the exercises opposite.

Left-hand agility

Any excess finger tension will hinder coordination and agility, so only use the minimum of pressure when you play. If you find yourself pressing too hard, try doing the opposite by practising with muted notes, then gradually increasing the pressure. The left-hand-coordination exercise, opposite bottom, will help.

Chromatic coordination exercise

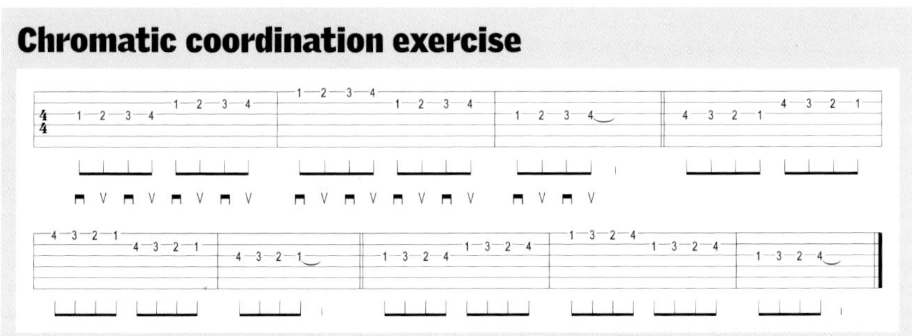

Extended coordination exercise

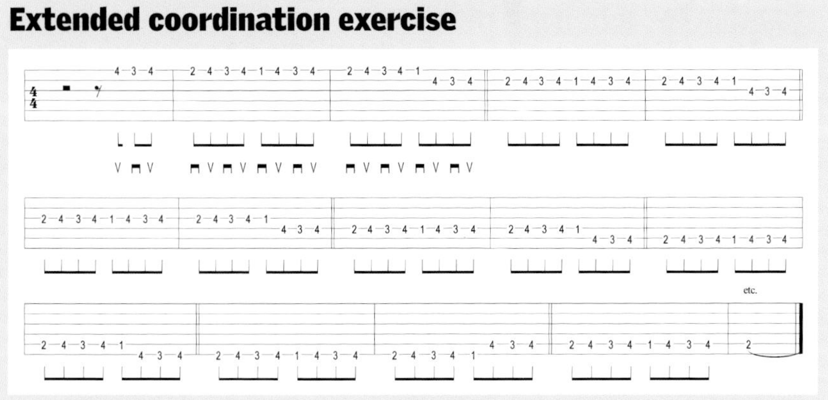

This exercise is an excellent workout for the fourth finger. Keep the left-hand fingers parallel to the strings at all times and play with as little pressure as possible.

Exercise in open-string sweep picking

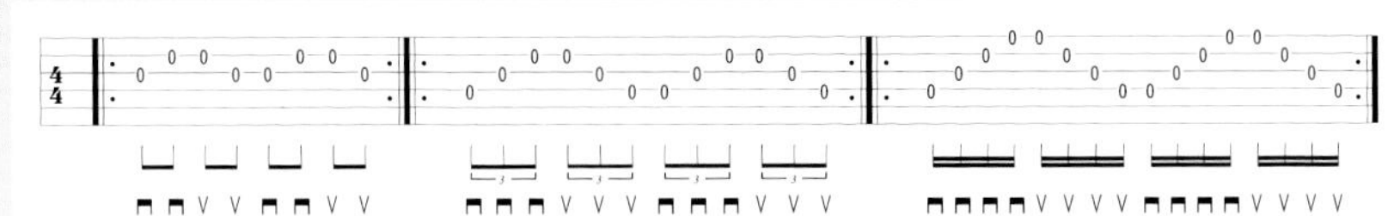

Control the speed and pressure of the plectrum as it passes across the strings. Each pass of the strings should be as fluid as possible.

Exercise in sweep picking with chords

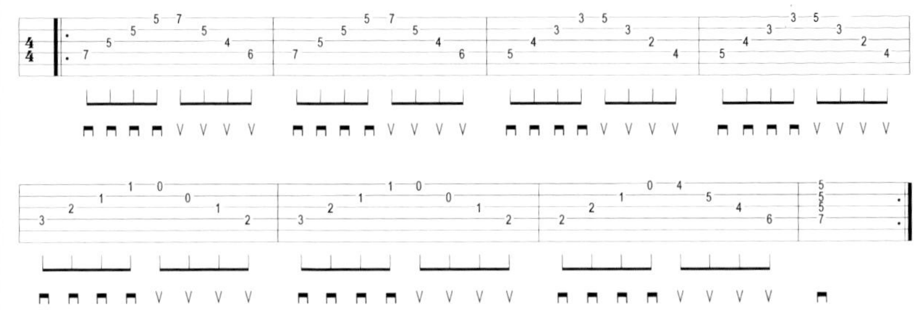

Practise the chord shapes before getting started on the right hand. In this exercise there are two chord shapes in each bar.

Exercise in left-hand agility

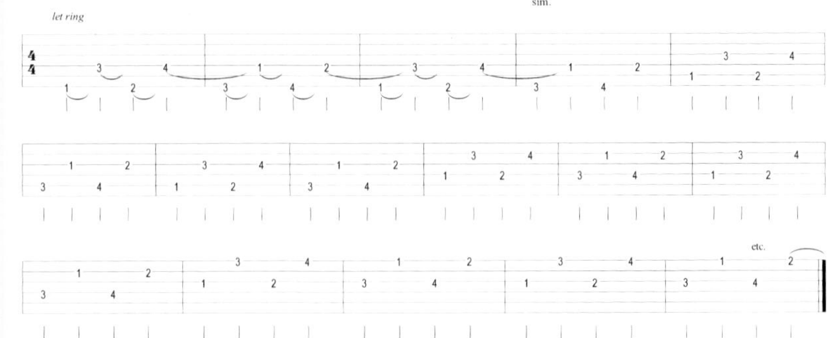

This is a tricky exercise that involves playing two chromatic scales at the same time. Let the notes overlap for as long as possible. For a more extended workout, move up one fret position at a time to cover the whole neck.

DAILY EXERCISE ROUTINE

The purpose of this daily exercise routine is to reinforce the basics of good technique. Once you get to know the drill, it should take no more than five minutes to run through the whole sequence. Use the routine as a regular warm-up before practising.

You should strive to play each of these exercises steadily, with an emphasis on control rather than speed. The aim is to make a good, solid tone, and to move smoothly and confidently between notes. Avoid rushing and having to go back over notes because you have made a mistake. Play within your limits.

Also, be aware of your body as you play. Press no harder on the strings than is necessary. Check and maintain the correct hand positions and be sure that your hands, arms and shoulders are relaxed. Concentrate throughout. In time you will reap the benefits of better control and consistency.

Step 1: Open strings

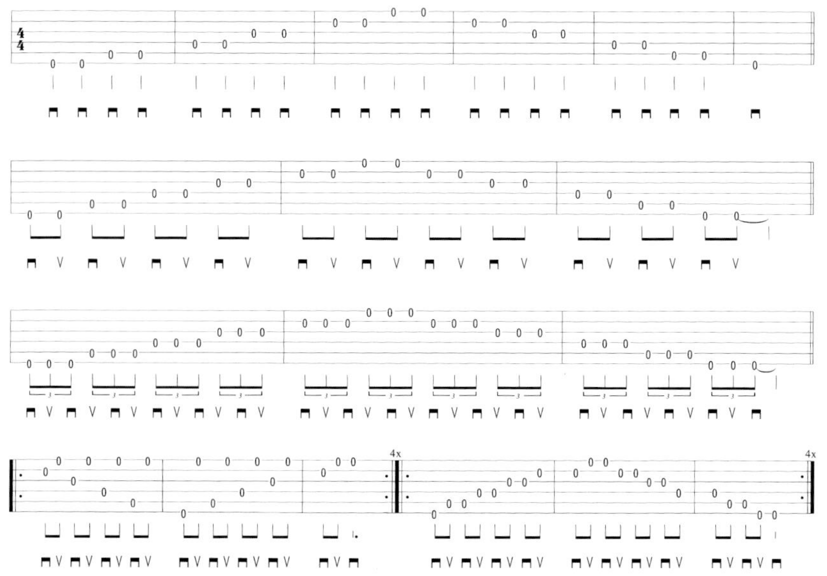

Step 2: Left-hand walking

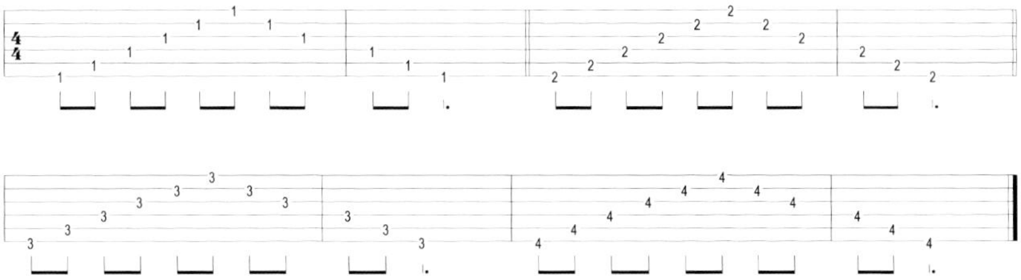

Hold the position of the left hand and focus on landing the fingertip of each finger on the strings. Hop cleanly across the strings without letting the fingers squash.

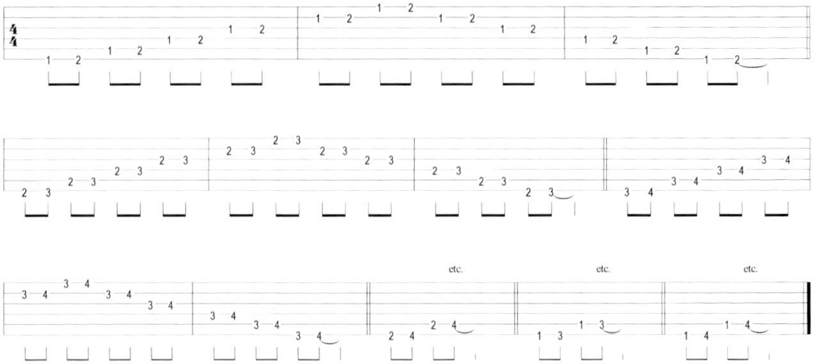

Walk the fingers carefully across the fingerboard. Lift each finger deliberately, and aim for a smooth transition between the notes. There should always be one finger in contact with the strings. Step across the strings; don't jump.

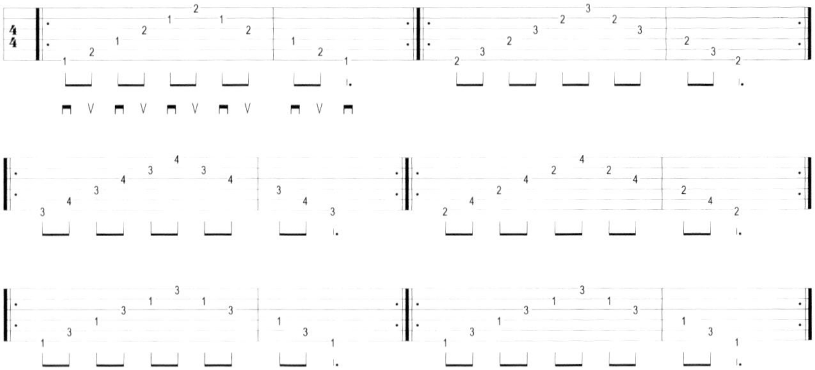

Cross the strings one at a time. Keep the left-hand thumb fairly stationary on the back of the neck.

Step 3: Hammer-ons and pull-offs

Keep all the fingers under control when playing hammer-ons and pull-offs. Hold the left-hand position – especially the fourth finger – and keep fingers parallel to the strings.

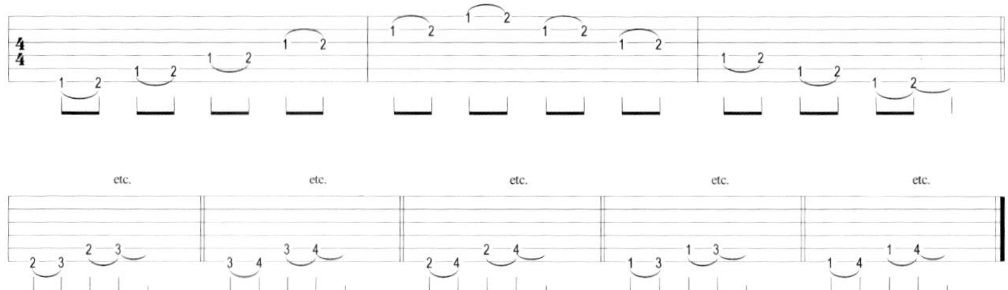

Daily hammer-on exercise Play this exercise continuously as a good workout for every combination of fingers. Experiment with different speeds and gauge your progress over time.

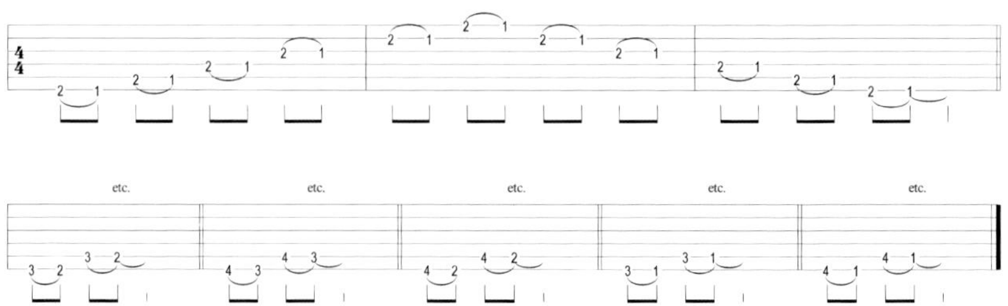

Daily pull-off exercise Place each pair of fingers together on the string and stay on your fingertips in order to clear the exercise without getting tired.

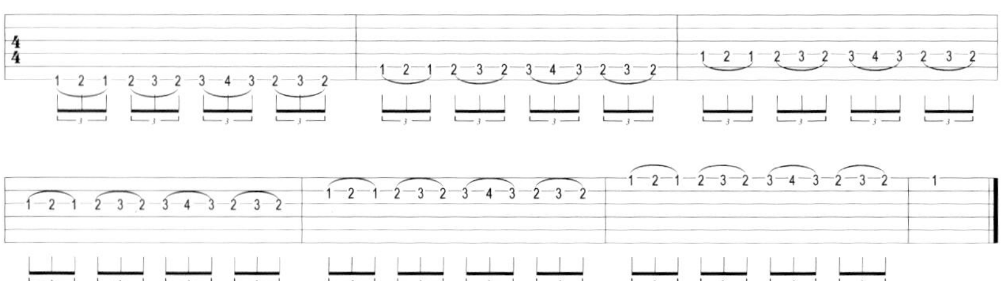

Daily hammer-on/pull-off exercise Pluck only the first note of each group. Add the left-hand fingers as you work up each string. This exercise can be placed anywhere on the neck.

Step 4: Scales

These scales can be positioned anywhere on the neck. To extend the exercises, move up one fret at a time. Repeat each pattern four times and aim for consistency rather than speed.

Chromatic exercise Keep your left-hand fingertips pointing at the string to be played – and no more than one centimetre away.

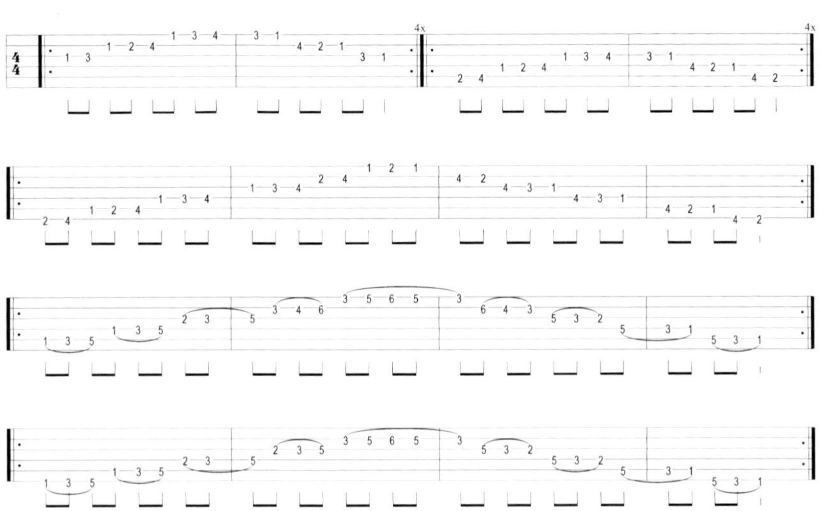

Major scales These scales can be played anywhere on the fingerboard. Start around the fifth, sixth and seventh frets before trying the same scale at a lower fret, where the stretch is more difficult. The last two scales use three fingers on each string – a popular technique used by speed metal guitarists.

Step 5: Opposing-motion exercises

These exercises are great for developing the left-hand stance. Try both the sweep picking and the fingerpicking patterns.

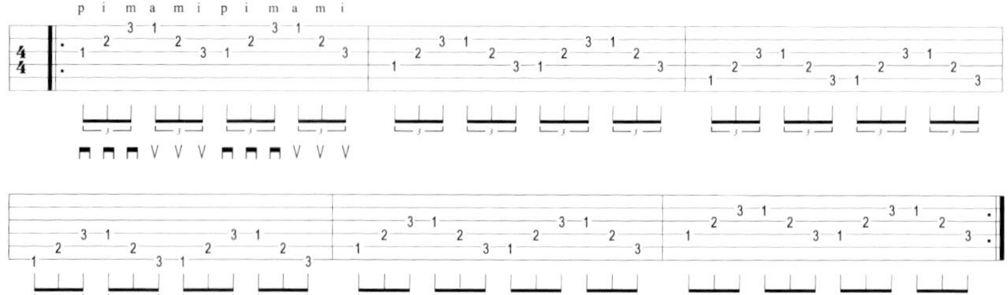

Three-finger opposing-motion exercise Keep the left hand very neat and on the fingertips. Place this pattern anywhere on the neck.

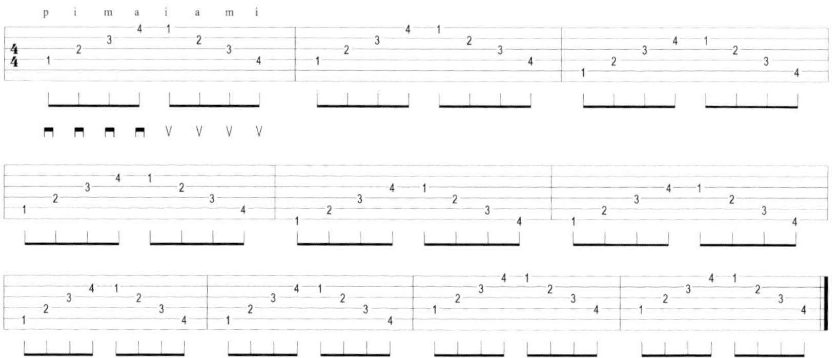

Four-finger opposing-motion exercise Focus on pressing very lightly on the strings, and on keeping all the fingers over the strings, ready to play. At first, try playing dead left-hand notes before gradually increasing the pressure.

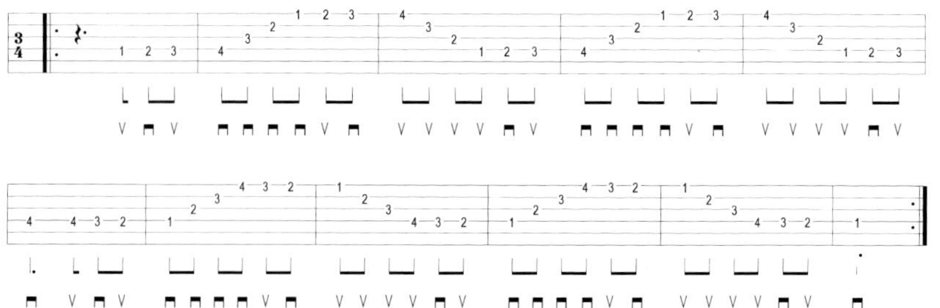

Advanced opposing-motion exercise This exercise is more challenging. It uses chromatic scales either side of the string-crossing pattern in order to reverse the direction. Play very slowly at first.

Step 6: Speed bursts

This exercise works best if you have a metronome handy. You can push up the speed gradually and keep a record of your progress. Repeat each section until it feels easy. Take care over the string crossings, and make sure that every note rings clear. You can practise finger patterns of your own devising with this method.

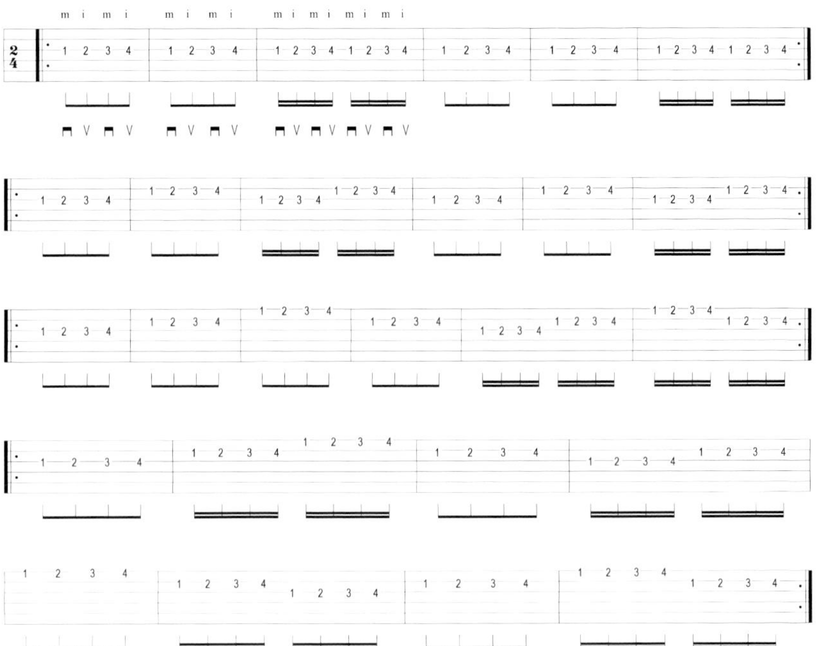

Left- and right-hand speed-coordination exercise Play very lightly in the left hand, and hold a strong stance. Use short strokes with the plectrum, and gradually increase the speed until the open notes sound like an independent line. Try the same exercise on the inside strings for more of a challenge.

THE NEXT STEP

Now that you have come to the end of the book, you might like to think about how to move on with your guitar playing. Playing regularly, alone or with friends, is one sure way to improve. You might also benefit from taking formal guitar lessons.

If you have followed this course all the way through – even if you have only got through the first two sections – then you are by now a pretty competent guitarist. You will be playing fluently, using your sound knowledge of chords of all kinds; you will be able to read tablature and basic music notation; you will be a dab hand at improvising solos, and you might know your way around some specialized techniques such as slide guitar.

This is a great start – but where to now? An excellent next step is to get some one-on-one instruction. A good teacher will be able to help you structure your learning, and will provide the kind of technical advice and correction that can come only from someone who has seen you play. Your choice of teacher might well turn out to be crucial to your development as a musician. Here are some ideas on how to find the right person for you.

Find a teacher

Your local music shop is a good place to start looking for a teacher. Many shops selling guitars or other instruments provide in-house lessons. Most will also have a list of teachers who live in the area, and will either visit your home or give lessons at their own. Some shops will have a noticeboard or other space where teachers advertise their services.

Instrumental teachers are not obliged to have an official qualification to teach, but you may find it reassuring to look for those with the right letters after their name. Most professional teachers will hold a music diploma or a degree in addition to their teaching qualifications.

Make the grades

A good teacher will be able to put you through accredited exams, and so will be familiar with the relevant syllabus. Working your way up the grades is a good way to keep track of your progress, and it will give structure to your learning.

Formal examinations are perhaps more associated with the classical guitar, but they are increasingly popular for the electric guitar, too. Exams in the pop and rock genres are administered by a body called Rockschool. The grade system has the same structure – from 1 to 8 – as for classical guitar and other instruments.

Younger students should be able to take lessons at school (at both junior and senior levels). This system suits students and parents alike, as lessons normally take place during normal school hours.

If you happen to live near a music college, it is worth seeing if it runs a scheme whereby tuition is provided to students outside the institution. Some colleges hold weekend classes, mainly for younger students.

Above all, make music

You may not like the idea of undertaking formal study – and that is fine. There are other great ways to learn more about the guitar. Forming a band and playing with others is one. There is a huge satisfaction to be had from playing music with other people, whether you are jamming at home or performing for a crowd. The 'in at the deep end' approach – playing in public and under pressure – might well teach you a lot more about what does and does not work than can be learned in hours of private study.

Remember that you don't need to be a virtuoso to play to an audience. Listen to some simple pop songs: with the knowledge you now have, you will see that many players make a living by strumming just a handful of easy chords. So whatever level you have attained or aspire to, be sure – above all else – that you take pleasure in making music, and that you share your enjoyment with other people as often as you can.

Band together Play with other people whenever possible. There is always something you can learn from another guitarist, and what is more, it is great fun.

REFERENCE

REFERENCE

CHORD GUIDE

These pages are a quick reference guide to the most common chord shapes in standard tuning. White circles in a red square indicate the location of the root note.

Open chords

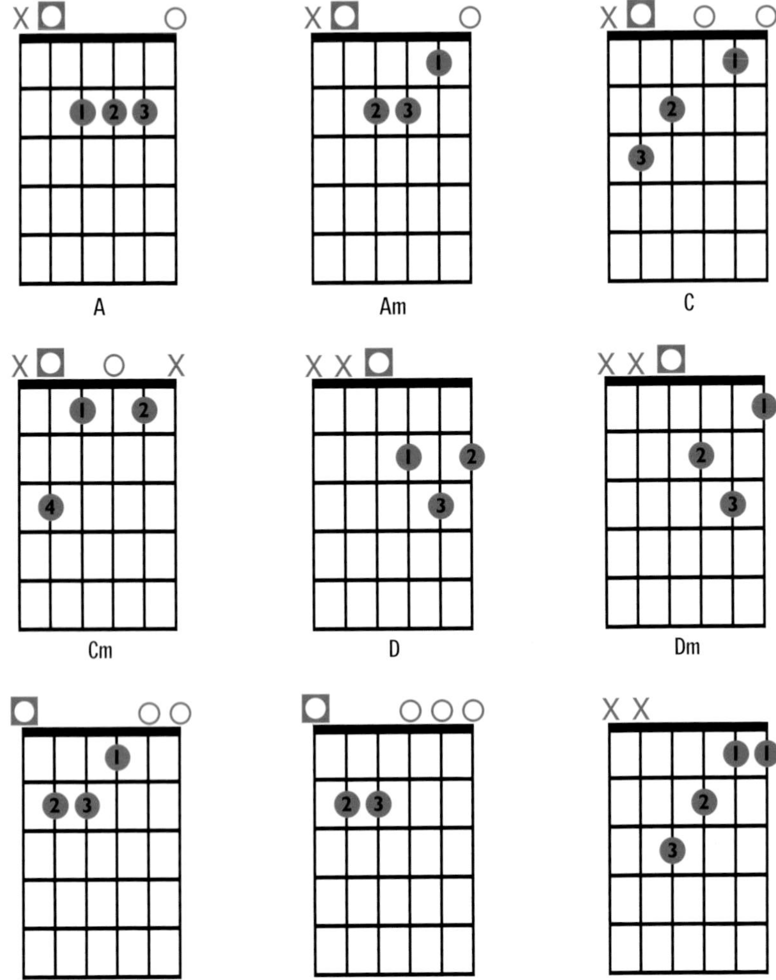

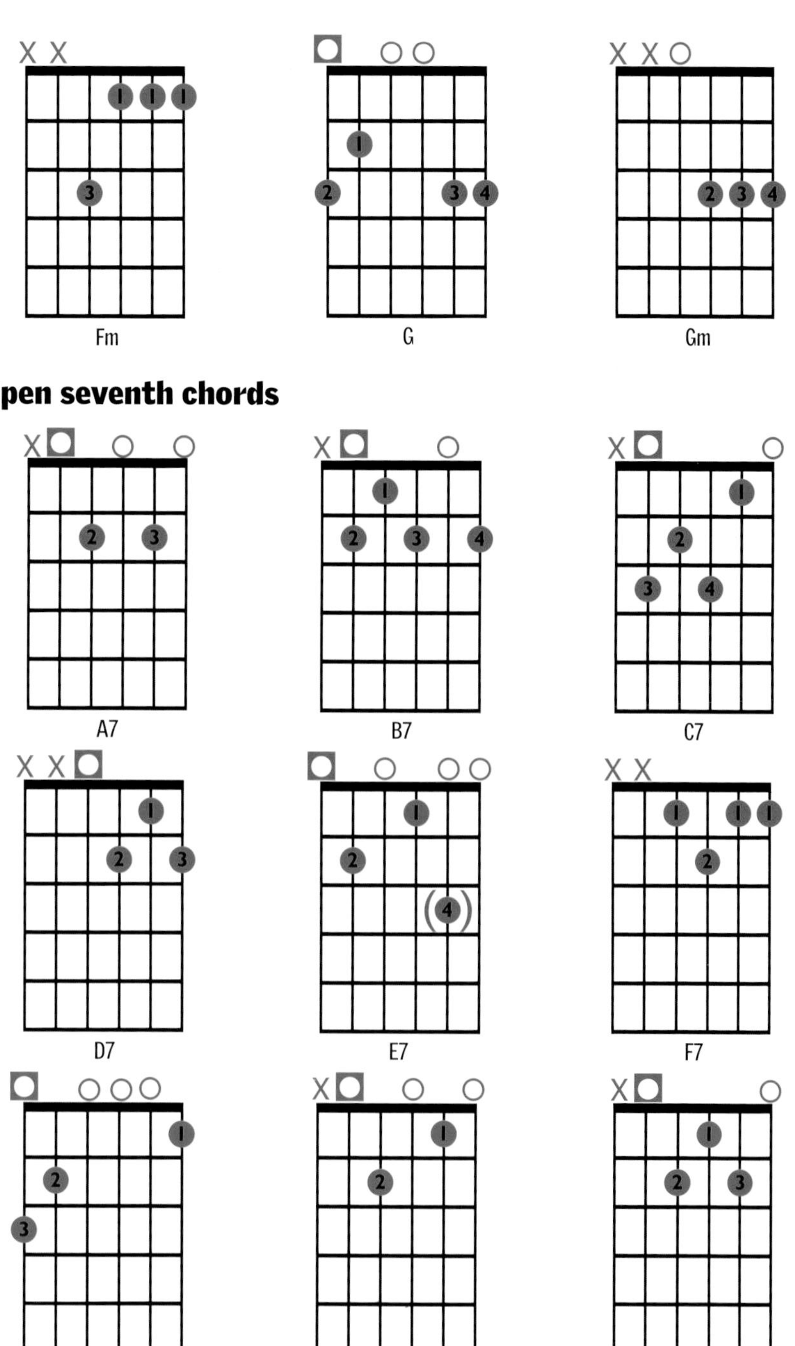
Fm
G
Gm
Open seventh chords
A7
B7
C7
D7
E7
F7
G7
Am7
Amaj7

REFERENCE

Open seventh chords (continued)

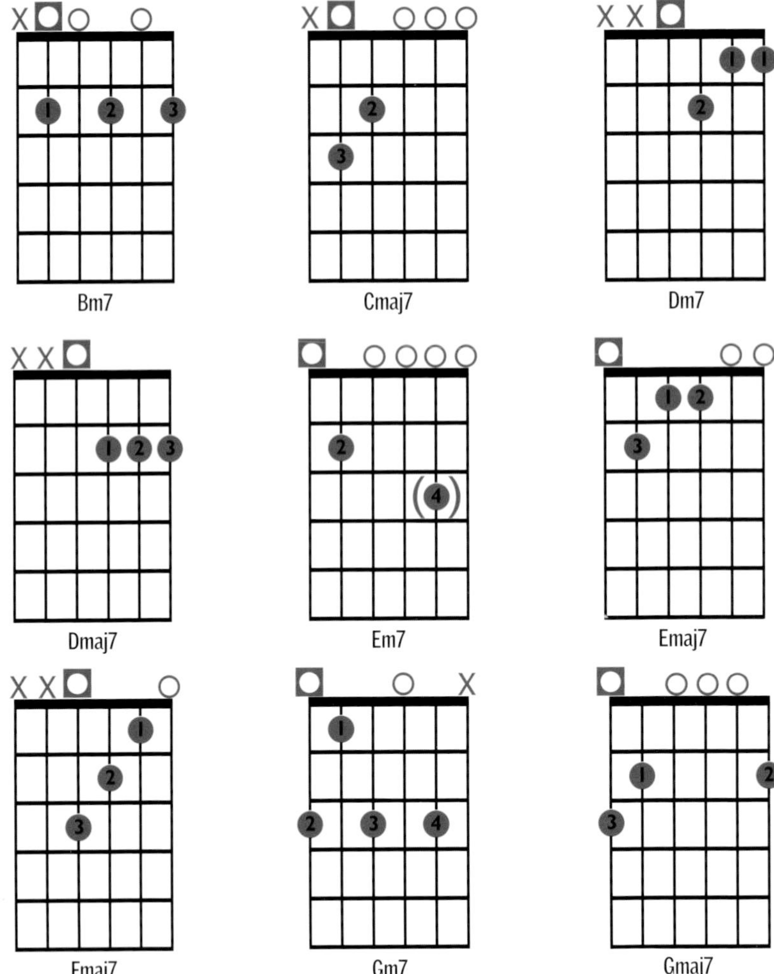

Moveable shapes

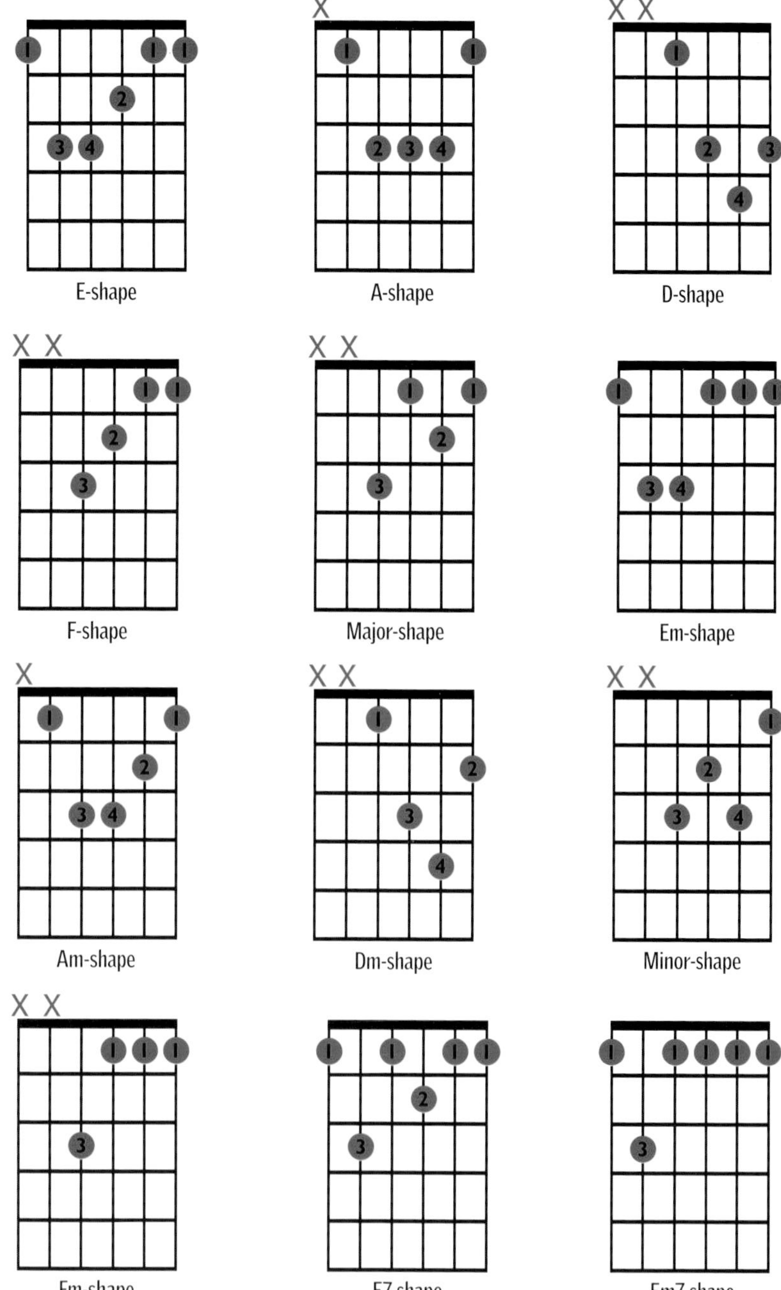

Moveable shapes (continued)

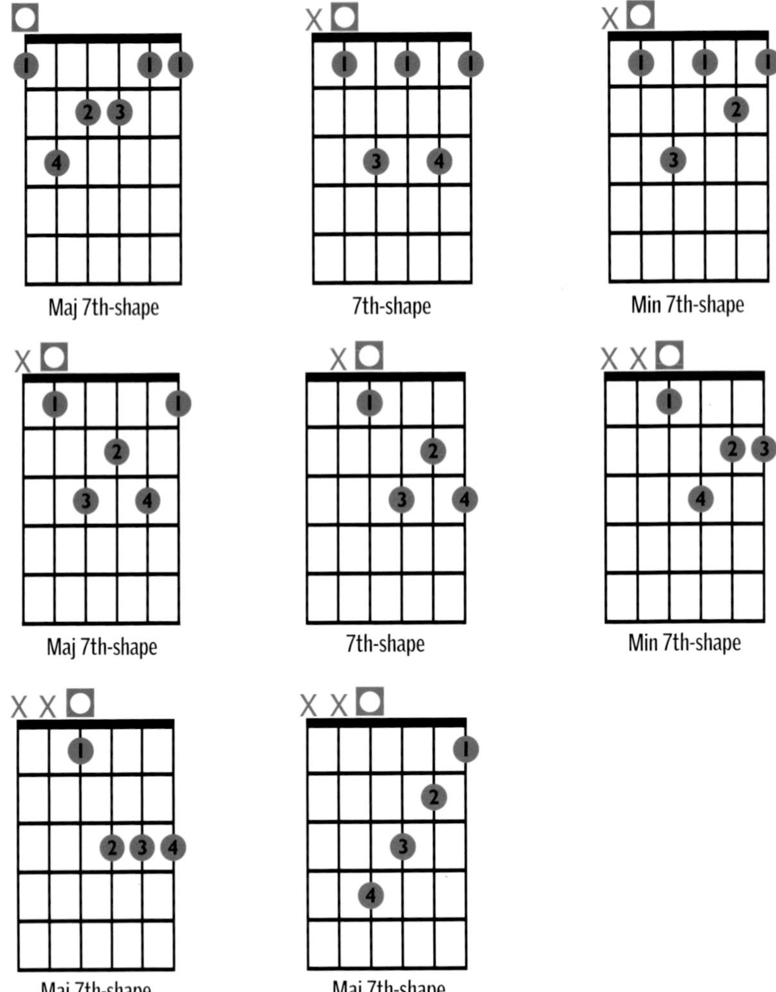

Jazz chords and extensions

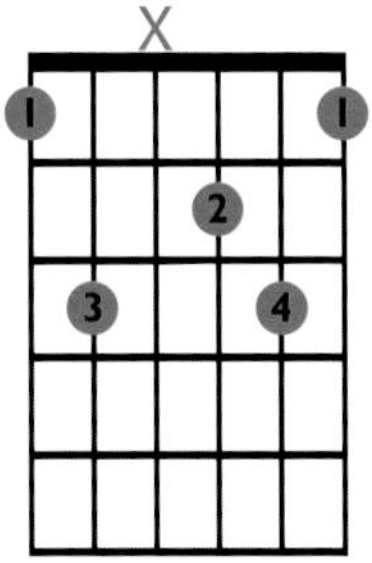

Maj 6th

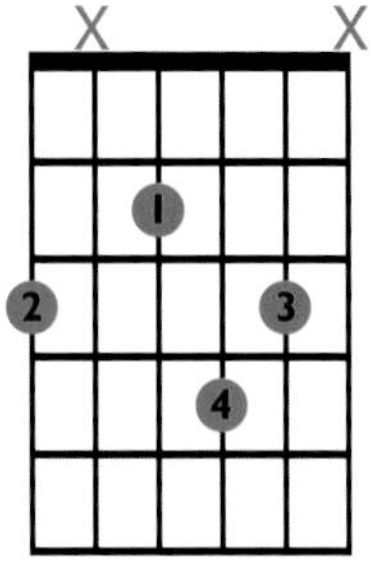

Maj 6th

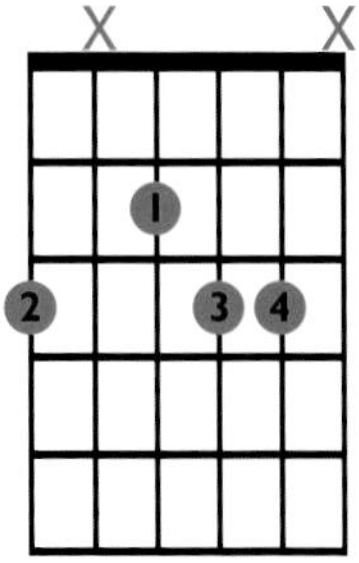

Min 6th

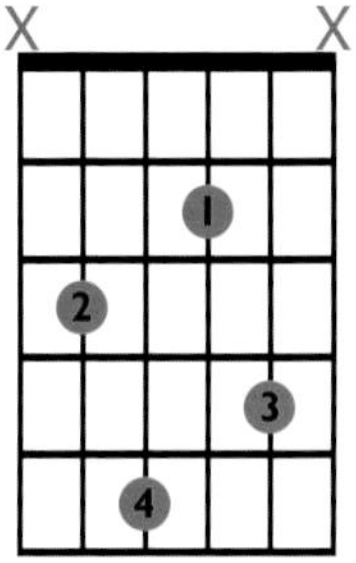

Min 6th

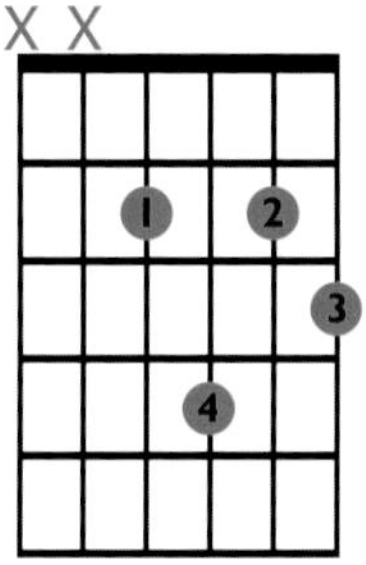

Min 6th

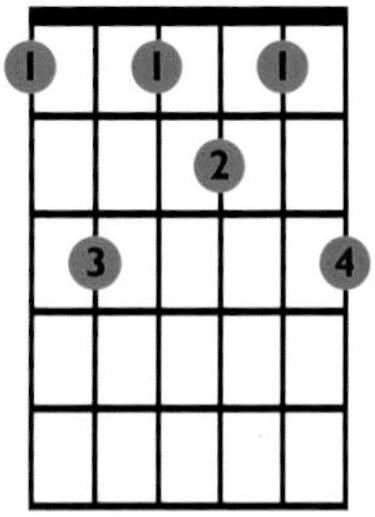

9th

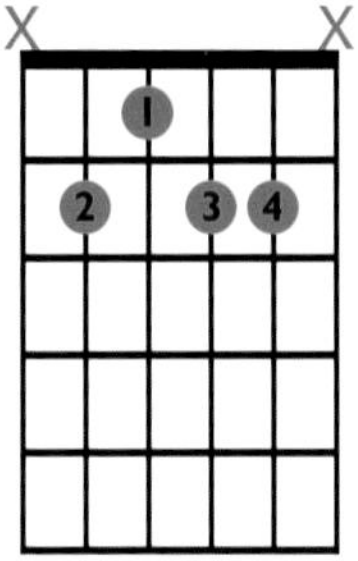

9th

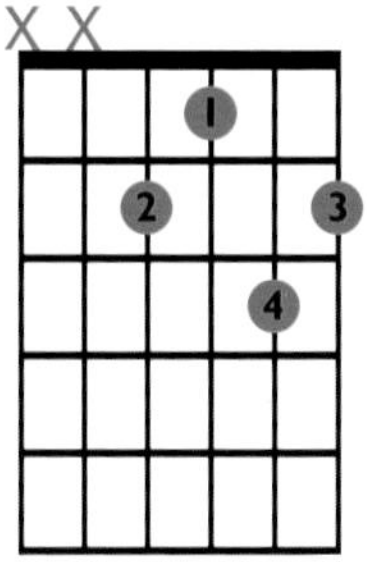

9th

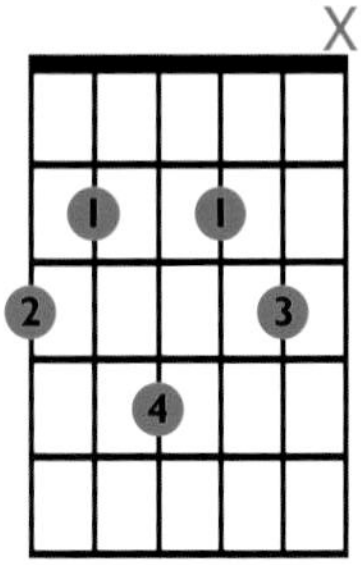

Maj 9th

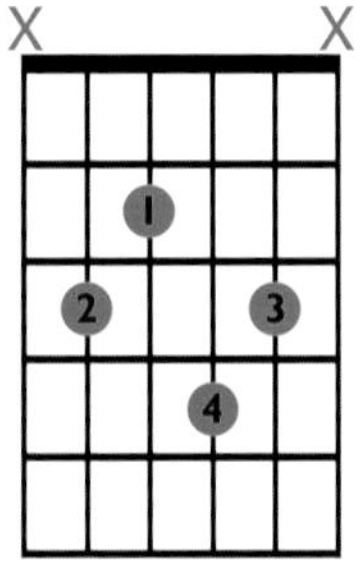

Maj 9th

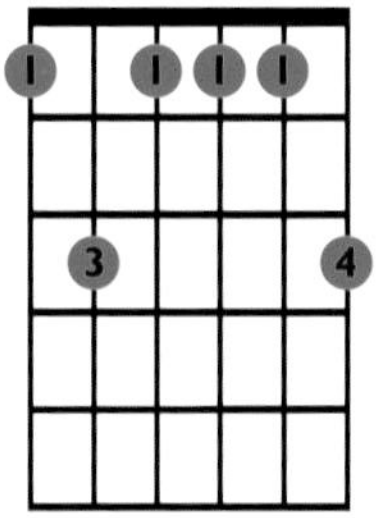

Min 9th

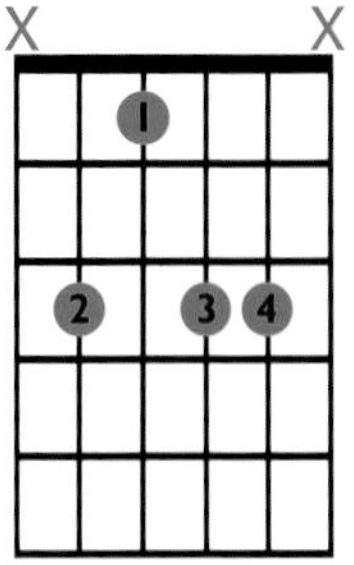

Min 9th

Jazz chords and extensions (continued)

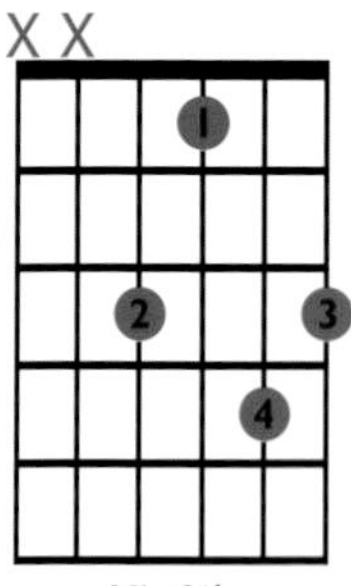
Min 9th

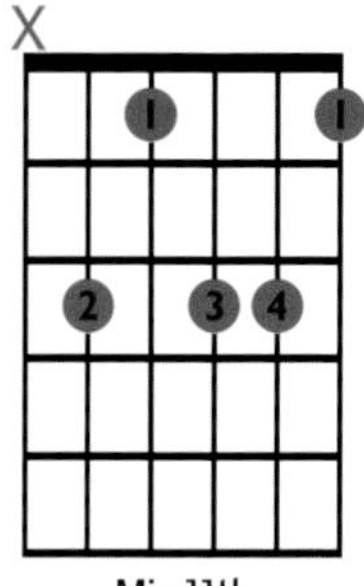
Min 11th

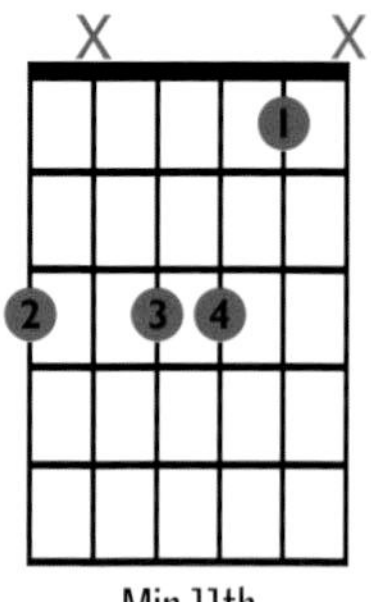
Min 11th

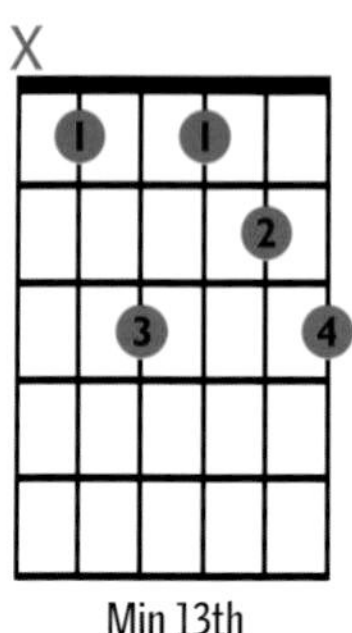
Min 13th

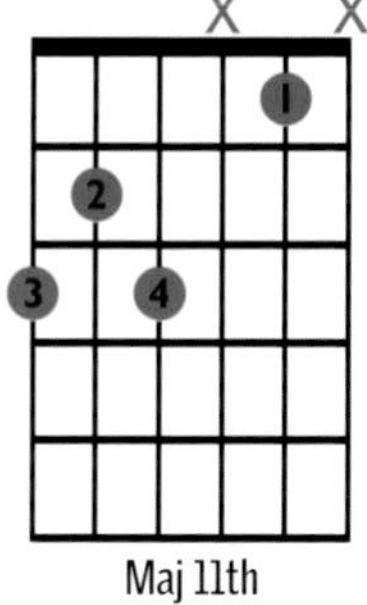
Maj 11th

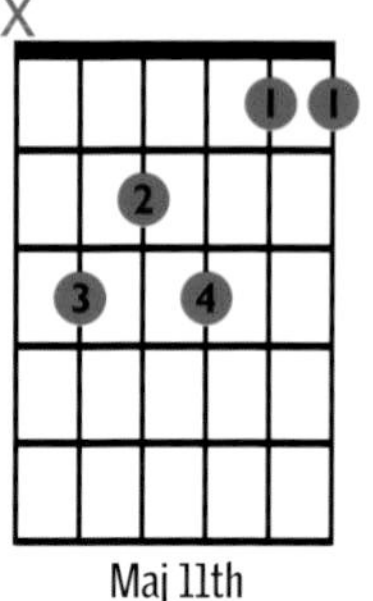
Maj 11th

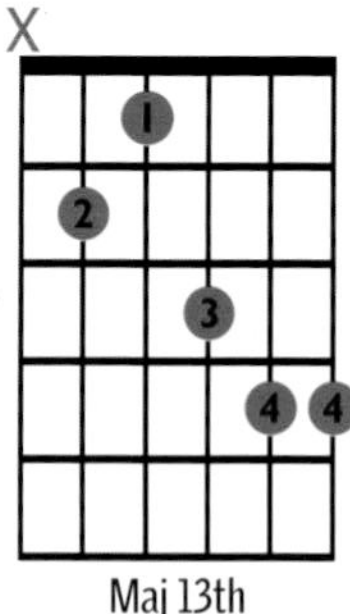
Maj 13th

Diminished and augmented chords

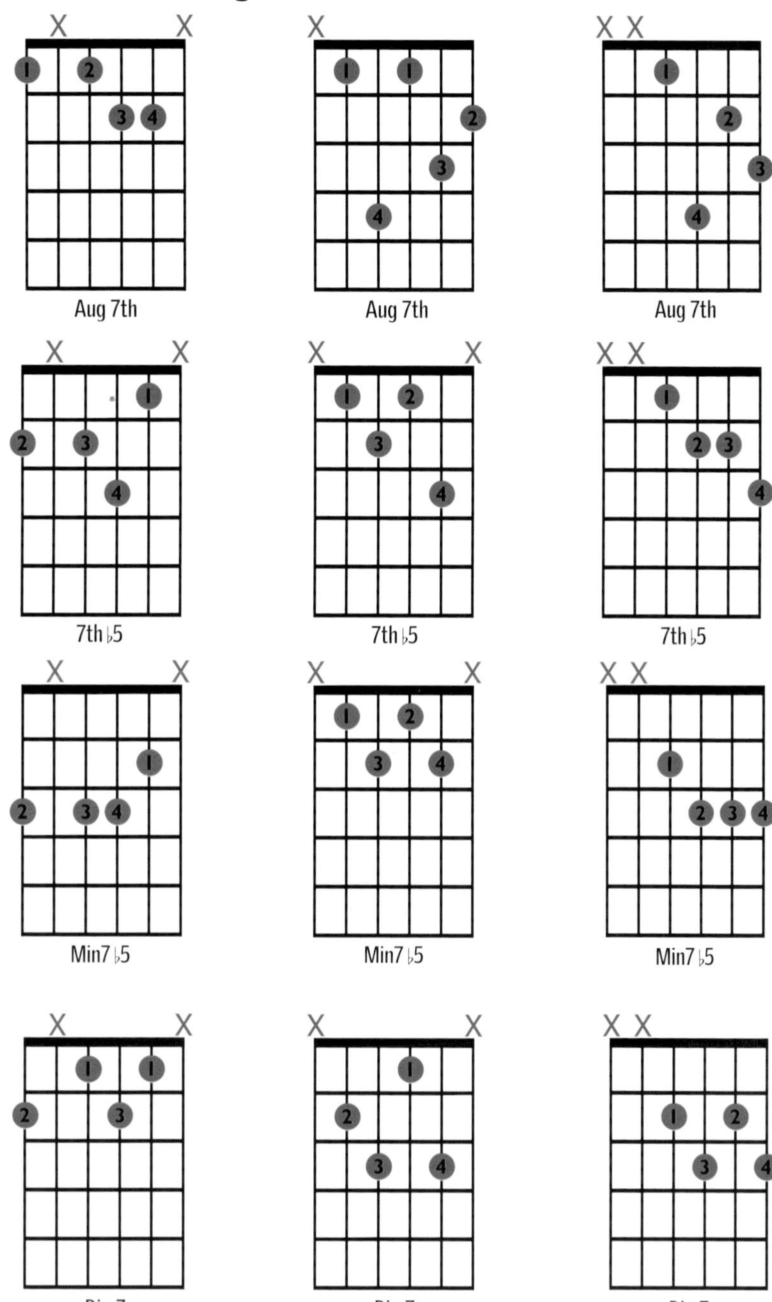

GLOSSARY

Action The distance of the strings from the frets. A guitar that is comfortable to play is said to have an 'easy action'.
Arpeggio The notes of a chord played in succession rather than together.
Bar chord A chord that involves using the first finger to cover all or most of the strings.
Bend A note that is altered in pitch by pushing the string upwards against the frets.
Blues scale A six-note scale used in blues music. It is similar to the pentatonic scale but has an additional flattened fifth (the 'blue note').
Broken chord An alternative term for an arpeggio. Also known as a 'spread chord'.
Capo A device that can be clamped to the neck of a guitar in order to raise the base pitch of the strings.
Capstan A rotatable drum, fitted to the headstock, around which the strings are wound.
Chord A set of three or more notes played together. The musical qualities of standard chords are described as major, minor, augmented or diminished.
Chromatic scale A musical scale with twelve pitches, each a semitone (or one fret) apart.
Counterpoint The interplay of two independent lines or voices in a piece of music.
Crotchet A note lasting one beat. Known as a quarter-note in the USA.
DADGAD A tuning used in folk guitar whereby the six strings are tuned (from sixth string to first) to the notes D, A, D,G, A and D.
Damping A technique for cutting the sound of the guitar strings while playing.
Dissonance An unstable, harsh-sounding clash of notes.
Double stopping The act of fingering two notes together with the left hand, usually in intervals of thirds or sixths.
Drop-D An alternative tuning whereby the sixth string is tuned downwards from E to D.
Extended chord A chord that has more notes than the three contained in standard or major or minor triads. The chord is generally described by this extra note, for example as a seventh, a sixth or an eleventh.
Fingerboard The front side of the neck in stringed instruments, the part that the strings lay over.
Finger-picking A fundamental and highly versatile style of guitar-playing in which the fingertips of the right hand are used to pluck the strings.
Fingertapping A technique, usually associated with the electric guitar, whereby notes are sounded by hammering on the string with the fingers of the left and right hands. Also known for short as 'tapping'.
First position The stance of the left hand when covering the first four frets. The first finger is assigned to the first fret; the second finger to the second fret, and so on.

Fixed finger A chord-change technique whereby one finger remains in position when the other fingers are moving from one position to another.
Fixed string bend A technique whereby one finger remains in place on a fret while another executes a bend on a different string.
Fourth position The stance of the left hand when the first finger is positioned at fret four.
Fifth position The stance of the left hand when the first finger is positioned at fret five.
Flat A term describing a note that has been lowered by one semitone (one fret).
Frets The metal strips that divide a fingerboard into intervals of a semitone.
Gauge The diameter of a string, usually expressed in thousandths of an inch (for example .008, .036).
Guide finger A finger used to connect two positions on the fingerboard by sliding along the string.
Hammer-on A means of playing legato on the guitar. The left hand produces the second note of a pair by hammering onto the string.
Interval The gap in pitch between any two notes.
Legato The slurring or tying two consecutive notes.
Major scale An eight-note scale widely used in Western music. A full tone follows the first, second, fourth, fifth and sixth notes; a semitone follows the third and seventh notes.
Minor scale An eight-note scale in which a full-tone follows the first, third, fourth, sixth and seventh notes; a semitone follows the second and fifth notes.
Moveable chord A finger-pattern that can be transposed to different areas of the fingerboard in order to make new chords.
Open chord Chord shapes that utilize the open strings of the guitar.
Open tuning An alternative tuning whereby the open strings form a chord such as D, G or C.
Palm muting A technique whereby the side or heel of the right hand is used to mute the strings.
Passing notes Notes used in melodic writing to bridge the gap between tones that belong to the underlying chord.
Pentatonic scale A five-note scale widely used for improvising in blues and rock music. The pentatonic scale is also found in traditional forms of music all over the world.
Pedal (1) A device that alters the signal from an electric guitar to the amplifier and so alters the sound; (2) A drone note that remains unchanged through one or more chord changes.
Pick-up A transducer fitted to an electric guitar; it captures the vibrations of the strings and turns them into an electrical signal.
Plectrum A small tear-drop-shaped disk used for strumming the strings.
Power chord A moveable chord shape containing only the root and fifth degrees

of the scale. The omission of the third gives it a characteristic 'bare' sound.

Progression A set of chords played in succession to make up a coherent musical phrase.

Pull-off A means of playing legato. The left hand produces the second note of a pair by plucking the string.

Relative tuning A method of tuning the guitar without a reference note. The strings are tuned to each other, so that the guitar is in tune with itself.

Riff A short series of notes, or a finger pattern, that is repeated as part of a melody or accompaniment.

Rolled chord The notes of a chord played successively, as in a slow strum.

Root note The fundamental note on which a chord is built. The root is usually, but not always, the bass note of a chord.

Second position The stance of the left hand when the first finger is positioned at the second fret, the second finger at the third fret, and so on.

Semitone The smallest musical interval commonly used in Western music; also called a half-step or a half-tone. On the guitar, all the frets are a semitone apart.

Seventh chord A chord consisting of a standard triad plus the seventh degree of the scale.

Sharp A term describing a note that has been raised by one semitone (one fret).

Slide A seamless shift of the finger between two notes along one string.

Slide guitar A style of guitar playing whereby the pitch of the notes is altered by sliding a glass or metal tube along the strings.

Slur An alternative term for legato playing, produced on a guitar using slides, hammer-on and pull-offs.

Spread chord An alternative term for arpeggio. Also known as a broken chord.

Standard tuning The most common tuning for a guitar whereby the six strings are tuned to E, A, D, G, B and E.

Stave The set of five spaced horizontal lines, on which music is written in standard notation.

String crossing The act of moving the fingers of the right hand from one string to another in the course of playing a musical phrase.

Suspended chord A chord in which the third of a triad is replaced by a fourth.

Tablature A system of musical notation in which fingering positions are indicated, rather than the pitches of notes.

Third position The stance of the left hand when the first finger is positioned at the third fret.

Three-chord trick A song that can be played using only three chords.

Timbre The tonal quality of an instrument or voice.

Time signature A marker at the beginning of a piece of music, indicating the length and number of beats in a bar.

Triad A chord consisting of the first, third and fifth notes of the scale.

Tuning pegs The geared knobs, connected to the capstans, that are used for tightening or loosening the strings of a guitar when tuning.

Vibrato An effect produced by rapid movement of the left-hand fingers on the strings, to give a note a wavering quality.

TABLATURE LEGEND

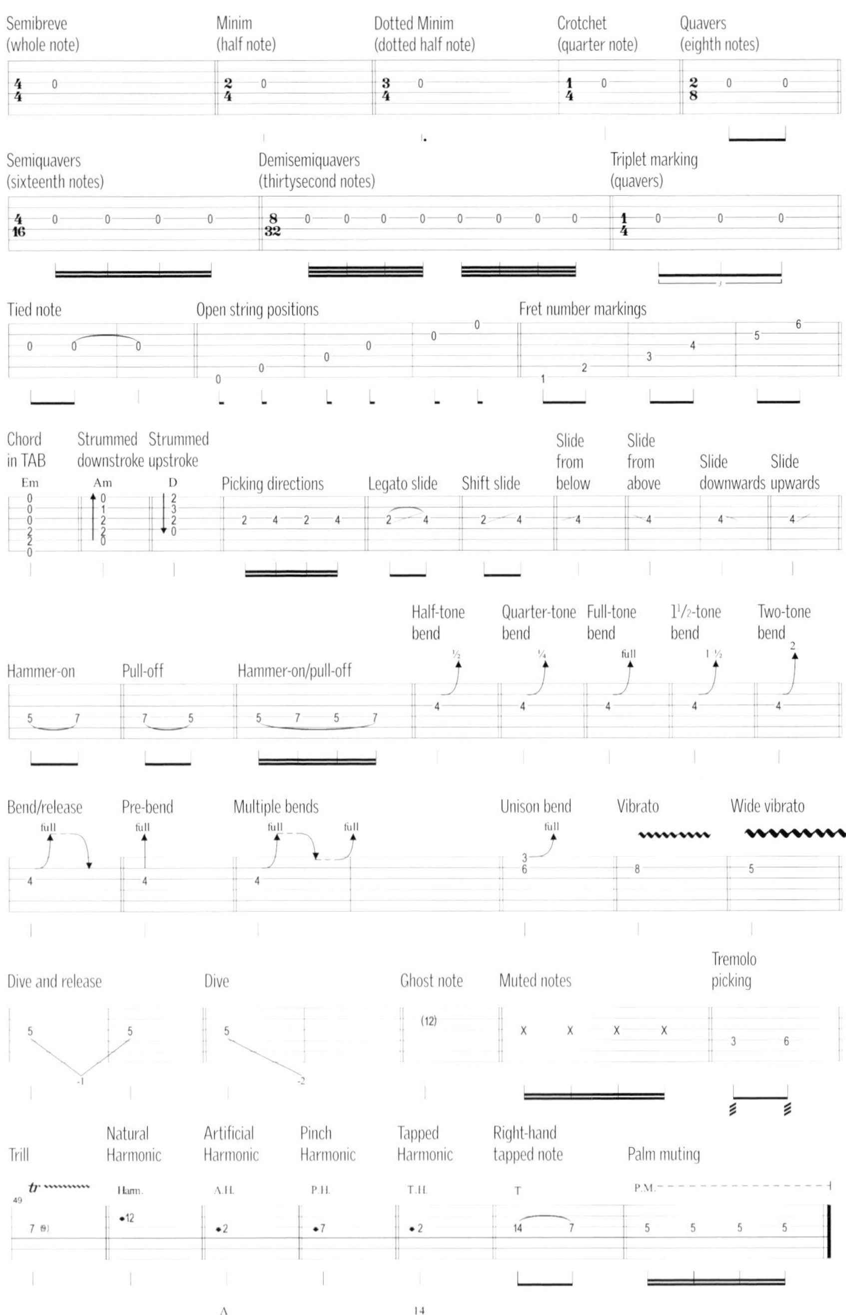

INDEX

Author

DAVID BLACK began playing the guitar at the age of ten and studied at the Royal Scottish Academy of Music and Drama and the Royal College of Music, London. He teaches guitar at several schools in southeast London and regularly performs solo, as one half of the Albach Guitar Duo. David is also a member of the contemporary music group Rarescale.

Picture credits

Corbis/Cultura: 175. **Fotolia**: 2, 4. **Getty Images**/Erich Auerbach: 156; CBS Photo Archive: 39; John Cohen: 100; Mick Hutson/Redferns: 73br; Joe Kohen/WireImage: 127; Neil Lupin/ Redferns: 77; Paul Natkin/WireImage: 84; Martin Philbey: 30; David Redfern/Redferns: 7; Peter Still/ Redferns: 67. **Greg Heet**: 115tr. **iStockphoto**: 8, 34, 54, 116, 176.

Photography by Laurie Evans
Illustrations by Richard Peters

Author acknowledgements

The author would like to thank the guitar students and music department staff of Crown Woods School, St Olave's Preparatory School, Blackheath High Junior School and Charter School. Also: Huong Black; Stephen Black of *Sweet Baboo*; Rebecca Baulch of the *Albach Guitar Duo*; Carla Rees of *rarescale*; David Braid; and Antenna Studios, Crystal Palace.

Quercus Publishing Plc
21 Bloomsbury Square
London
WC1A 2NS

First published in 2010

This edition produced by Ivy Contract

Text by David Black and Jonathan Bastable

A catalogue record of this book is available from the British Library

UK and associated territories
ISBN: 978 1 84916 484 9

USA and associated territories
ISBN: 978 1 84866 049 6

Printed and bound in China

10 9 8 7 6 5 4 3 2 1